A volume in the Hyperion reprint series
THE RADICAL TRADITION IN AMERICA

HYPERION PRESS, INC.
Westport, Connecticut

Robert M. La Follette

Edmonston Studio,
Washington, D. C.

The Political Philosophy

OF

ROBERT M. LA FOLLETTE

As Revealed in his Speeches and Writings.

Compiled by
ELLEN TORELLE
Assisted by Albert O. Barton and Fred L. Holmes.

In the Valley of Decision,
Down the Road of Things-that-are,
You gave to us a vision,
You appointed us a star
And through Cities of Derision
We followed you from far.

On the Hills beyond Tomorrow,
On the Road of Things-to-do,
With that strength of hand we borrow,
As we borrow soul from you,
We know not sloth nor sorrow
And will build your vision true.

William Ellery Leonard.

MADISON, WIS.
THE ROBERT M. LA FOLLETTE CO.

Published in 1920 by The Robert M. La Follette Co., Madison, Wisconsin
Copyright 1920 by Robert M. La Follette Co.
Hyperion reprint edition 1975
Library of Congress Catalog Number 75-348
ISBN 0-88355-252-3
Printed in the United States of America

Library of Congress Cataloging in Publication Data

La Follette, Robert Marion, 1855 - 1925.
   The political philosophy of Robert M. La Follette as revealed in his speeches and writings.

   (The Radical tradition in America)
   Reprint of the ed. published by Robert M. La Follette Co., Madison, Wis.
   Includes index.
   1. United States — Politics and government — 20th century — Collected works. I. Torelle, Ellen, 1870 -   II. Barton, Albert Olaus.   III. Holmes, Frederick Lionel, 1883 - 1946.   IV. Title.
E660.L332   1975   320.9'73'091   75-348
ISBN 0-88355-252-3

The Inspiration of a Life

There is looming up a new and dark power. I cannot dwell upon the signs and shocking omens of its advent. The accumulation of individual wealth seems to be greater than it ever has been since the downfall of the Roman Empire. The enterprises of the country are aggregating vast corporate combinations of unexampled capital, boldly marching, not for economic conquests only, but for political power. For the first time really in our politics money is taking the field as an organized power. * * * Already, here at home, one great corporation has trifled with the sovereign power, and insulted the state. There is grave fear that it, and its great rival, have confederated to make partition of the state and share it as spoils. * * * The question will arise, and arise in your day, though perhaps not fully in mine, "Which shall rule—wealth or man; which shall lead—money or intellect; who shall fill public stations—educated and patriotic free men, or the feudal serfs of corporate capital?"

Chief Justice Edward G. Ryan, Speech to Graduating Class, Wisconsin Law School, 1873.

CONTENTS

I.	REPRESENTATIVE GOVERNMENT	13
II.	PRIMARY ELECTIONS	27
III.	POLITICAL MACHINE AND THE BOSSES.	53
IV.	TAXATION	61
V.	RAILROAD REGULATION AND GOVERNMENT OWNERSHIP	72
VI.	TRUSTS AND MONOPOLIES	104
VII.	LABOR AND ITS RIGHTS	129
VIII.	BIG BUSINESS AND GOVERNMENT	148
IX.	THE TARIFF	160
X.	MONEY AND BANKING	166
XI.	INITIATIVE, REFERENDUM AND RECALL.	173
XII.	FEDERAL JUDGES AND INJUNCTIONS	179
XIII.	THE PROGRESSIVE MOVEMENT	182
XIV.	MILITARISM	190
XV.	WAR	200
XVI.	DRAFT AND CONSCRIPTION	215
XVII.	WAR TAXES AND PROFITEERING	220
XVIII.	FREEDOM OF SPEECH AND PRESS	231
XIX.	THE PEACE TREATY AND THE LEAGUE OF NATIONS	251
XX.	INTERNATIONAL RELATIONS	270
XXI.	THE AMERICAN SOLDIER	275

Contents

XXII.	Agriculture and Co-operation	280
XXIII.	Education and Public Service	289
XXIV.	Economic Problems	314
XXV.	Conservation	325
XXVI.	Equal Suffrage	338
XXVII.	The Press and the Public	345
XXVIII.	Miscellaneous	350

Appendix 380
Index 421

FOREWORD

HE moral issues before the people of this country at the present time are more momentous than at any other period since the foundation of the government.

The Civil War solved the problem of secession and resulted in the emancipation of three million slaves. Today, violations of the Constitution are more flagrant and more dangerous to our institutions than was the attempt at secession, and the liberty of a hundred million people, white as well as black, is in jeopardy. The assurance that a higher and nobler democracy would be a result of the Great War has been found to be a mockery, the reverse of democracy being realized in a reign of terror and oppression. Public disillusionment has been followed by doubt and indecision, and men and women are reaching out for the guidance of a political philosophy which is founded on principles of truth and justice and competent to meet the needs of the times.

It is the purpose of this book to indicate where such a philosophy may be found and to present it in epitome. To the many busy men and women who cannot spare the time to read the entire articles or addresses, it will prove a valuable compendium. For the student or social worker it may serve as an inspiration to a more extended study of the subject. The citizen who wishes to understand the progressive movement in order that he may use his suffrage more intelligently will find much to ponder over in these pages. To those who are familiar with the clear, simple, and forceful style of the author, nothing needs to be said in commendation or amplification. For those to whom this book may be an introduction we predict great interest and pleasure in further acquaintance with the man and his work.

Robert M. La Follette has led the progressive movement in this country during the last thirty years. Its development may be said to be co-incident with his public career. He was the first to secure progressive legislation, and the political structure which was reared in Wisconsin as a result of his self-sacrifice and devotion, was so well founded on sound economic principles that it has withstood the attacks of its enemies, the supporters of corrupt machine and corporation rule.

La Follette's position as the pioneer of the progressive movement was secure long before 1912, but in that year his leadership was strikingly acknowledged by Bryan, Wilson, and even by Roosevelt, prior to the latter's candidacy for a third presidential term.

To Bryan, La Follette was the "prince of progressives." Roosevelt wrote of La Follette's five years as governor:

"Thanks to the movement for genuinely democratic government which Senator La Follette led to overwhelming victory in Wisconsin, that state has become literally a laboratory for wise experimental legislation, aiming to secure the social and political betterment of the people as a whole."

Foreword

It remained for Woodrow Wilson to pay the most fulsome tribute to La Follette, in a speech at Wilmington, Del., in October, 1912:

"Now there arose in Wisconsin that indomitable little figure of Bob La Follette. I tell you ladies and gentlemen, I take off my cap to Bob La Follette. He has never taken his eye for a single moment from the goal he set out to reach. He has walked a straight line to it in spite of every temptation to turn aside. * * I have sometimes thought of Senator La Follette climbing the mountain of privilege * * taunted, laughed at, called back, going steadfastly on and not allowing himself to be deflected for a single moment, for fear he also should hearken and lose all his power to serve the great interests to which he had devoted himself. I love these lonely figures climbing this ugly mountain of privilege. But they are not so lonely now. I am sorry for my own part that I did not come in when they were fewer. There was no credit to come in when I came in. The whole nation had awakened."

Since 1912 Senator La Follette has seen the progressive principles he sponsored swept aside in the unchecked growth of monopoly. He has seen monopoly control of industry and government bring increased living costs and encroachments on individual liberty: the evils against which he warned the people. The war gave La Follette's foes their opportunity to attempt his destruction, but the logic of his principles could not be destroyed and today, erect, unyielding, La Follette stands on the ground the other leaders have abandoned, still fighting for the old principles, with the confidence of the people in his progressive leadership unshaken.

Throughout this book the reader will be impressed, not only with the unusual mental power and vision of the man, but with the moral elevation of his spirit. He views problems of state as well as problems of the individual in the clear, white light of ethics, and no compromise with expediency is permitted in any case. It is this which gives his work high and permanent value. It is in line with social evolution.

The excerpts vary in length, but each expresses concisely a principle of government, a political method to be followed, or calls attention to unjust or harmful conditions which need to be remedied. For convenience, reference is made to the article or discourse from which each is taken so that the original may be consulted at leisure.

In the compilation of this work I have been assisted by Albert O. Barton, a former secretary of Senator La Follette, and Fred L. Holmes, managing editor of La Follette's Magazine.

The work of compilation and classification has been a pleasure which is surrendered with regret since additional material of surpassing interest is continually being made available.

Ellen Torelle.

MADISON, WIS.,
July 15, 1920.

I.
REPRESENTATIVE GOVERNMENT

Democracy is a Life

E have long rested comfortably in this country upon the assumption that because our form of government was democratic, it was therefore automatically producing democratic results. Now, there is nothing mysteriously potent about the forms and names of democratic institutions that should make them self-operative. Tyranny and oppression are just as possible under democratic forms as under any other. We are slow to realize that democracy is a life and involves continual struggle. It is only as those of every generation who love democracy resist with all their might the encroachments of its enemies that the ideals of representative government can even be nearly approximated.
Introduction to Autobiography, 1913.

Political Parties

Political parties are not organized or maintained upon the personality or strength of individuals, but around certain deep-seated ideas which lay hold of the convictions of men. These ideas when formulated and proclaimed become the party's declaration of principles, its promise to perform. This declaration of principles, this promise to perform, is of the highest importance to each citizen. When so proclaimed it enables him to determine his party affiliation. He well understands that one political party or another will control government, will make and administer the laws. Hence, he gives his support to that party which promises to do the specific things that he regards of the highest importance to the state and to the welfare of every citizen. The party promise, therefore, is a covenant with the voter upon which he has staked his faith and his interests. He has given his support; he has invested the party with his authority; he has made it possible for the party to control in government. Upon its promise and his support the party has become the custodian of his political rights as a citizen, of his property right as a man.

But the party obligation goes still further. The obligation of the party is made the more binding because it has sought out the citizen, urged acceptance of its pledges, pressed them upon his consideration, proclaimed again and again its purpose to keep them in letter and spirit. It has made the citizen its solicitor and secured his good offices to repeat its promises, proclaim its principles, and enlist in its ranks his neighbors and friends. Having received his vote, his influence, his devotion, the party is bound to keep its pledged word. This is its title to confidence. This measures its value as a power for good in representative government.

Every established practice and custom which tends to impair in any degree the citizen's right of suffrage subverts the principles of representative government and undermines the foundations of democracy.

It is a plain proposition that the right of suffrage is much broader and more comprehensive than the mere physical act of casting the ballot without interference, and having it returned, as cast, without fraud. All of the guarantees of the constitution, all of the acts of legislation, are designed to secure and record the will of the citizen; to make it certain that, untrammeled and uninterrupted, the influence of his judgment may be felt in matters pertaining to government. If this be the real substance of the right of suffrage, then it becomes an equally sacred obligation on the part of the lawmaking power to so safeguard every step and proceeding which constitutes any element of the right of suffrage that the citizen shall be protected with respect to it.

Through the succession of generations human nature is the same, and when De Tocqueville declared that "the most powerful, and perhaps the only, means of interesting men in the welfare of the country is to make them partakers in the government," he uttered a truth which applies quite as forcibly to the primary step in suffrage, as to the secondary step in suffrage,— to the nomination of candidates as to their election after nomination. And the interest and influence of the voter can be as well and as certainly secured in the one as in the other, if the same means are taken to guarantee to him the same certainty of result respecting the one as the other.

Message to Legislature, 1903.

Right to Equal Voice

It is a fundamental principle of this republic that each citizen shall have equal voice in government. This is recognized and guaranteed to him through the ballot. In a representative democracy, where a

citizen cannot act for himself for any reason, he
must delegate his authority to the public official
who acts for him. Since government, with us, is
conducted by the representatives of some political
party, the citizen's voice in making and administering the laws is expressed through his party ballot.
Hence, to preserve his sovereign right to an equal
share in government he must be assured an equal
voice in making his party ballot. This privilege
is vital. This is the initial point of all administration. It is here government begins, and if there
be failure here, there will be failure throughout.
Control lost at this point is never regained; rights
surrendered here are never restored. As the foundation is laid, so will the structure be reared. The
naming of the men upon the party ticket is the
naming of the men who will make and enforce the
laws. It not only settles the policy of the party,
it determines the character of the government.
Inaugural Message, 1901.

I do not believe that it lies in the power of any one
man or group of men successfully to proclaim the
creation of a new political party, and give it life,
and being, and achievement, and perpetuity. New
parties are brought forth from time to time, and
groups of men have come forward as their heralds
and have been called to leadership and command.
But the leaders did not create the party. It was the
ripe issue of events. It came out of the womb of
time, and no man could hinder or hasten the event.
No one can foretell the coming of the hour. It
may be near at hand. It may be otherwise. But if

it should come quickly, we may be sure strong leadership will be there; and some will say that the leaders made the party. But all great movements in society and government, the world over, are the result of growth. Progress may seem to halt; we may even seem to lose ground, but it is my deep conviction that it is our duty to do, day by day, with all our might, as best we can for the good of our country the task which lies nearest at hand. The party does not consist of a few leaders or of a controlling political machine; it consists of the hundreds of thousands of citizens drawn together by a common belief in certain principles.

A political party is not made to order. It is the slow development of powerful forces working in our social life. Sound ideas seize upon the human mind. Opinions ripen into fixed convictions. Masses of men are drawn together by common belief and organized about clearly defined principles. From time to time this organized body expresses its purpose and names candidates to represent its principles. The millions cannot be assembled. Until direct nominations and the rigid control of campaign expenditures shall prevail they must seek to express their will through the imperfect agencies of congressional, state, and national conventions. These agencies are not the party. They are temporarily delegated to represent the millions who constitute the party. If recreant to their trust the party may suffer the temporary defeat of its purposes.

Autobiography, 1913.

Platform Pledges

Mr. President, a platform promise is a covenant with the voter, upon which he stakes his faith and his interests. He gives the party his support; he invests it with his authority; he makes it possible for the party to control in government. The obligation of the party is made the more binding because it seeks out the citizen, urges acceptance of its pledges, presses them upon his consideration, proclaims again and again its purpose to keep them in letter and spirit. The party makes the citizen its solicitor, secures his good offices to repeat its promises, proclaim its principles, and enlist in its ranks his neighbors and friends. Having secured his support, his influence, his vote, the party is in honor bound to keep its pledged word.

When the citizen, relying upon the pledges made in the platform of the party, aids to place a representative in the public service to the end that he may fulfill and perform in letter and spirit the promises for legislation and administration promised in the platform, the official is solemnly bound to the execution of his sacred trust. He cannot play fast and loose with party promises and preserve a semblance of official or individual integrity.

Any legislation which does not proceed upon the basis that it is a wise, just, and safe exercise of legislative power cannot achieve any enduring good. Without these supporting considerations, such legislation can be urged only on grounds of political expediency. But let no man be misled by the expectation

that any half-way measure will serve even the end of political expediency.
"Regulation of R. R. Rates and Services,"
U. S. Senate, April 19-21, 1906.

The Iniquity of the "Conference" System

Mr. President, a system of rules giving into the hands of a conference the power to make legislation is destructive of democracy.

I hope that as a member of this body I shall live to see the rules with respect to conference reports so changed that it will not be possible for two or three men to dictate and put through legislation. This is a democracy. We are supposed to be the representatives of the people.

Our work upon this floor and the work of our associates at the other end of the capitol is supposed to represent public opinion and the interests of the great masses of this country. But I need not say to the senators what everybody knows, that very often the public will is defeated, that public interest is perverted, and democracy is shackled in legislation as we enact it.
U. S. Senate, July 26, 1916.

Never Know Defeat in a Good Cause

There is no difference in principle in pressing the same issue before the people in successive campaigns and in presenting the same issue to the legislature in successive sessions. Our direct primary law, equalization of taxation, our railroad commission, our control of public utilities and other advanced measures were ultimately secured after a number of hard-fought campaigns. It was for that very reason that they won so completely. We not only struck while the iron was hot, we made it hot and kept it so by striking. That is what the new spirit of American politics has taught us—never to know defeat in a good cause.

Speech in U. S. Senate on Railroad Regulation, April 26, 1913.

The Supreme Issue

With the changing phases of a twenty-five year contest, I have been more and more impressed with the deep underlying singleness of the issue. It is not railroad regulation. It is not the tariff, or conservation, or the currency. It is not the trusts. These and other questions are but manifestations of one great struggle.

The supreme issue, involving all others, is the encroachment of the powerful few upon the rights of the many. This mighty power has come between the people and their government. Can we free ourselves from this control? Can representative government be restored? Shall we, with statesmanship and constructive legislation, meet these problems, or shall we pass them on with all the possibilities of conflict and chaos, to future generations?

There never was a higher call to greater service than in this protracted fight for social justice. I believe, with increasing depth of conviction, that we will, in our day, meet our responsibility with fearlessness and faith; that we will reclaim and preserve for our children, not only the form but the spirit of our free institutions. And in our children must we rest our hope for the ultimate democracy.

It is my settled belief that this great power over government legislation can only be overthrown by resisting at every step, seizing upon every important occasion which offers opportunity to uncover the methods of the system. It matters little whether the particular question at issue is the tariff, the railroads, or the currency. The fight is the same. It is not a question of party politics. The great issue strikes down to the very foundation of our free institutions. It is against the system built up by privilege, which has taken possession of government and legislation, that we must make unceasing warfare.

Autobiography, 1913.

Pledges of Political Platforms

What is a political platform? What is its purpose? What is its importance in democratic forms of government?

In every republic, government is practically certain to be administered by some political party. The citizen gives his support to that political party, the principles of which most nearly meet his approving judgment. These principles are placed before the citizen for his consideration in a platform expressing the will of the majority of the party. The method of ascertaining that will having been agreed upon, the platform then becomes the law of the party to which all of its members owe faith, support and allegiance. The promulgation of a platform of declared principles, upon which the voters are asked to entrust a political party with the government of the state or the nation, must be as binding upon the party conscience as though it were the sealed bond of every individual of the party The obligation is two-fold: first, to the party itself; second, to the citizen whose support is sought. Violation of the party promise is an assault upon the party honor, destroys the confidence of its membership, and endangers the existence of party organization. It is a betrayal of the public, a fraud upon the citizen who supported it, and who, relying upon it, has been deprived of a sovereign right. To secure the support of voters upon any promise, express or implied, and then to refuse to fulfill the promise deprives the citizen of his right of suffrage as completely for the time being as though he were disfranchised by legislative enactment.

Manhood suffrage is a precious right, and in a democracy it lies at the foundation of all personal and property rights. Without it the citizen has no protection for home or liberty. If it be denied to him, the citizen becomes a serf. A party platform is, therefore, of the highest importance to the individual voter. When it has been formulated by the party and promulgated as its declaration of principles, as its pledge to do certain things, to administer the government in a certain way, to enact certain legislation, the citizen is then placed in a position where he can easily determine whether he desires to support the party promising that kind of government. It is the party platform which enables him to choose in making his party alliance. He understands that one party or the other will control, and will make and will administer the laws Guided, then, by the promises made in the party platform he casts his ballot, gives his support, works for the triumph and success of that party whose platform principles most strongly appeal to his judgment. The party's tender of its platform, the citizen's tender of his support upon that platform, makes, therefore, a solemn compact, a covenant, which binds the party to the voter, who has staked his faith and placed his interests upon its honor and in its keeping. The party, therefore, has become the trustee of the citizen's right, and it cannot violate the obligation which it has assumed.

But, more than this, the party summons its members to go forth bearing its banners and proclaiming its principles. It seeks out the citizen, it enlists him in its service, it urges him to accept its pledges, and appeals to him to go forth and repeat its promises and proclaim its good faith, multiplying, on every hand, its obligations to keep its word and make good every promise in its platform. Its willingness to do this is the test of its integrity of purpose.

No fear need ever be entertained that the party itself will ignore or repudiate its platform obligations. Great bodies of men constituting party organizations are drawn together by deep-seated convictions, lasting in character, and appealing strongly to the sentiments of loyalty and patriotism. The mass of men composing party organizations can always be relied upon to support party platforms. There will be no failure through lack of fidelity on their part. But a political party can only work out a practical application of the principles of the party platform through legislation and administration.

To accomplish this it must, out of all its members, choose agents to represent it and execute its will.

These members of its organization are placed before the public as its candidates for office, its honored and trusted spokesmen. In the nature of things, the party can only execute its will through its chosen representatives. They are clothed with its authority; they are the custodians of its pledges. Upon them rests the double obligation to execute this trust; as individual members of the party they share in its responsibility, but, as the representatives of the party deputed to perform its promises, its honor is placed in their keeping. When the citizen, relying upon the pledges made in the platform of the party, gives his support to the representative of the party and aids to place him in the public service to the end that he may fulfill and perform, in letter and in spirit, the promises for legislation and administration embodied in the platform, the official has become yet more solemnly bound to the faithful execution of his sacred trusts.

Upon all matters, not covered by the platform, in his official capacity as the agent of his party and the representatives of the public, he may exercise his best judgment; but in all matters upon which his political party has spoken in its platform, when that party has put him before the public as its nominee, representing the principles embodied in its party declaration, he has no right to exercise an independent judgment. He cannot play fast and loose with party promise and preserve a semblance of official or individual integrity.

The enactment of legislation which has been pledged by the party and endorsed by the people cannot be defeated, in whole or in part, without a violation of obligation. It becomes an express trust, the terms clearly defined, and the public official has no more moral right to quibble and evade, to say that he will perform a part and repudiate the rest, than he would have to use a part of trust funds committed to his keeping as a private trust.

If government is to be representative government, then it must truly represent the will of the majority; both of the party when it has spoken in its platforms and of the people when they have spoken through the right of suffrage, as expressed in their ballots. For a minority to obstruct or delay or defeat the will of the majority is destructive of the principles upon which a republican form of government is founded.

Speech Accepting Nomination for Governor,
May 19, 1904.

The Reformer

It is incumbent upon the reformer who seeks to establish a new order to come equipped with complete mastery of all the information upon which the established order is based. And it is for this reason that the thoroughgoing, uncompromising, Progressive movement is essentially a safe one for the public and for all legitimate business.

Reformers often stop fighting before the battle is really won; before the new territory is completely occupied.

I have always felt that the political reformer, like the engineer or the architect, must know that his foundations are right. To build the superstructure in advance of that is likely to be disastrous to the whole thing. He must not put the roof on before he gets the underpinning in. And the underpinning is education of the people.

While much has been accomplished, there is a world of problems to be solved; we have just begun; there is hard fighting, and a chance for the highest patriotism, still ahead of us. The fundamental problem as to which shall rule, men or property, is still unsettled; it will require the highest qualities of heroism, the profoundest devotion to duty in this and in the coming generation, to reconstruct our institutions to meet the requirements of a new age. May such brave and true leaders develop that the people will not be led astray.

Autobiography, 1913.

II.

PRIMARY ELECTIONS

Ballot at Bottom of Reform

HE existence of the corporation as we have it today was not dreamt of by the fathers. It has become all-pervasive; has invaded all departments of business, all activities of life. By their number and power and the consolidation oft-times of many into one, corporations have practically acquired dominion over the business world. The effect is revolutionary and cannot be overestimated. The individual as a business factor is disappearing, his place being taken by many under corporate rule. The business man and artisan of the past gave to his business an individual stamp and reputation, making high mental worth an essential element of business life. Gathered in corporate employ men become mere cogs in the wheels of complicated mechanism. The corporation is a machine for making money, demanding of its employes only obedience and service, reducing men to the status of privates in the regular army.

It is but just to say that no legislature has assembled in Wisconsin in many years containing so many good men as the last. But when a bill to punish corrupt practices in campaigns and elections is destroyed by amendment; when measures such as the Davidson bills requiring corporations to pay a just share of the

taxes go down in defeat; when bills to compel millions
of dollars of untaxed personal property to come from
its hiding place and help maintain government fail of
adequate support; when republicans and democrats
unite in defeating the Hall resolution to emancipate
the legislature from all subserviency to the corporations by prohibiting acceptance of railroad passes,
telegraph and express company franks; when these
things and many others of like character happen and
are made matters of public record which no man may
deny, then that man is untrue to his country, his party
and himself who will not raise his voice in condemnation—not in condemnation of the principles of the
political party in which he believes, or of the great
body of its organization, but of the men who betray
it and of the methods by which they control, only to
prostitute it to base and selfish ends.

The remedy is to begin at the bottom and make one
supreme effort for victory over the present bad system.
Nominate and elect men who will pass a primary election law which will enable the voter to select directly
candidates without intervention of caucus or convention or domination of machines. Thus may a permanent reform greater even than the reform effected by
the Australian ballot which has so revolutionized the
conduct of elections be brought about. Apply the
method of the Australian ballot as embodied in the
Cooper law to the primary election and let it take
the place of both the caucus and convention. Furnish
the primary election booth with ballots as under the
Australian system and print on the ballot for each
party the names of the different candidates proposed
for its nominee as candidates for judicial offices are

Primary Elections 29

now proposed; provide for the selection of a committee to represent each party organization and promulgate the party platform through such committee composed of party committeemen elected by and for the voters of each party in every assembly district of the state. Provide severe penalties for any violation of the primary election law. Prohibit corrupt influence in or about the election booth and insure an honest count and return the votes as cast. Provide that each man receiving the highest number of votes cast in the ballot box of his party for the office for which he is a candidate shall be the nominee of that party in the general election to follow. In short pass such a measure as the Lewis primary election bill. Under this system you will destroy the machine because you destroy the caucus and convention system through which the machine controls party nominations. You will place the nominations directly in the hands of the people. You will restore to every state in the union the government given to this people by the God of nations.

Address "Menace of the Machine,"
Chicago University, Feb. 22, 1897.

Direct Nominations Fundamental

Under our form of government the entire structure rests upon the nomination of candidates for office. This is the foundation of the representative system. If bad men control the nominations we cannot have good government. Let us start right. The life principle of representative government is that those chosen to govern shall faithfully represent the governed. To insure this the representative must be chosen by those whom he is to represent. This is fundamental. A system built upon any other foundation is not a representative government. By no other means can it be established or maintained. The moment that any power or authority over the representative comes between him and those who have selected him to be their representative that moment he ceases to be their representative. His responsibility is at once transferred to the intervening power or authority. He becomes the trustee of this new authority and to it he must render account for his actions. It is vital then in representative government that no power or authority shall be permitted to come between the representative and those whom he is to represent. To secure this every complication of detail and method, in any system, behind which such intruding power or authority might be concealed must be torn down and cast aside. The voter, and the candidate for nomination who desires to represent the voter, must be brought within reaching distance of each other, must stand face to face.

To accomplish this we must abolish the caucus and convention by law, place the nomination of all candidates in the hands of the people, adopt the Australian ballot and make all nominations by direct vote at a primary election.

With the nominations of all candidates absolutely in the control of the people, under a system that gives every member of a party equal voice in making that nomination, the public official who desires re-nomination will not dare to seek it, if he has served the machine and the lobby and betrayed the public trust;

Primary Elections

if he has violated the pledges of his party and swapped its declared principles to special interests for special favors.

But under a primary election the public official who has kept faith with the public can appeal to that public for its approval with confidence. He will then have every incentive to keep his official record clean. If he have no loftier standard than mere personal success he will nevertheless so administer his office as to earn the commendation "Well done thou good and faithful servant."

The nomination of all their candidates by the direct vote of the people is the spirit, the very life of representative government. It is plain, simple, practical. It is their right. It will come. Whoever seeks to thwart or defeat it is an enemy of representative government. Let him beware! Whoever would control as the agent of the machine will encounter lasting defeat. Let him beware! The country is awakening, the people are aroused. They will have their own. The machine may obstruct, misdirected reform may temporize, but "be of good cheer, strengthen thine heart," the will of the people shall prevail.

I appeal to you, young men and old, plain citizens and politicians. You are confronted with a great responsibility. In this contest you must either stand for representative government or against it. The fight is on. It will continue to victory. There will be no halt and no compromise.

Address at Ann Arbor, Michigan,
March 12, 1898.

Means Higher Standards of Service

For many years there has been a growing demand for ballot reform. Intelligent, patriotic men of all parties have weighed carefully the influence of the ballot upon both government and party. The public official who can count on party loyalty to carry him through, grows indifferent and dishonest in the public service. The political party which is strongly intrenched in power behind a blind partisan majority, scorns public opinion and claims its share of graft to enrich bosses and maintain the party machine. To control the selection of candidates for office, to hedge the party organization about with a sentiment that the party is a sacred thing, to so arouse partisan feeling in the campaign as to fuse the mass of voters together, and make them vote as one man, has made possible the era of official dishonesty, which seems to have taken possession of the public service everywhere. Out of it there came to political bosses a sense of security which made them bold in dealing with the agents of the captains of industry, who have found it to their interests to make politics and government a matter of business.

Whatever conduces to make the voter as he enters the election booth free to exercise an independent judgment, to consider the public welfare, the integrity of the state and the country first of all, will at once establish higher party standards and better public service.

Message to Legislature, Special Session, 1905.

Primary Elections

Caucus Reform Idle Dream

Corporations, exacting large sums from the people of this state in profits upon business transacted within its limits, either wholly escape taxation or pay insignificantly in comparison with the average citizen of Wisconsin.

Owning two-thirds of the personal property, evading the payment of taxes wherever possible, the corporations throw almost the whole burden upon land—upon the little homes and the personal property of the farmers.

While this is getting to be somewhat understood, yet a rigid investigation of this whole subject of evasion of taxation by corporations and the possessors of great wealth in every state, would awaken the just wrath of the people and inaugurate a reform which might reach even to the machine-made legislators of the day.

But in a government where the people are sovereign, why are these things tolerated? Why are not the remedies promptly applied and the evils eradicated? It is because today there is a force operating in this country, more powerful than the sovereign in matters pertaining to official conduct. The official obeys whom he serves. Nominated independently of the people and elected because there is no choice between candidates so nominated, the official feels responsibility to his master alone; and his master is the political machine of his party.

Between the people and the representative there has been built up a political machine which is the master of both. It is the outgrowth of the caucus and convention system.

Experience has proved it to be almost idle folly to attend caucuses and conventions with the hope of defeating the machine until today, after a century of statesmanship and of struggle and sacrifice, after all the triumphs achieved under the stars and stripes, thousands and thousands of good citizens in every state stand aloof from the caucus and convention with the settled belief that representative government is a failure.

When the solemn promise of a great political party to prohibit the issuing of railway passes to officials is not only broken but attempted to be repudiated, when these things, and many others of like character, transpire and are made matters of public record, which no man can deny, then that man is untrue to his state, his party and himself who will not raise his voice in condemnation—not in condemnation of the principles of the political party in which he believes, nor of the great body of its organization, but of those men who betray it and the methods by which they control only to prostitute it to base and selfish ends.

When legislators will boldly repudiate their constituents and violate the pledges of their platforms, then, indeed, have the servants become the masters and the people ceased to be sovereign. Gone the government of equal rights and equal responsibilities, lost the jewel of constitutional liberty.

Speech at Lodi, Wisconsin, 1898.

Second Choice Voting

I congratulate you, and through you, the people of Wisconsin upon the adoption of a law for the nomination of all candidates for office by direct vote. The demand of the voters of this state for such a law had been made many times in a clear and explicit manner. Its defeat, against the will of the majority, was the clearest impeachment of the caucus and convention system which made it possible for a minority to control.

When after years of delay the people of Wisconsin were granted the opportunity finally to determine the question, they wrote the law upon the statutes of Wisconsin by more than 50,000 majority. The perfection of legislation can only be determined by the practical test of experience. With respect to any modifications in the existing statute during the present session, I have no recommendations to make further than to repeat a suggestion heretofore made.

In the first message submitted to the legislature of 1901 upon the subject, after discussing the possibility of the vote being so divided among a number of candidates for the same office that no one of them might receive a majority of all the votes cast, I said:

"If, however, upon trial, it should be found desirable or if, in your judgment, it should be deemed wise at the outset, this objection can be effectively met by providing that the voter at the primary shall indicate upon his ballot his first and second choice of the candidates presented for each office. And that if no candidate has majority over all candidates of first choice, then the candidate having the largest number of first and second choice votes shall be accorded the nomination."

The application of this principle may be carried still further, insuring a nomination by majority vote.

Upon this, or any other branch of this great subject, the best thought of your honorable body will be well bestowed. For it is our duty to unite at all times to give to the people of this state the best statute which can be framed upon any subject.

Message to Legislature, 1905.

Primary as Citizen's Right

But, gentlemen of the convention, with all of your good work, nothing which you have done, nothing which has been done by any convention in a quarter of a century, will give to every man who has had a share in this work, such enduring honor when it shall have ripened into statutory law, as the declaration made here today, for the nomination of all candidates by direct vote at a primary election under the Australian ballot. The tests of experience will doubtless be required to perfect all the working details of a primary election law. It would be strange indeed if it were not so. But your great achievement is in having established the principle and begun the overthrow of a system that is undermining the representative government throughout the land. No longer in Wisconsin will there stand between the voter and the official a political machine with a complicated system of caucuses and conventions, by the easy manipulation of which it thwarts the will of the voter and rules official conduct. No valid reason can be given for continuing the caucus and convention another day. If the voter is competent to cast his ballot at the general election for the official of his choice, he is equally competent to vote directly at the primary election for the nomination of the candidates of his party. It is his right as a citizen and taxpayer and who will dare to gainsay or deny it?

Inspired with confidence by the great reformation accomplished in our general elections through the Australian ballot, we advance the standards of reform and demand the application of the same method in making nominations together with the sovereign right that each citizen shall for himself exercise his choice by direct vote, without the intervention or interference of any political agency.

Into the life of every generation comes some great opportunity for great public good. It has come to you today and, with high courage and patriotism, you have marked the way to restore to the people the pure form of representative government given them by the fathers in the beginning.

Accepting Nomination for Governor,
August 8, 1900.

Equal Voice Essential

Commissioned by the suffrages of the citizens of this state to represent them, you will have neither in the session before you nor in any official responsibility which you may assume, a more important duty than that of perfecting and writing upon the statute books of Wisconsin a primary election law.

It is a fundamental principle of this republic that each citizen shall have equal voice in government. This is recognized and guaranteed to him through the ballot. In a representative democracy, where a citizen cannot act for himself for any reason, he must delegate his authority to the public official who acts for him. Since government, with us, is conducted by the representatives of some political party, the citizen's voice in making and administering the laws is expressed through his party ballot. This privilege is vital. This is the initial point of all administration. It is here government begins, and if there be failure here, there will be failure throughout. Control lost at this point is never regained; rights surrendered here are never restored. The naming of the men upon the party ticket is the naming of the men who will make and enforce the laws. It not only settles the policy of the party, it determines the character of the government.

For many years the evils of the caucus and convention system have multiplied and baffled all attempts at legislative control or correction. The reason for this is elementary. The evils come not from without but from within. The system in all its details is inherently bad. It not only favors, but, logically and inevitably, produces manipulation, scheming, trickery, fraud and corruption. The delegate elected in caucus is nominally the agent of the voter to act for him in convention. Too frequently he has his own interests alone at heart, and, for this reason, has secured his selection as a delegate. As a consequence, he acts not for the voter, but serves his own purpose instead. This fact in itself taints the trust from the outset, and poisons the system at its very source. No legitimate business could survive under a system where authority to transact its vital matters were delegated and redelegated to agents and sub-agents, who controlled their own selection, construed their own obligations, and were responsible to nobody.

The officials nominated by the machine become its faithful servants and surrender judgment to its will. This they must do in self-preservation or they are retired to private life. Wielding a power substantially independent of the voter, it is quite unnecessary to regard him as an important factor in government. He can usually be depended upon in the elections, because campaigns are so managed as to make strong appeal to party feeling, and he has to vote his party ticket or support that of the opposition nominated by the same method. Under our system of party government the selection of the candidate is the vital question.

A political convention is never a deliberative body. It is impossible from the brevity of its life, the confusion of its proceedings, the intangible character of its records, to fix or attach any abiding sense of responsibility in its membership. Its business is rushed through under pressure for time. Excitement and impatience control, rather than reason and judgment. Noisy enthusiasm outweighs the strongest argument. Misstatements and misunderstandings will defeat the best candidate. The plain truth can hardly keep pace with hurrying events. It is rare, indeed, that the results of a convention are satisfactory to anybody excepting the few who secure some personal advantage or benefit from it.

It is the essence of republican government that the citizen should act for himself directly wherever possible. In the exercise of no other right is this so important as in the nomination of candidates for office. It is of primary importance that the public official should hold himself directly accountable to the citizen. This he will do only when he owes his nomination directly to the citizen. If between the citizen and the official there is a complicated system of caucuses and conventions, by the easy manipulation of which the selection of candidates is controlled by some other agency or power, then the official will so render his services as to have the approval of such agency or power. The overwhelming demand of the people of this state, whom you represent, is that such intervening power and authority, and the complicated system which sustains it, shall be torn down and cast aside. This is your duty, and high privilege as well, to accomplish it in the session before you. This, it is well understood, cannot be accomplished by any temporizing measure or so-called caucus reforms. The defects of the caucus, convention and delegate system are fatal because organic. It cannot be amended, reconstructed or reorganized, and its perpetuation secured. Its end is decreed by the enlightened moral sentiment of the entire country. It can no more resist the development which is sweeping it aside than could the adoption of the Australian ballot be successfully opposed a short ten years ago. It may secure trifling delays by temporary expedients. Its advocates may insist on making it a fetich and being sacrificed with it. But its knell has been sounded in Wisconsin, where it is already defeated, and a decade will leave scarcely a trace of its complicated machinery in existence in any State of the Union.

Message to Legislature, 1901.

Primary Deserving of Fair Test

I herewith return without approval bill No. 73, originating in the senate, entitled "An act relating to nominations of county officers by direct vote." The history of the effort to secure a primary election law in this state, the character of the opposition, and the means employed to defeat it demand a permanent place in the legislative record of this session. It is therefore from a controlling sense of obligation that I submit the following in connection with specific reasons for interposing the executive veto to prevent this bill from becoming a law.

More than four years ago the contest for nominations by direct vote of the people began in this state. The principle was then clearly defined. The plan under which it could be accomplished was then fully presented. More than that, the foundation and framework for a primary election law were at that time set forth and submitted to the people of this state as follows:

"Substitute for both the caucus and the convention a primary election held under all the sanctions of law which prevail at general elections, where the citizen may cast his vote directly to nominate the candidates of the party with which he affiliates, and have it canvassed and returned as he cast it.

"Provide a means of placing the candidates in nomination before the primary and forestall the creation of a new caucus system back of the primary election.

"Provide a ballot for the primary election and print on it the names of all candidates for nomination who have previously filed preliminary nomination papers with a designated official.

"Provide that no candidate for nomination shall have his name printed on the primary election ticket who shall not have been called out as a candidate by the written request of a given percentage of the vote cast at the preceding election in the district, county or state in which he is proposed as a candidate, in the same manner that judicial candidates are now called out in many states.

"Provide for the selection of a committee to represent the party organization and promulgate the party platform by the election at the primary of a representative man from the party for each county in the state.

Measure Fully Discussed

"Under severe penalties for violation of the law, prohibit electioneering in or about the election booth, punish bribery or the attempt to bribe, and protect fully the canvass and return of the votes cast."

Excepting as to the manner of making the platform, which is not the same, this presents fairly all the essential provisions of the primary election bill as originally introduced at this session. It would be difficult, indeed, to cite another instance in the history of the state where a great measure, of such fundamental importance in government, was more fully and clearly outlined and more generally discussed so long in advance. No haste was anywhere shown to urge legislation. Whatever was done was solely with the view of stimulating thought and

Primary Elections 43

argument of the measure upon its merits. From platform and pulpit, before agricultural societies, good government clubs, political clubs, debating societies, in the schoolhouses and public halls, wherever men were gathered together, the dangers which threaten representative government were discussed, the cause plainly traced to the selection of candidates by the bosses, the vital importance of election by the people by direct vote, and the necessary provisions of a primary law were fully and fairly presented. The press of the state, almost without exception, gave the subject editorial treatment from time to time, while the leading periodicals and magazines of the country, widely read by our people, devoted much space to its consideration. Hundreds of thousands of pamphlets and addresses presenting every phase of the issue and meeting the arguments and objections of the opposition were distributed throughout the state. The entire matter was thoroughly well understood. Indeed, so plainly were the provisions of the primary election bill outlined, so fully was the principle and its application discussed, so emphatically approved by the voters of Wisconsin in the last election, that the defeat of the bill is a plain violation of the principle upon which is based a "government of the people, by the people, and for the people." It was so overwhelmingly approved by the voters because they were everywhere ready for it. The machine had prepared the way. Not a county, not a community but had its boss and master, who in turn had his, higher up in the feudal system which then controlled the commonwealth. State officers and members of

the legislature were named by less than half a dozen
gentlemen equal in authority, absolutely at their
pleasure. Such was the sense of security which
unopposed power inspires, that nominations were
settled sometimes months in advance of conventions called merely to "ratify" the same. In state
conventions delegates were bribed to betray their
constituents by men who had held high official station. So brazen and reckless did their agents become in approaching decent men who spurned their
offers that good citizenship was everywhere ready
for open revolt. Representative government was
being practically undermined. The men were not
the candidates of the voters but of the machine.
The official was no longer the servant of the people,
but the abject tool of the men who fought the nomination and owned the official. These gentlemen
had from time to time manifested their power in
debauching legislation and their evil work is found
today in many statutes, affecting adversely the interests of every citizen of the state.

The remedy proposed—the nomination of all candidates by direct vote of the citizen—went straight
to the heart of the trouble. It brought the business
of choosing candidates back to the basic principle
of pure democratic government. It eliminated the
boss and the machine. It left no place for either.
It was a new declaration of independence. It proclaimed to the world that the people proposed to
take charge of the business of government for themselves. It was so manifestly right, so plainly necessary to rescue representative government from absolute overthrow by machine control, which is al-

ways minority control, that it quickly received the approval of the thoughful and patriotic citizenship of the state without respect to party alliance.

Clearly understanding the meaning and full scope of their action, each of the great political parties of the state—the Democrats in 1898 and the Republicans in 1900—adopted in their respective platforms, without qualification or limitation, the principle for the nomination of all candidates by direct vote of the people at a primary election, in lieu of nominations by delegates through the machinery of caucuses and conventions.

Platform Pledge Important

In every republic the laws are very certain to be made and administered by the representatives of some political party. It therefore becomes a question of deep concern to every citizen to determine with what party he will affiliate. This is all-important to him, and to guide him in deciding, political parties present their purposes and their promises to perform, in the declarations adopted as the party's pledge or platform. This is offered to the voter for his consideration.

Otherwise he cannot know for what kind of government he is casting his vote. It is a contract pure and simple. The party which adopts it, the candidate who accepts a nomination upon it, is solemnly bound by its obligations. If he is not in accord with it he has neither moral nor political right to be a candidate. To stand as the candidate of a party not agreeing with its platform, to solicit the suffrages of the citizen, and when elected to violate the promises of that platform is to cheat and betray the voter. It is an evasion unworthy of the grave character of this great question to say that the constituent trusts to the independent judgment of his representative. In those matters as to which the party and its representatives have been pledged he has no right afterward to set up an independent judgment. If he has independent opinions not in conformity with his party platform he should assert them before the party and the voter have accepted him as the representative of the principle embodied in the platform. As to those matters it is too late to talk of "independent judgment." That for which he stands—the declarations and promises of his party to the public—is a sacred public trust, and to its faithful execution as a man and public official he is in honor bound.

These observations are submitted because the consideration of legislation, to control in any way party nominations, embraces within its scope and emphasizes in a marked way the relation of political parties to government, of the citizen to his political party, and of the public official to his constituent, his party and the state. These relations and the obligations imposed must in matters of special importance be defined by platform declarations. This is even more imperative in state government where the issues are not political, in that sense which distinguishes where national politics are involved. In matters of national legislation and national administration political policies are expected to control. The issues are clearly defined on all the principal subjects of legislation. This would be generally true in the absence of platform declarations. The traditions of parties and the fundamental principles upon which they were organized point the way they are certain to go. For these reasons the voter does not feel bound to consider so critically the construction of the national platform of his party, unless there be incorporated in it some new and unorthodox party creed. But state legislation deals with the subjects of taxation, the maintenance and regulation of our system of jurisdiction, the support and care for the charitable and penal institutions, the nurture and development of our educational system, the regulation of banking and insurance, and other purely domestic affairs, where political division is impossible. Indeed, it may be said that substantially all state legislation is strictly nonpartisan in character. Hence, if political lines cannot be drawn in the legislature because the subjects of legislation are not political, then the voter cannot anticipate what action will follow the election of a given set of officials upon the matters in which he is most deeply interested, excepting as the candidates are committed in advance by pledges of the respective parties. It therefore becomes imperative that the proposed policies of state government should be clearly defined in platform declarations and fully presented to the people of the state, that they may decide by their sovereign voice what kind of state government they are to have, and in so far as practicable what laws are to be enacted and what general policies shall be pursued.

Veto Message, May 10, 1901.

Transfer of Power Weakens Authority

Compelling the citizen to hand his sovereign right, to vote directly for the candidates of his choice, over to some caucus delegate, to be turned over to some convention delegate to barter for something for himself, impairs the voter's right of suffrage, and its evil effects in representative government are more strikingly manifest in the actions of the public official than of the private citizen.

The official well understands that his nomination through delegates invariably is secured without the consent of a majority of the voters of his party, or indeed, without the consent of even a fair minority of his party. He well knows the value of the powerful influence of public-service corporations through the caucus and convention, and this knowledge bears strongly upon his official action. He reasons that under ordinary circumstances the unlimited use of money, the support of purchasable newspapers, the maintenance of perfect organization, all attainable through the vast resources of such corporations, will, under ordinary circumstances, enable him to succeed in politics.

No man can have witnessed the protracted struggle in this state to secure legislation equalizing the burdens of taxation, no man can have witnessed the defeat of bills increasing the taxation of the railroads to more nearly their justly proportionate share, and escape the conviction that the present method of selecting candidates for office is radically defective. It cannot be seriously doubted that under a system of nominations by direct vote of the people, their influence upon the official could not fail to be very much more pronounced and direct. He would well understand that in order to secure their approval and support to continue him in public life, he must win that approval upon the merit of his record in their service. He would know that every vote cast, every act as a representative in aid of measures or opposed to measures affecting the public interest, would be canvassed and reviewed when he came to seek re-nomination; hence, his record as a public official would be made day by day with that sense of personal responsibility, arising from a knowledge of direct and certain accountability to the people, pointing the way he should go.

This is the one thing needful in a republican form of government, and the one thing which cannot be dispensed with in any of the affairs of life where one man performs services for another. No trust would be safe, unless the trustee knew that he would be required to render an account of his stewardship to one having authority to terminate it. In no other trust positions are the opportunities for evading responsibility so many or the temptations for betrayal so great and the likelihood of confusing and befogging the issue so favorable as in the public service. Hence it is imperative that the trustee be required to account directly to those whom he represents in the discharge of his trust.

This is the fatal defect in the caucus and convention system of selecting candidates to be elected to office. Even if men chosen as delegates in the caucuses and conventions were never guilty of a wilful and corrupt betrayal of trust, if bargains and deals and bribery could be eliminated, nevertheless the entire plan should be abolished because it removes the nomination too far from the voter, the trustee too far from him for whom he bears the trust, the agent too far from the principal. Every transfer of delegated power weakens authority and diminishes responsibility until the candidate nominated represents nothing that the voter wanted, feels under no obligation to the voter for his nomination, nor is he directly accountable to him for his acts as a public official.

The momentous importance of discarding the delegate system and securing the personal responsibility of the official to the citizen is rapidly coming to be accepted through the country. Already legislation recognizing the principle of nominating by direct vote of the people has been applied in making nominations in a dozen different states, while the legislatures of twenty-two others have taken hold of the subject in an earnest way within the last two years. The demand for direct nominations was recognized in the platforms of both political parties in several states in the recent campaign, and the progressive movement is commanding strong support throughout the country.

Will of the People

To secure a more direct expression of the will of the people in all things pertaining to the people's government is the dominating thought in American politics today. The citizen will no longer surrender to delegate, agent, or substitute, any political control which he may properly exercise for himself.

He understands that in some matters pertaining to government he must be represented by a public servant. The citizen is resolved to participate directly wherever he can, and in all matters where he must be represented by another, to bring that representative as near to him as possible. The fundamental principle upon which this government was established can no longer be subverted. No more striking manifestation of this could be found than in the current volume of the Congressional Record. For the first time in history the house of representatives passed, without one dissenting vote, and sent to the senate a resolution for the election of United States senators by direct vote. The spirit of democracy is abroad in the land. Government is to be brought back to the people.

The nomination of all candidates by direct vote under the Australian ballot should appeal to the patriotism of all legislators and lift them above partisan and personal prejudice, in a united effort to give the people of Wisconsin a system of electing public officials truly representative of public interests: in restoring to the people in full measure this principle of pure democratic government. This is required particularly of republicans by every obligation which can be made binding upon the honor of the representatives of any political party in the public service.

The party itself will not fail. Men in masses are not drawn together in support of principles which endure the strain of protracted contest without fixed convictions. The party is the aggregation of citizens bound together by an agreement of opinion respecting the declared principles of the party. They are for maintaining the principles and keeping faith with one another. Fixed convictions are the foundations of good faith. The party honor is safe with the party. It will not betray itself.

But the party must select men as its medium of expression in government from the members of its organization and make them public officials to execute the will of the majority. Upon the public official then there falls the full weight of this double obligation. He represents the individual citizen in person. He is the custodian of the party honor. He cannot play fast and loose with clearly understood personal and party obligations and maintain a semblance of official integrity. He has no more moral right to quibble and evade, to say that he will perform a part and repudiate some of the specific promises of the party, than he would have to use in part trust funds committed to his keeping. If this be counted too exact a standard of public duty today, be sure that it will not be so regarded tomorrow. The citizen is being rapidly schooled by experience throughout the entire country, and is fast acquiring definite ideas of the right relation of the political party to government, of the citizen to his political party, and the duty of the public official to the citizen, to his party, and to the State.

Message to Legislature, 1903.

III
POLITICAL MACHINE AND THE BOSSES

Legitimate Organization and Machine Contrasted

TO enlist the interest of every individual, encourage research, stimulate discussion of measures and of men, prior to the time when the voter should discharge this primary duty of citizenship, offers political organization opportunity for the highest public service. Teaching the principles of the party, reviewing political history, discussing pending and proposed legislation, investigating the fitness of candidates for office, quickening the sense of obligation and personal responsibility in all the duties of citizenship, commanding the continuous, intelligent, personal interest of the individual voter —and when the campaign is on, conducting the canvass—these are the legitimate functions of political organization.

Such organizations cannot be used as political machines for individuals or factions. Whenever such organizations are maintained political slates are shattered and political bargains fail of consummation. Cliques, rings, machines, thrive upon the citizen's indifference to the plain duties of representative government.

There is no likeness or similitude between a political organization that appeals to every voter in the party and a machine that appeals only to the most skilled and unscrupulous workers of the party.

This is the modern political machine. It is impersonal, irresponsible, extra legal. The courts offer no redress for the rights it violates, the wrongs it inflicts. It is without conscience and without remorse. It has come to be enthroned in American politics. It rules caucuses, names delegates, appoints committees, dominates the councils of the party, dictates nominations, makes platforms, dispenses patronage, directs state administrations, controls legislatures, stifles opposition, punishes independence and elects United States senators. In the states where it is supreme, the edict of the machine is the only sound heard, and outside is easily mistaken for the voice of the people. If some particular platform pledge is necessary to the triumph of the hour, the platform is so written and the pledge violated without offering excuse or justification. If public opinion be roused to indignant protest, some scapegoat is put forward to suffer vicariously for the sins of the machine, and subsequently rewarded for his service by the emoluments of machine spoils. If popular revolt against the machine sweeps over the state on rare occasions and the machine finds itself hard pressed to maintain its hold on party organization, control conventions and nominate its candidates—when threats and promises fail—the "barrel" is not wanting and the way is cleared.

It is independent of the people, and fears no reckoning. In extreme cases where it becomes necessary to meet arraignment it has its own press to parry

The Machine and the Bosses

or soften the blow. Having no constituency to serve, it serves itself. The machine is its own master. It owes no obligation and acknowledges no responsibility. Its legislatures make the laws by its schedule. It names their committees. It suppresses bills inimical to its interests, behind the closed doors of its committee rooms. It suppresses debate by machine rule and the ready gavel of a pliant speaker. It exploits measures with reform titles, designed to perpetuate machine control. It cares for special interests and takes tribute from its willing subjects, the private corporations. There was a time when the corporation lobbyist was an important functionary, and the mercenary legislator a factor with whom it was necessary to make terms. The perfect political machine is fast superseding the lobbyist. The corporation now makes terms direct with the machine and the lobbyist now attends upon the legislature to look after details and spy upon the action of members.

It is as much the interest and as plainly the duty of the state, to as carefully perfect and guard a system of nominating candidates as it perfects and guards the system of electing them.

The reformation effected in our elections by the Australian voting system should inspire us with confidence in advancing the lines of attack. Recall for one moment the change wrought wherever the Australian system has been adopted. Formerly the polling place was the scene of wrangling, dispute, disorder, often of violence and collision; weak men were badgered, corrupt men were bought. The employer often followed his men to the ballot box, voting them in a body, and the political boss was always present. Today the voter, freed from all annoyances, all espionage, all intimidation, goes alone into the quiet of the election booth and exercises his right without fear of punishment or hope of reward, other than his own conscience affords and the general good secures. Here rich and poor, employer and employed, meet on the same level. That which had become mere theory under the old plan of voting is transformed into an assured fact under the new, and the state maintains in this place the equality of its citizens before the law.

Is there any good reason why a plan so successful in securing a free, honest ballot and fair count in the election, will not work equally well in the nomination of candidates?

Then every citizen will share equally in the nomination of the candidates of his party and attend primary elections, as a privilege as well as a duty. It will no longer be necessary to create an artificial interest in the general election to induce voters to attend. Intelligent, well-considered judgment will be substituted for unthinking enthusiasm, the lamp of reason for the torchlight. The voter will not require to be persuaded that he has an interest in the election. He will know that the nominations of the party will not be the result of "compromise," or impulse or vile design—the "barrel" and the machine—but the candidates of the majority honestly and fairly nominated.

To every generation some important work is committed. If this generation will destroy the political machine, will emancipate the majority from its enslavement, will again place the destinies of this nation in the hands of its citizens, then, "Under God, this government of the people, by the people and for the people shall not perish from the earth."

Address, "Menace of the Machine," Chicago University, February 22, 1897.

Iniquity of Secret Caucus

Mr. President, if the senate shall determine to make the precedent which the senator from New York seeks to raise here, it may take notice now that such a precedent will return many times to plague it hereafter.

I do not recognize, sir, the right of any senator here, directly or indirectly, to make against me the criticism that I am voting against my party because that vote is against the action of members of this senate regarding the public business in a secret meeting held in some place outside this chamber. I deny the right of any secret caucus held outside of the senate chamber behind closed doors, with no reporters present, to dispose of the public business or anything which may exercise an important or controlling influence upon the public business.

I regard the election of a president pro tempore of this great body as of great importance in the conduct of its business. It is of tremendous importance at times, Mr. President, in determining what measures shall pass this body. I do not propose to be read out of the republican party because I cannot conscientiously support some man whom a number

of my party associates have agreed upon in a secret meeting as their choice for president pro tempore of the senate.
Speech in U. S. Senate, 1911.

Platform Pledges Sacred

Platform pledges express the convictions of the party and are the inducements offered by the party for the votes of the people. They are the party's promise to do specific things. They are the voter's guide in determining with what party he will affiliate. They constitute a written contract deliberately entered into with every man who casts his vote for the candidate of his party. Neither the party nor the official representative of the party can with honor change or repudiate that contract. The candidate who is unwilling to be bound by the platform of the party has no moral or political right to accept a party nomination. If having accepted a nomination he finds that he is not in accord with the pledges of his party, if he cannot carry out its promises as an official, if he decides to be independent of platform obligation, he is then in honor bound so to announce, at once to withdraw as a party candidate and stand, if at all, upon his individual declaration as a candidate for office independent of party support.

These propositions require no argument. They are the unwritten but unchangeable law of political ethics. They enforce themselves between the candidate and the party, the official and the public.
Acceptance of Nomination for Governor, 1902.

The Machine Politician

The psychology of a certain type of machine politician is a most interesting study. It is characteristic of him to win if possible, but to appear to win in any event. He has a quick, almost prophetic eye for the loaded wagon. He has one rule: beat the opposition man, but if he cannot be beaten, support him. Claim credit for his victory, and at all hazards, keep in with the successful candidate. He believes that if he cannot get what he wants for himself by opposing a candidate, he may possibly succeed in getting what he wants by supporting him.

Never in my political life have I derived benefit from the two sources of power by which machine politics chiefly thrives—I mean patronage, the control of appointments to office, and the use of large sums of money in organization.

Autobiography, 1913.

Honesty in Politics

The politician cannot exist without absolute, unyielding, uncompromising honesty. The same high regard for right conduct which earns confidence in business and professional life commands like tribute in politics. There is no call to party or public service where it is wanting; there is no continued success where it is not held and cherished.

The politician and the statesman stand, the representative of this principle or that party, only so long as he stands erect in honor. One deviation, one relaxation, one bending of principle, and he falls, and falls forever. Nay, woe to him though he yield only to weakness, evincing the slightest want of moral discrimination! Under the scorching breath of public suspicion, a shining record of honor and integrity withers to dust and ashes. There is no escape, no appeal. His office is either a sacred trust or the poisoned shaft of Nesus. Vain the defense of personal friends, vain the previous clean public life! Hunted from his high place by a betrayed people, retribution soon closes his career and gives his name to the ensuing generation abhorred. No! No! politician or statesman, more than any other man, must he ever bend a "vaulting ambition" to meet the last exaction of the moral law.

Speech, House of Representatives,
March 25, 1886.

IV

TAXATION

Complete Valuation Essential

I RECOMMEND that you so legislate as to require the commission not only to have a general supervision of the system of taxation, but to take such measures as will enforce the provisions of law, that all property be placed on the assessment roll at the actual cash value; that it be required to institute proper proceedings enforcing penalties provided for public officers whose duties pertain to the assessment and collection of taxes, and against individuals and the officers of corporations failing to comply with the provisions of the law with respect to the disclosure of property for assessment; to prefer charges for the removal from office of any assessor who has violated the law respecting assessment, and, in the prosecution of the same, authorize the commissioner to call upon the attorney general or any district attorney of the state to prosecute any violation of the law respecting the assessment and collection of taxes; to visit, through some members of the commission, each county in the state, personally, and investigate the work of assessors, with authority to summon the assessors of the county to appear before such commission, or any member thereof, and to submit to examination respecting the performance of their duties as such

assessors; to have full power and authority to take testimony and examine individuals and officers of corporations, and require the production of books and papers; and where the offices and books and papers and any of the witnesses are located outside the state, whenever necessary, to be empowered to take deposition in order to procure such information as may be useful either in enforcing the law or in enabling the commission to recommend legislation; to examine upon their own motion, or upon the information of any individual, into any complaint as to property liable to taxation that has not been assessed, or has been improperly assessed, or to take such proceedings as will insure its assessment under the law, whether such property be owned by an individual, a co-partnership or corporation.

Message to Legislature, 1901.

Equal Taxation Fundamental

Uniformity of valuation lies at the foundation of equal taxation as between individuals and localities, and a complete listing of all taxable property is not less essential.

No student of the subject, however, is unmindful of the difficulties encountered in the administration of laws to secure the direct taxation of all intangible property. While the subject is not a new one, thoroughgoing, scientific investigation of it conjoined with practical test has still a wide field to explore.

The question of railway taxation is a practical one and it is expected that as public officials we will

Taxation 63

deal with it in a practical way. As men of experience, some of you men experienced in legislation, you will understand, as the public likewise understands, the opposition which has been made by the railroad companies, to any increase in their taxes. It is a matter of common knowledge among those who have encountered the railroad lobby that this opposition was so determined as to announce the declared purpose of the railway companies to increase their freight rates enough to offset any increase in taxation. The ease with which this menace might be enforced can very readily be seen. An increase in the fraction of a per cent, in freight rates, or a slight readjustment of the classifications, would enable railroads to collect from their patrons in Wisconsin more than enough to balance any increase in their taxes.

Indeed, since legislation has been pending in this state to require railroads to pay their proportionate share of taxation, freight rates for Wisconsin have been increased, indicating a forehanded determination to be prepared against legislation to equalize taxation.

It becomes apparent at once that legislation compelling the railroads, and other public-service corporations, to pay their proportionate share of the taxes will fail utterly in its object unless it be supplemented with legislation protecting the public against increased transportation charges.

This is not a question of policy. The railroad companies of this state owe the state more than $1,000,000 a year. For many years, because of the postponement or defeat of legislation requiring them to pay their proportionate share of the taxes, the other taxpayers of Wisconsin have paid for them $1,000,000 annually. The case has been tried; the hearing has been full. Judgment has been given again and again. Pledges have been made by political parties and repeated by candidates for office, over and over again. The question is not an open one. There is no opportunity for misunderstanding. There is no room for speculation. The truth is ascertained. The truth is known. It is lodged in the public mind to stay. The people want $1,000,000 a year because it is the sum owing. They are not to be wheedled by any soft phrases about "conservation." There is nothing to compromise. Equal and just taxation is a fundamental principle of republican government. The amount due as taxes from railroads and other public-service corporations should be paid, and paid in full, and I am confident that legislation to secure that payment will be promptly enacted.

Message to Legislature, 1903.

Dog Tax Discrimination

I return herewith, without approval, bill No. 267, originating in the assembly, entitled, "An act to provide for licensing dogs and for the collection of said license."

The bill proposes to exact a license fee of from one to three dollars from every owner or keeper of a dog. Residents of cities and villages can escape payment of such a tax by ceasing to own or keep dogs. Upon the farm, however, the watch dog and shepherd are as much a necessity as the other domestic animals which they protect and guard, and the license fee would amount to an increase in taxation. The fee or tax proposed may not be esteemed by the legislature a serious burden in itself, but it would add to burdens borne by a great majority of the people which are already out of all proportion to those borne by others whose influence would seem to be more potent in shaping legislation.

For many years there has been a well-settled belief in the minds of a great majority of people of this state that quasi-public corporations were paying less than a fair share of the taxes necessary to maintain government. That belief was fortified by the absolute knowledge that certain corporations were not taxed at all, and that certain other corporations were paying but a nominal tax in the form of a license fee. In 1898 this belief had become a conviction in the public mind so strong that it found clear and emphatic expression in each of the platforms of the political parties of this state, and the legislature of 1899 assembled under a solemn pledge to equalize the burdens of taxation. The corporations not taxed resisted taxation in any form. The corporations then paying taxes in the form of license fees opposed any increase. It is a matter of legislative history that after the enactment of the express company, life insurance and sleeping-car legislation, and after passing through the assembly a bill increasing the rate of the license fee on railroads from four to five per centum upon their gross earnings, which was defeated in the senate, the entire subject was committed to a tax commission created by a bill originating in the senate. That bill was passed under the pretext that the pressing work of legislative sessions prevented members and senators from giving the subject that thoroughness of investigation which would insure fairness to every interest, and for that reason the people of this state acquiesced in the establishment of the commission to determine the rights and duties of all respecting taxation. Thus this question, of great and pressing interest to every citizen, was placed in the hands of the able gentlemen comprising the tax commission two years ago, and the public was required to wait upon their decision. The disappointment incident to the further delay was borne with patience by the people, upon whom fell the added burden occasioned by the creation of these new offices. They assented, however, to the postponement which this plan necessitated, because, and only because, they were assured and persuaded to believe that the report of the tax commission would settle the disputed question. They submitted without a murmur to the increased taxation necessary to pay the Commission to do its work, believing that those who offered this solution of the controversy were acting in good faith. They had been promised equal and just taxation for years, and had borne repeated disappointments and delays in the fulfillment of those promises with great fortitude. They agreed to this form of legislative arbitration, confident that the right would prevail because they demanded nothing more than just and equal taxation for all. They were led to believe that when the disinterested gentlemen comprising that commission determined the questions and made their rec-

Taxation 67

ommendations to the legislature, action would follow in accordance therewith.

After long continued arduous labor and research, the tax commission reported to this legislature that there do exist gross inequalities in the tax burden placed upon the different classes of property in this state, and they made clear and definite recommendations for a better equalization of these burdens.

The proposition of the tax commission, like its statistics, are too plain and simple to permit misunderstanding or doubt in intelligent minds which give them consideration. They cannot be obscured by a selfish plea that property which can be reached by the tax gatherers should be allowed to escape a part of its just share of the cost of government, at the expense of property now paying a still greater share, until that very uncertain and remote time when campaign promises and legislative procrastination conjoined will result in bringing hidden and intangible property within reach of the tax officers. Nor is it probable that a majority of the people of Wisconsin can be satisfied by framing appropriation bills in accord with the theory that citizens will bear the imposition of unjust and unequal taxation so long as the increase in their burden is made to appear to be due to the betterment and support of the public schools. When the taxpayer comes to compute profit and loss it cannot change the result because the increase in his taxes, caused by neglect properly to tax powerful corporate interests, comes through a bill making increased appropriations for common schools.

The tax commission has formulated and presented to you bills which would increase the state's revenues from railroad companies, street railway companies and from telephone companies. These bills are still pending before the legislature, or its committees. The commission has presented facts and reasons which have not been discredited, showing that the increases proposed in these several bills would impose less than the full share of taxes due from such companies in comparison with the tax charges imposed upon the property and individuals carried upon the tax rolls of the state.

I am aware that members of the legislature are desirous of an adjournment of this session at the earliest possible day, but I am very certain that the people of this state are more anxious for an approximately equitable distribution of the tax burden, even if the session should be protracted thereby.

For the reasons herein stated, I am unwilling to present to the people of this state, in lieu of the legislation to equalize taxation which has been promised to them, and which they have a right to expect from representative government, a scheme which, in a general way, may be described as an act to relieve the farmer or city home-owner of a small measure of increased tax upon his realty by imposing a license fee upon his dog.

Veto Message, May 2, 1901.

Ad Valorem Tax Most Just

The license fee system if fairly adjusted as between railroads and other taxable property of the state today upon an agreed percentage would fur-

Taxation

nish no assurance of a fair division of tax burden a year hence. Conditions arise from time to time in the commonwealth requiring an increase in the rate upon taxable property. At such times property taxed under the ad valorem system must bear all of the increased burden, while the percentage upon which the license fee is based remains the same. No valid reason can be assigned why railroad property, remunerative as it is, its value increasing with the development and growth of the state, should not bear its relative proportion of whatever befalls other property by reason of increases in taxation to meet emergencies and exigencies that come in the ordinary course of human events.

Legislative appropriations from year to year are increased as the expansion and development of the state create proper and unanswerable demands therefor. Public buildings for properly housing and caring for the state's dependents, its criminal classes, its schools, and courts, and university, must be erected, renewed and enlarged repeatedly. It is but just that railroad property should bear its share of such appropriations.

The railroad companies under the license fee system have no interest and no concern respecting the money appropriated by the legislature. It is a fact within the knowledge of every legislator of experience that the influence of the railroad lobby is often employed to pass legislation resulting in an increase of general taxes in exchange for the votes of those interested in such appropriations to defeat other legislation obnoxious to the railroads. Doubtless millions of dollars have been unnecessarily expended through such combinations. This could not have occurred if the railroads had been taxed under the ad valorem system and possessed the same general interest that other taxpayers have in keeping appropriations within reasonable limits.

But in addition to all of the other objections to the license fee system, when it is remembered that they are permitted in effect to fix the amount of the taxes which they will pay, without any practical check or supervision by the state, no excuse or justification can be given for continuing a plan of taxation so unjust to other taxpayers of the state. Investigations which have been conducted by the interstate commerce commission in the courts leave no room to doubt that millions of dollars are paid back to shippers in rebates under arrangements deemed advantageous, directly and indirectly, to both the railroads and the favored shippers. That these rebates in Wisconsin alone amount to vast sums of money annually is beyond dispute. Not one dollar of this sum rebated to shippers, and properly a part of the gross earnings of railroad companies, is reported to the state. That a valid claim exists against the railroad companies for the amounts so withheld from their reported earnings, does not admit of question, whatever difficulties lie in the way of making proof of the same. I do not believe that you will fail to follow the recommendations of the tax commission and abandon a system of taxation so obnoxious to every principle of fairness to those who must maintain government.

Message to Legislature, 1903.

Taxation

Results of Ad Valorem Tax

The regulation bill did not pass at that session, (1903) nor did we expect it to pass. But the contest accomplished the purposes we had chiefly in mind. It stirred the people of the state as they had never been stirred before, and laid the foundations for an irresistible campaign in 1904. It also gave the lobby so much to do—as we had anticipated—that it could not spend any time in resisting our measures for railroad taxation. It also forced some members of the legislature who were really opposed to us, and who intended to vote against the regulation bill, to vote with us on the taxation bill as a bid for the favor of the people of their districts

So, at last, after all these years of struggle, we wrote our railroad tax legislation into the statutes of Wisconsin. As an immediate result, railroad taxes were increased more than $600,000 annually. When I came into the governor's office, on January 1, 1901, the state was in debt $330,000 and had only $4,125 in the general fund. But so great were the receipts from our new corporation taxes, and from certain other sources, that in four years' time, on January 1, 1905, we had paid off all our indebtedness and had in the general fund of the treasury $407,506. We had so much on hand, indeed, that we found it unnecessary to raise any taxes for the succeeding two years.

Autobiography, 1913.

V

RAILROAD REGULATION AND GOVERNMENT OWNERSHIP

Railroad Commission a Necessity

HE duty which confronts this legislature respecting this phase of railroad legislation is two-fold: First, to enact a law creating a state railway commission with full authority to act in the premises, and second, to so advise the representatives of Wisconsin in the United States senate and house of representatives by memorial, and in such other ways as may tend to impress them with this importance, that the business interests of Wisconsin demand that the oft-repeated appeal of the inter-state commerce commission, supported as it has been by the messages of the president, for authority to regulate rates and prevent discriminations' should be promptly given to the inter-state commerce commission.

Upon the necessity of the establishment of a commission to protect the shipping interests of Wisconsin, there would seem to.be no need of argument. The rates in themselves make the demand stronger than any form of words can express it. It must come, and it ought to be the care of those charged with the responsibility of making the law, that Wisconsin should not be compelled to travel

Railroad Control

over the same ground, by the same devious and circuitous route which the resisting railroad companies have compelled other states to take. We should in this, as in all other matters, secure the benefits and advantages accruing from the ripe experience of other states and step out abreast of those enjoying benefits derived from many years of experience. And if in any respect it is possible for us to improve upon the legislation of any state by combining the best factors, or improving upon the systems of all, it is our duty so to do.

By providing that the commissioner of railroads elected under the existing laws shall be a member of a state commission, and that at the expiration of his present term of office, the elective member of the commission shall be elected for a term of six years, and by further providing that the two remaining members of the board shall be appointive officers, appointed by the executive, subject to confirmation by the senate, the terms of the two appointed commissioners to expire in two and four years respectively, and thereafter that their successors shall be appointed for terms of six years each, would give to the state a commission to fix rates, combining the elective and appointive features, in support of which the strongest reasons can be urged.

It would scarcely be possible for the law-making power of the state under a representative form of government to be more strongly obligated than is the law-making power of Wisconsin to write upon the statute books at this session of the legislature the necessary laws to secure the payment of taxes in full due from the railroad corporations to this state. The railroad companies have by their own opposition made legislation for the establishment of a commission to regulate transportation rates a necessary concomitant of tax legislation, and added to this, investigation of existing transportation charges in Wisconsin has disclosed conditions making the appointment of a commission to regulate railroad rates an imperative necessity in the interests of the whole commonwealth. That these conditions have existed, as it cannot be doubted that they have, throughout many years but strengthens and makes more irresistible the demands for prompt action in accordance with the dictates of absolute justice and fair dealing as between these corporations and the people. It is not a case where some fatwitted genius may find a happy medium. It stands side by side with the people's cause for equal and just taxation, out in the open, clear as the sun at noonday.

Justice Must Apply to All Alike

For many years with each recurring legislative session it has been the comforting assurance conveyed to the people of this commonwealth that the relations existing between the people and the railroads were "pleasant" and "harmonious." It would indeed have been cause for congratulation had it been a fact that those relations were grounded upon conditions that were just to the people and the railroads alike. But if the people of Wisconsin are to pay a million dollars of railroad taxes annually in order to maintain pleasant relations with these

Railroad Control

companies, and if they are also to pay many millions of dollars a year in transportation charges more than other States pay for like service for the continuation of harmonious conditions agreeable to the railways, then it is high time that the people of Wisconsin see to it that instead of "pleasant" and "harmonious" relations of that character, there should be established sound business relations based upon business principles of exact justice to public-service corporations and the citizens as well.

We know from the experience in other states, we have learned the lesson in a way to remember here in Wisconsin, that these measures cannot be secured without encountering the most vigorous opposition from the railroad interests. It may be quite as well for us to be admonished at this time that opposition to the establishment of a commission to regulate transportation rates will not be limited to the corporation and their lobby agents before the legislature. They will be able to summon to their support every shipper in Wisconsin who is, or who thinks he is, at this time receiving some special favor or concession from the railroads, or who has, or thinks he has, assurance which will give him exceptional rates and advantages over his rivals and competitors in business for the future. The shippers will be able through organized effort to make their influence felt as a commanding one, but it is well for us to remember that we stand here representing the interests of all the people of Wisconsin, the thousands of merchants and manufacturers who are not receiving special rates and concessions, and the hundreds of thousands of producers and

small shippers who are being grossly wronged in
the millions of dollars exacted from them in excessive
and exorbitant transportation charges, year
after year.

They are entitled to an equal chance with the
merchants and manufacturers and farmers of adjoining
States. I submit that it is our duty to secure
this for them and to secure it now.

Message to Legislature, 1903.

Granger Legislation and Railway Regulation

The Potter law was repealed in the early part
of 1876, after having been in force less than two
years. The reasons for this are not far to seek.
The law, as explained, was the subject of constant
attack. It was lied about early and late.
Newspapers were more influential then than they
are now in Wisconsin. In consequence of the
constant assaults upon the law, many came to the
conclusion that it was really bad. They reasoned
that where there was so much smoke, ther must be
some fire. Some reaction always follows every successful
achievement, and the railroads relied upon
the usual abatement of interest. The public having
seen to it that the laws were placed upon the statute
books, felt that its responsibility had been discharged,
and in security turned its attention to private
affairs. With the people generally, the question
was taken to be settled. Furthermore, as the
railroads were not observing the law, many of the
worst abuses continued. This also had its effect,
and caused disappointment on the part of many who
had otherwise been hearty supporters of the prin-

ciple. The railroads took advantage of this situation, and in the preceding election, with men active in every assembly and senatorial district they were able to elect members who favored the repeal of the statute. Accordingly, the present commissioner system was substituted for the Potter law.

The repeal of the Potter law is now generally regarded as a mistake by the best modern writers on the railway problem. It has at last dawned upon them and others that the law was just, and that, above all, it was a step in the right direction. It did not do away with discriminations. But this was because the roads declined to observe the law, and because adequate machinery for its enforcement had not been provided. The practice of discriminations against both persons and places had already become so firmly rooted in the policy of the roads, that nothing but the most vigorous sort of enforcement by the best men, and the most stringent of laws could have abolished it. To expect that this power, so dear to the officers of the roads, could be taken from them by simply making it illegal, was irrational. More than this is required. Discrimination will never be abolished until the state takes complete control of the rate-making power.

But even if the Potter law did not accomplish all that was expected of it, it taught railway managers many useful lessons. They learned for the first time that there was a higher authority. This law also brought the question before the courts, and by the decisions that followed, all doubt was forever removed as to the authority of the state to fix rates and exercise control over the railroads. This alone was probably worth many times more to the people than the cost of the movement.

A law such as that adopted at the last session of the legislature, providing for assessing the property of railroads in Wisconsin at full value, and taxing them upon that value at the same rate which other taxable property in the state bears, and thus compelling them to pay from ten to twelve hundred thousand dollars additional taxes, would be of little value to the state if the railroad companies are at liberty to add enough to the freight rates paid by the people of Wisconsin to compensate them for the ten or twelve hundred thousand of dollars of additional taxes. That they could readily increase the freight charges upon the producers and consumers of Wisconsin without let or hindrance under existing law, no man will for one moment dispute. That this would be the course which they would pursue, if not prevented by additional legislation, was openly threatened by their lobbyists during the legislative session of 1901.

Railroads Fight Freight Reductions

Therefore the people of this state must either tamely submit, and allow the railroad companies to go untaxed to the amount of a million or more annually, or provide against their regulating freight charges within this state at their pleasure, regardless of public interest and public justice.

That for several years, and until very recently, freight rates have been gradually advanced in this state, every student of the subject well knows. That it was the fixed intention of the railroad of-

Railroad Control

ficials controlling traffic rates in this state to make advances until less than a year ago, there is unmistakable proof. When submitting their bids to the state board of control for furnishing coal to the state institutions of Wisconsin less than a year ago, coal dealers were warned directly from the railroad offices to submit their bids conditioned upon an increase in freight charges. And the bids were submitted subject to variation with reference to freight charges. This was the first time that such an intimation had been received by the coal dealers bidding for state business, and the first time that such bids were ever made in that form.

The attention of the legislature was directed to that fact by special message, which I submitted, and the recommendation was made that if no law could be passed creating a railway commission with authority to reduce rates generally in Wisconsin to a reasonable basis, at least the legislature ought, in fairness to the people and to protect them against increased transportation charges as an offset by the railroads against increased taxation of their property, to pass a law prohibiting the possibility of such advance being made.

The attorneys and lobbyists of these railroads had previously placed themselves on record before that same legislature, while opposing the establishment of a commission to reduce transportation charges, as being satisfied with existing rates. They further protested before legislative committees that no advance was contemplated in Wisconsin. It nevertheless is true that immediately following the presentation of the message recommending a law prohibiting any increase in freight charges, there was, within twenty-four hours, sent from the general freight departments in Chicago of the principal railroads in Wisconsin, telegrams to their agents along their lines in this state directing them to cause local merchants and shippers to sign telegrams addressed to their assemblymen to vote down the measure recommended by the governor.

Publicity Spoils Sinister Game

If they contemplated no increase in transportation charges why, then, did they warn the coal dealers bidding for the large coal business of the state? Why, then, did their attorneys and lobbyists oppose the passage of a bill that merely would have prevented such an increase? Why, then, did they summon all of their station agents in this state to cause the local merchants and shippers at each station to flood the legislature with telegrams protesting against the measure designed to save those shippers and merchants from paying increased freight charges?

Aye, but, says the leading organ of the corporations of this state, with all the croaking from the executive office, warning the people that their transportation charges would be increased, no increases have been made and nearly a year has gone by.

I answer that it would have been strange, indeed, after their plans had been exposed, after their secret warnings to their shippers have been made the subject of executive message, after the telegrams which they had sent to their station agents throughout Wisconsin had leaked out and been printed in full, after every citizen of the state had been warned and made vigilant and every shipper was alert for the advances, with another legislative session approaching and the question still pending, it would have been strange indeed if the managers of these interests should have taken the chance of being detected in sliding up the scale of rates in Wisconsin.

In fact, there are some evidences of these corporations being temporarily on their good behavior, and of their bearing just at this opportune time fruits meet for repentance. But, as will appear, I think, upon investigation and reflection, there is likewise special reason for this, and small hope to believe that the fruitage will be either a large or a steady crop.

I am persuaded to believe that with the information already before the people of this state upon the subject bearing on the control of railway transportation; with the clear knowledge they now have of the injustice which they have suffered for many years in the matter of railway taxation; remembering that these corporations away back in 1899 publicly promised before the legislature that if a bill to investigate the subject by a commission were passed instead of the bill to increase their taxes, they would pay promptly whatever was found to be due upon the report of that commission; with the memory of their obstruction, delay, and defeat of taxation measures based upon and designed to carry out the recommendations of that commission, which they asked to have created at public expense, fresh in the public mind; with the assurance made doubly certain by their past record, that they will contest the assessment which the tax commission is now engaged in making and carry it to the supreme court for its decision;—I say, knowing all these things, I do not believe that the people of Wisconsin will be misled or befooled by any plea, however, specious or plausible or conciliatory, coming from those whose record marks them as hostile to the interests of the taxpayers of this state.

If the work of the years that have recently passed is not to be wasted, if the large sums of money already spent on investigations pertaining to taxation shall not be squandered, if the producers and consumers of Wisconsin are to be saved from paying a million dollars of additional taxes for the railroads in the form of higher freight rates whenever the railroads deem it safe to increase these rates, then it will be because, and only because a railway commission, with full power to control freight rates, stands between the railroads and the people of Wisconsin.

Speech at Milton Junction, on "Granger Legislation," January 29, 1904.

Granger Regulation not Destructive

Any review or consideration of government regulation of railway transportation must deal with state and federal regulation, in a measure, independently. The states were years in advance of the nation in moving for control of railway services and railway rates. As Wisconsin, Illinois, Iowa and Minnesota led in broadly asserting the right of the state legislature to control transportation rates and services, a consideration of the results attained in these states is important and necessary to an intelligent understanding of the whole subject.

In the early '70's these states enacted legislation for the regulation of railroad transportation. The legislation was then designated, and will for all time be known as "Granger Legislation." The granger statutes were at that time and have ever since been violently denounced as radical, revolutionary, and a hindrance to the development and prosperity of the country. And yet the granger legislation in those four states of the Old Northwest was simply a protest of a conservative and law-abiding people in the name of the law, against a railroad management which violated the rights of individuals without pretense of excuse or justification.

The granger statutes were far from perfect, especially in respect to provisions for their enforcement. But they were essentially correct in principle and reasonable in their terms, so far as the railroads were concerned, and in so far as they sought to regulate services and rates between the public and the public-service corporations. They were in no sense "an unwarranted and irrational interference with the laws of trade and economic conditions." They simply applied a principle as old as the common law. They were enacted with the purpose of enforcing just and equitable rates to individuals and communities. They expressed in legislation an effort to escape from arbitrary and tyrannical control on the part of common carriers.

This was the first great struggle between the railroads and the public to determine which should be master. It was a battle royal, and established as the law of this country the right of the people through legislation to regulate transportation charges upon the railroads of the land.

The ability with which the railroads conducted their opposition to the granger legislation is interesting and instructive at this time. It was an indication of their sincerity and a measure of the value of their representations with respect to the disaster to the railway business and the industrial interests of the country, which they assert is certain to follow the legislation now proposed in some of the states for state regulation, and in congress for an enlargement of the powers of the interstate commerce commission, as demanded by the people, and suggested by the president in his recent message to congress.

Alarmist Predictions Not Borne Out

Upon the enactment of the granger laws, harrowing accounts of "Railroad Construction at a Standstill," of the "Collapse of Railroad Business," the "Spoliation and Ruin of Railway Property," and the "Checking of All Development in the Granger States" were published and re-published as the dire and awful consequences following as a logical result of that legislation.

From the enactment of the law in Wisconsin until its repeal, two years later, when the railroads regained control of the legislature, and long after, the highest talent which money could command was employed in assailing the Wisconsin law, and the laws passed in Illinois, Iowa and Minnesota, as well, and in misrepresenting the effect of the legislation upon railway and all other business within the state. Reports as to the financial condition of the roads were suppressed or destroyed, and the corporations caused to be published broadcast that not only had their business fallen off, but that they had been obliged to suspend all construction and improvements, and that even maintenance of existing lines was threatened, while the railroad business, and all other business dependent upon it, was prostrate and languishing in consequence of the legislation which "violated all the laws of trade."

Even economic writers of eminence and fairness of purpose accepting the railroad figures then put forth and the railroad conditions then reported by the companies, were misled into partisan and violent denunciation of granger legislation. In all of the criticism and attack made at the time, and since, it seems almost incredible that no independent investigation should have been made by any of the writers dealing with this subject. This is especially true of those whose criticisms should have been based upon thoroughgoing and critical study, in conformity with the character of the work then and afterwards turned out by them as authors and writers upon economic subjects. Strangely enough, it is manifest that their argument was based upon false premises furnished, and misleading statements published by the interested railroad authorities. In so far as my research extends, I have been unable to find that any one of them ever made an independent, critical analysis of the facts involved.

Notwithstanding all that has been written and the authorities which may be quoted to the contrary, I venture here to declare that, in so far as the granger laws were enforced in either of the four states, they were helpful and not harmful to the interests of the state and of its citizens and of the railway companies as well.

Speech, Milton Junction, Wisconsin, 1904.

Government Control Vital

No power other than the government itself is equal to that of these industrial combinations always in close association, and often identified in interest, with railroad and transportation companies. Their tremendous political influence is shown by the mere recital of the history of the interstate commerce act, and by an examination of the records of congress for the last seven years. Which has had the stronger hold upon the state and national legislation during the last twenty years, the corporations or the people? Whose interests have been the more safely guarded? Where is the power lodged which has for seven years been strong enough to bar national legislation, designed to enlarge the powers of the interstate commerce commission? It is not necessary to charge venality anywhere, but that the public-service corporations have been steadily undermining representative government in national, state and municipal legislation, no thoughtful man can question. They come between the people, and the chosen representatives of the people.

I would in no wise disparage either the rights or the interests of the railroad side of this legislation.

The question is one of very great magnitude. The amount of property involved is very large. The owners of railroads, and the holders of railroad securities must be protected in all of their rights. They must not be wronged in any way. They are entitled to such remuneration as will enable them to maintain their roads in perfect condition, pay the best of wages to employees, meet all other expenses incident to operation, and in addition thereto enough more to make a reasonable profit upon every dollar invested in the business. To preserve all of these rights, they are entitled to the strongest protection which the law can afford.

But the public, each community, and every individual, has rights equally precious. Upon the railway companies rendering an adequate and impartial service at reasonable rates, all general prosperity is dependent. Deprived of either, every community is checked and limited in its growth; every business of whatever nature must languish and fail. The denial of an impartial service at reasonable rates, is the denial of equal opportunity, the denial of a· square deal.

Message to Legislature, 1904.

Must Control Railroads

Let it be remembered that the plan developed and consummated in building up the anthracite coal trust, the grain trust and the meat trust is indicative of the power of the railroads in combinations. There is not an important trust in the United States which does not have the assistance of the railroads in destroying its competitors in business. The limitation and control of these public-service corporations within their legitimate field as common carriers is of primary importance in the practical solution of the trust problem which confronts the people of this country. It is manifest that any trust legislation to be effective must go hand in hand with a control over railway rates by the federal government on interstate commerce, through an enlargement of the powers of the interstate commerce commission, and a like control of railway rates on state commerce by each of the states through a state commission. Added to this, the railroad companies must be prohibited from using the extraordinary powers conferred upon them by the state for any other purpose than conducting efficiently and impartially the transportation business for which they were organized.

When we consider the magnitude of the railroad question and the industrial question, and their combined influence upon industrial and political independence, it becomes apparent that it is impossible to overstate or exaggerate the dangers with which we are menaced. These great combinations of wealth, owning most of the natural produce of the earth, controlling what they do not own, created and nourished by the railways and in combination with them, are already making their powerful influence felt in municipal, state, and national legislation. More than all other national questions with which we have to deal should this question be placed above party consideration. The sentiment of the American people is unanimous that it should be solved, not in any spirit of blind, irrational prejudice, but with an enlightened public policy that employs all the power lodged in state and federal government against the wrongful usurpation of the rights of the people.

"Railway Regulation," 1904.

Carriers Have But One Duty

Whenever and wherever persons engage in the business of public carrying the law says to them: "You must provide efficient service, you must be fair and impartial, your charges must be just and reasonable. Your legitimate function is transportation. In your capacity as a public servant, you must know nothing of persons, things, or places. You are legally bound to treat all alike. Discrimination and favoritism are forbidden."

While it has been commonly understood that the railways of the country have overridden law, and, in a measure, controlled legislation, it is doubtful whether any considerable number of the people of Wisconsin have until very recently had any conception of the enormity of the wrong which they have suffered in discriminating rates at the hands of railroads through this Commonwealth.

Railroad transportation is a tax upon the commerce of the country. It is a tax from which no one can escape. Every producer, every consumer, every man who buys, every man who sells, must pay railroad transportation. It pervades every phase of our existence; it is a part of every hour of our daily life. It is an important element in the cost of our clothing, our food, our fuel. It is a tax upon that which nourishes our intellectual and spiritual life as well, the books we read, the schools and churches we build. It adds materially to the price of everything we purchase. Each article of manufacture, every pound of butter and cheese, or pork and beef, every produce of the soil, must pay its part of the forty-five millions and more that constitute the gross amount paid as transportation charges to the railroads of Wisconsin every twelve months.

How essential it is that this tax imposed by the railroads should be fairly and justly levied. It must be just and reasonable in amount. It should be justly and fairly distributed. Each individual, every class of business, and every town, city, and section of the state is entitled to equitable transportation charges under a system which shall be open to public inspection and controlled by public justice instead of private interest.

Message to Legislature, Jan. 15, 1903.

Evils of Discrimination

No man, no body of men, wrongfully amassing riches out of the toil and savings of others, ever willingly relinquished such tribute, no matter how unjustly levied. Throughout history the struggle has continued between the few, vigilant, aggressive, persistent, well organized, rich, and powerful, and the many, unorganized, though strong in individual numbers, and irresistible in concerted and continuous effort. The long possession of any power or source of gain, no matter how unjustly and unlawfully acquired or exercised, comes sooner or later to be regarded as rightfully belonging to the possessor, whose indignation is at once aroused against the man or the laws compelling the surrender of such power or source of gain. Legislation designed to require men and corporations to pay a just share of the taxes in support of government is declared to be persecution. Argument and recommendation in plain, direct language in support of such legislation is denounced as violent and revolutionary. The presentation of evidence proving indefensible and unjust discrimination in the performance of a service to the public by a common carrier under every obligation to deal with all alike,—a discrimination so unjust and so sweeping as to amount to a wrong against all the people of a great commonwealth,— the proof of this to the legislature and the public is decried as tending and intended to arouse prejudice and is complained of most bitterly as radical and populistic.

There is an aphorism, the truth of which has long been accepted; that no member of that class which has always found difficulty in distinguishing as to the ownership of property, "e'er felt the halter draw with good opinion of the law"—or of the advocate of the law.

Special Message to Legislature on State Regulation of Railroad Rates, April 29, 1903.

Regulation a Duty

The government has a duty to perform in the regulation and control of railway transportation, because the service is a public service and essentially a function of government. But there are other reasons.

The railway corporation is a natural monopoly. Its lines once established in a given territory naturally excludes other capital from investment in a field which it covers. People living along its line, and in the country tributary to it, must market their products and receive their supplies over its road. They have no choice. The government had empowered the railway company to take their land on which it has built its road. They must accept their services, or they must "walk." The government has placed the corporation in a position where, uncontrolled, it can tyrannize over individuals and entire communities. It is therefore bound to protect them against any wrong or injustice at the hands of its creatures. Nay, more, the government is under obligation to see to it that the corporation performs its full duty to all persons and all places, efficiently, impartially and upon reasonable terms. The government cannot divest itself of this responsibility. One of the ablest of the United States Supreme Court judges, speaking for that court, said:

> "But a superintending power over the highways and the charges imposed upon the public, for their use, have always remained in the government. This is not only its indefeasible right, but it is necessary for the protection of the people against extortion and abuse."

The duty which the state owes to protect the commerce of the state, the federal government owes to protect the commerce of the country.

Message, Railroad Regulation, 1904.

Railroad Control 93

Wages and Rates

Whenever the public complains that rates are unjustly increased, we are at once told in sweeping, though somewhat indefinite way that the advances have been made to meet increased expenses and higher wages paid to employees. The corporations well understand the public regard for all the men employed in this hazardous calling, and that such an explanation will go a long way to quiet criticism. It is true that material is somewhat higher. It is likewise true that the companies are paying higher wages or rather higher salaries. The total wages paid by the roads of late years have increased, owing mostly to the increase in the number of men employed to handle the traffic or business. But the total wages per mile of road from 1897 to 1902 did not increase over 32 per cent which is a much lower ratio of increase than the increase in both gross and net earnings.

Message, Railroad Regulation, 1904.

Ownership As Alternative

(Note: The following interview with Senator La Follette is taken from an unpublished work dealing with the reform movement in Wisconsin:)

About the time that La Follette was first elected governor he was visited by a man who had stumped the west for the people's party and who had been one of the "intellectuals" in the first Oregon movement in the 90's. Said the visitor: "Our movement has gone down; I am a man without a party."

"The time for great souls is when all is lost," said La Follette; "You belong with us."

"But I believe in the initiative and referendum. Can I be a republican and hold such views?"

"You can; I believe in them myself."

"I am also for the popular election of senators."

"So am I," said La Follette.

"I also favor government ownership and control of railroads."

"We may have to come to that; but we must first obtain and try regulation. If that fails the people will no doubt take over the common carriers."

"But I am against monopoly-breeding tariffs, although I am a protectionist. Can I hold such views and still be a republican?"

"I am also a protectionist, but favor a tariff that in general shall measure the difference between the cost of production at home and in the competing foreign countries."

"I had not thought of tariff legislation in that light," said the visitor. "If I can be that kind of a republican I am with you."

Government Control and Regulation of Railways

Sir, I say to the Senate here today that nothing, absolutely nothing, can prevent the ultimate government ownership of the railroads of this country except a strict government control of the railroads of the country.

There is today in the stock and bond valuation of the railroads of this country upward of seven billions of water. If the American people are expected to continue to pay transportation charges that will make a return upon that valuation, the temper of the people of this country is not understood here. Until there is invested in this commission or some other authoritative body the power to determine the real, true valuation of the railroads of this country and the authority to fix rates so that they shall bear only a fair return upon that fair value, senators may as well understand now that you will have this question constantly before you. It will not be possible to suppress it or keep it within the closed doors of committees for nine years to come. At every session, until an adequate measure is adopted, while I remain a member of this body the demand will be made here for legislation that will insure to the people of every state fair treatment at the hands of the common carriers of the country.

Speech in U. S. Senate,
April 19–21, 1906.

Valuation as Basis in Rate-Making

Mr. President, there is no reason for us to hesitate. You cannot wrong the railroads in this matter. The courts will not permit it. They guard the property of the railroads at every step. All the decisions of the supreme court from 1870 down to the present time stand like a bulwark, like a breastwork, like a stone wall around the railroad property. It is not in the power of congress, it is not in the power of any state legislature to do harm or wrong to a railroad company in the states or in the United States. I repeat, the courts will not permit it.

Here is a fair, plain proposition, one so simple that it seems to me no man can hesitate to accord it his support; and I appeal to the senate to put on the records after all these years this rule of measuring reasonable rates and of ascertaining the true value of the property of railroads for that purpose sanctioned by the supreme court of the United States, urged by the interstate commerce commission for a decade, and approved by the judgment and conscience of this country.

The amendment provides for a valuation from time to time covering extensions and improvements. It is necessary, if we are to follow the rule of the supreme court and are to deal fairly by these companies, that we should make and maintain a valuation that completely covers the property, and it is necessary, if we are to deal fairly by the public, that we should not leave it to the railroads to fix the value of their property at any sum which they choose to name.

It is the duty of this government, Mr. President, to see that the people of this country receive reasonable rates, impartial rates, and adequate services. These three things belong to the public at the hands of every transportation company that is given a franchise, and the government owes it to the public to guarantee those three things—reasonable rates, impartial rates, and adequate services. On the other hand, it owes it to the railroad company to see that it has a fair return on the fair value of its property—no more and no less.

Speech in U. S. Senate,
May 31, 1910.

To Strengthen Railway Bill

Mr. President, the people protest against the ever increasing burdens of railway transportation. They know enough of railroad finance to understand that there is no justification for advancing rates. They will not be satisfied with the postponement of rate increases for a few months. They cry out with one voice for substantial and permanent relief. They want justice from their government.

No man who has vision and outlook can fail to see what is coming in this country unless these great and powerful organizations are brought into subjection and control. Within a decade and a half we have seen competition in all the industries wiped out and markets and prices placed under a common control. Within the same period of time we have seen the railroad lines consolidate and merge until there is scarcely a trace of competition left in transportation. There is nothing to stay the increased cost of living except the ability of the consumer to pay. Need anybody marvel at the public unrest—the growing feeling of resentment?

Mr. President, with all of the improvement we have been able to make in this bill, to me it is a matter of deep and profound regret that we still fall far short of having discharged our plain duty to the people who trust us to represent them in this body. Every senator on this floor knows that the interstate commerce commission is powerless to do the very things for the public which the law imposes upon the commission as a duty. We require the railroads to file with the commission all changes in rates, ostensibly to enable the commission to keep some check upon rate changes. Then we refuse to equip the commission with sufficient help to enable it to examine a fraction of one per cent of the rate schedules filed with it week after week.

More than 5,000 men, the best and highest paid men in the railway service, are making rates, working out an increase here, another there; watching the tonnage and pushing transportation charges a notch higher wherever the traffic will bear the burden. And Congress furnishes the commission of seven men one cheap, low-priced clerk to check over the work of 50 high-priced rate experts employed by the railroads. We require the commission to fix reasonable rates, and then vote down an amendment to authorize them to get the value of railway property, without which they cannot take the first step to ascertain reasonable rates. Sir, it is a travesty—a farce. It is more than that—it is a betrayal of those who have confided in us; of those who honor us.

Speech in U. S. Senate, 1911.

On Esch-Cummins Railway Bill

Long before we entered the war, the railway transportation system of the country was on the verge of total collapse through mismanagement and corruption. The railroads from the beginning were grossly over-capitalized, and the public was burdened with constantly increasing rates to pay dividends on watered stocks. Added to this, the railroads were unlawfully permitted to collect from the

Railroad Control

public a further excessive rate for the accumulation of billions in surplus. Out of these vast sums, thus wrongfully levied upon traffic and pocketed as surplus, the railroads built extensions and made permanent improvements. They then over-capitalized these improvements as a basis for further wrongful exactions from the public.

Moreover, the managers openly robbed the railroads from the inside. Construction and supply companies were organized by railway officers and managers. From these companies the railroads bought supplies of all kinds at exorbitant prices. Unrestrained greed exacted such profits on purchases by these insiders from themselves that there was always a shortage of funds for properly equipping the roads. This inside graft ate up the revenues of the railroads and furnished a perennial excuse for still further increasing rates upon the public. It goes without saying that a transportation system honeycombed with official graft and dishonesty was certain to be supplied—in so far as supplied at all—with inferior and defective equipment.

The result was inevitable. When the European war came on, with its stimulus to increased production and traffic, the roads, already short of engines, cars and all manner of equipment, at once disclosed the rottenness and inefficiency of the whole transportation system. By the summer and fall of 1916—months before we entered the war—to quote Director General McAdoo, "they had reached such a point that traffic was almost paralyzed, through inability to furnish but a small part of the cars necessary for the transportation of staple articles of commerce."

When in 1917 the government was forced to seize the roads it took over a ramshackle and utterly demoralized railway system. The operation of railroads in such a state of disrepair was very expensive and wasteful under the most favorable conditions and excessively so under the extraordinary demands the war imposed.

We are now urged to enter upon another protracted period of attempting to combine the conflicting and warring elements of private ownership and public regulation. If our past experience teaches us anything, is it not plain that this means another era of enormous profits for the private owners at the cost of an enormous and unwarranted expense to the public?

Is it rational to believe that in a few short months a small group of senators and representatives—no one of us an expert in railway transportation—has discovered some magic by which the miserable failures of seventy years are to be converted into a marvelous success?

Speech in U. S. Senate, 1919.

Esch-Cummins Bill Analyzed

No more important measure ever came before the senate of the United States for consideration. Yet public hearings were held upon the bill before the committee which framed it, and not one-fifth of the members of the senate have been in their seats during the few sessions that the bill has been debated in the senate.

Railroad Control

The bill is at once revolutionary and reactionary. All its essential features are to be found in the plans submitted by the committee of railway executives and the committee of railway security holders, and they were opposed with substantial unanimity by the labor organizations, farm organizations, and representatives of various other organizations that were accorded a hearing before the interstate commerce committee.

Instead of the preposterous scheme of railway legislation embodied in this bill which I have only hastily sketched, I propose simply that the railroads shall stay where they are under federal operation for some years to come. I suggest that the period be five years after the termination of the war. I understand that both the former and the present director general of the railroads favor the continuation of government operation for the same period. Within that time we can give government operation a fair trial.

La Follette's Magazine, December, 1919.

The Iniquity of the Esch-Cummins Law

I shall presently show how the whole system of railway accounting has been built up with a view of concealing these illegal transactions and of concealing the earnings of the railways from year to year up to the present time. Sir, I should not care to trespass upon the time of the Senate, to present the facts of the false and fraudulent capitalization of the railroads of these earlier years, except that the villainous system still survives.

You may dull your ears to that, you may deaden your consciences to it, you may set your face to go through with this thing no matter what the showing or what the argument, but let me say to you that you will not bury this fraud by your votes today. Like Banquo's ghost, it cannot be buried. It is an iniquity that will live until the scales of justice are fairly balanced.

Speech in U. S. Senate, on Railroad Control,
December 20, 1919.

The Darkened Glass

MR. McCORMICK, Mr. President—

THE PRESIDING OFFICER. Does the Senator from Wisconsin yield to the Senator from Illinois?

MR. LA FOLLETTE. I do.

MR. McCORMICK. I only wanted to observe that there are some of us who perhaps have as little taste for this bill as the Senator from Wisconsin, but we do not see clearly to the end of the passage along which he would lead us. We see "through a glass darkly," as the Scripture has it.

MR. LA FOLLETTE. I know. I do not wonder at that. The railroads and the railroad press have been darkening that glass for two years and distorting the facts through it. If the Senator could have the patience to follow me, I believe that I can produce facts here that will entirely sustain my proposition to leave this matter for at least two years in the hands of the Federal Government.

It has been admitted by practically every speaker in behalf of this bill—I think by every speaker—that it will be three years before the interstate commerce commission can report upon railroad valuation. In the meantime the book value, as I contend, must be accepted; and, Senators, the remarks in behalf of this bill of all except the Senator from Iowa (Mr. Cummins), clearly show that they expect book value to be accepted, and they are arguing for the validity of book value; and never before this session did anybody ever argue, here or at any other place, unless he was a retained attorney for the railroad companies before the interstate commerce commission, for the validity of book value.

Speech, U. S. Senate, on Railroad Control,
December 20, 1919.

VI.
TRUSTS AND MONOPOLIES

The Greatest of Issues

THERE is just one issue before the country today. It is not trust regulation. It is not banking and currency. It is not tariff. It is not railroad regulation. It is not conservation. These and other important questions are but phases of one great conflict.

Let no public servant think he is not concerned; that his state or his constituency is not interested. There is no remote corner of this country where the power of special interest is not encroaching on public rights.

Let no man think this is a question of party politics. It strikes down to the very foundation of our free institutions. The system knows no party. It has long supplanted government. Without risk of being misunderstood, at least by those of whom I speak, I may say that I know something of the sentiment of the people of this country.

There is no difference of opinion among them as to existing conditions and causes underlying it all. In Wisconsin, and from New York to the Pacific States, the people hold one opinion, have one conviction. They are deeply concerned. They understand. Men back of the system seem to know not what they do.

In their strife for more money, more power—more power, more money—there is no time for thought, for reflection. They look neither forward nor backward. Government, society, and the individual are swallowed in the struggle for greater control. The plain man living the wholesome life of peace and contentment has a better prospective, a saner judgment. He has ideals and conscience and human emotions. Home, children, neighbors, friends, church, schools, country, constitute life. He knows very definitely the conditions affecting the rights guaranteed him by the constitution, but he longs for expression, he longs for leadership.

Blind, indeed, is he who does not see what the time portends. He who would remain in public service must serve the public, not the system. He must serve his country, not special interests.

La Follette's Magazine, July 11, 1914.

Failure of Anti-Trust Laws

The operation of federal and state anti-trust and conspiracy laws has been productive of flagrant inequalities. The laws have been circumvented by the most dangerous and powerful of monopolies and trusts, which, through their control of banks, money and credit centered in Wall street, are able to control the natural resources, the food, clothing and highways of the nation. The money power taking refuge under corporation law, in order to defy or evade the conspiracy laws, has crushed competitors and has built up financial monopolies in the interest of speculators and against the interest of bona fide investors, producers, wage-earners and farmers.

These very laws that have failed to prevent financial and industrial monopoly have been used to suppress the unions and co-operative efforts of wage-earners and farmers in their struggle to protect the value of their labor against moneyed interests. Under the pretense of equal treatment of capital and labor, the farmer and the laborer whose capital is their labor and their savings from their labor, have been compelled to pay toll to those whose capital is their political power and their power to withhold money and credit from the commerce and industry of the country.

Republican State Platform, 1910.

Unions and Farmers' Organizations Should Be Exempt

We favor such classification of unions, associations, monopolies, trusts and corporations as shall abolish this pretense and shall establish real equality before the law. Where monopoly is inevitable we favor complete regulation by government. But we are opposed to any change in the laws against trusts and monopolies except as herein stated, until the people have regained control of government, and have been able to assert complete control over all questions of monopoly and corporation law.

Republican State Platform, 1910.

Price Control and Restraint of Trade Criminal

The evils to be reached by legislation on trusts and monopolies are such combinations and confederations as are organized to control prices, create

Trusts and Monopolies

monopolies and destroy competition, or which, in their practical working, have that effect.

It is not because a corporation has a large capital or transacts a large and profitable business that it is an injury to the community or a menace to its prosperity. On the contrary, the development and growth of modern business have made large aggregations of capital absolutely necessary, and such capital is fairly entitled to a reasonable legitimate profit. The wrong is done and the injury inflicted when such combinations of capital are enabled, by means adopted for that purpose, to control prices, stifle competition, and create a monopoly.

I think legislation should be adopted providing that, if any corporation organized under the laws of this or any other state, or any partnership or association of individuals, or any individuals, shall enter into, or become a member of, or a party to, any trust, agreement, combination, partnership, person, or association of persons, to regulate or fix the price of any commodity or to limit the amount of any commodity to be manufactured, mined, sold, transported or placed on sale or disposed of, or to do, or to refrain from doing, any other thing with the intent to control and fix the price of any commodity to be manufactured, mined, sold or transported in this state, such corporation and the officers and agents thereof, and such partnership, individuals and associations of persons, shall be deemed guilty of a conspiracy to defraud, and shall be subject to such prosecution and punishment and such penalty or forfeiture as may, in the judgment of the legislature, be proper.

Such enactment should also contain suitable provisions making all such contracts and agreements void, and provide machinery for the collection of such penalties and forfeitures and for the annulment of the charter of such offender, if a domestic corporation, and for the forfeiture of the right to do business in this state if a foreign corporation, and imposing such penalties on the individuals convicted of violating the law, as may be appropriate.

Message to Legislature, 1901.

The "Interests" or the People?

It seems to me now, as I look back upon those years, that most of the lawmakers and indeed most of the public, looked upon congress and the government as a means of getting some sort of advantage for themselves or for their home towns or home states. River and harbor improvements without merit, public buildings without limit, raids upon the public lands and forests, subsidies and tariffs, very largely occupied the attention of congressmen. Lobbyists for all manner of private interests, especially the railroads, crowded the corridors of the capitol and the Washington hotels and not only argued for favorable legislation, but demanded it.

At the time I was in congress, from 1885 to 1891, the onslaught of these private interests was reaching its height. I did not then fully realize that this was the evidence of a great system of "community of interest," which was rapidly getting control of our political parties, our government, our courts. The issue has since become clear. Whether it shows itself in the tariff, in Alaska, in municipal franchises, in the trusts, in the railroads, or the great banking interests, we know that it is one and the same thing.

And there can be no compromise with these interests that seek to control the government. Either they or the people will rule.

Autobiography, 1913.

Positive Action on Trusts

Foreign competition will not, therefore, cure the trust evil: indeed, it will encourage the movement, already strongly in evidence, toward the organization of international and worldwide monopolies.

No, the constructive statesmen of those times saw clearly that there must be positive action of government either to prevent or to control monopolies. Two very significant laws, both of which I supported heartily, were therefore passed in those years. In one of these—the Sherman anti-trust act—the keynote was prohibition, the effort to prevent combination and to restore competition by drastic laws. In the other, the act establishing the interstate commerce commission for the control of railroads, the keynote was regulation.

Autobiography, 1913.

The Making of America

For, after all, the glory and achievement of our country is men, not things. We build railroads and bridges and factories and markets, and outstrip the nations of the earth in trade and commerce. And what does it all signify? Is it the mere indication of the fatness of our land? or has it a deeper meaning? Manifestly these material things represent the energy, the ingenuity, the intelligence, the courage, of four generations of men, inspired with the conviction that they were born free and equal. Take the spirit of our free institutions out of the life of this nation and we would be compelled to re-write the history of our material progress. No just conception of the making of America from the beginning, no rational understanding of her present and future, can ignore the relation of man to the material development of our country and the influence of modern business methods upon the citizen and his government. * * *

So long as industry, thrift, prudence, and honesty underlie our vast material development, there is nothing to fear in the making of America. Every man who loves his country must rejoice to see those basic qualities of good citizenship rewarded. There can be no national property without individual prosperity. Property, whether the modest home of the artisan or farmer, or the great fortune of the masters of finance, if it be honorably acquired and lawfully used, is a contribution to the stability of government, as well as to material progress. * * *

The basic principle of our government is the will of the people. The representative elected by the people should be the people's representative. If the city alderman, the state legislator, the member of congress, or the United States senator represents privilege, he is not the servant of the people, but the servant of the special interest he represents. The people are not represented, but wealth in combination. * * *

America is not made. It is in the making. It has today to meet an impending crisis, as menacing as any in the nation's history. It does not call a sound to arms, but it is none the less a call to patriotism and to higher ideals in citizenship, a call for the preservation of the representative character of government itself. If we would preserve the spirit as well as the form of our free institutions, the patriotic citizenship of the country must take its stand, and demand of wealth that it shall conduct its business lawfully; that it shall no longer furnish the most flagrant examples of persistent violation of statutes, while invoking the protection of the courts; that it shall not destroy the equality of opportunity, the right to the pursuit of happiness, guaranteed by the constitution; that it shall keep its powerful hands off from legislative manipulation; that it shall not corrupt, but shall obey, the government that guards and protects its rights.

Mere passive good citizenship is not enough. Men must be aggressive for what is right, if government is to be saved from those who are aggressive for what is wrong. The nation has awakened somewhat slowly to a realization of its peril, but it has responded with gathering momentum. The reform movement now has the support of all the moral forces that the solution of a great problem can command. The outlook is hopeful. There is no room for pessimism. Every man should have faith. Advance ground has been secured which will never be surrendered by the American people. There is work for every one. The field is large. It is a glorious service, this service for the country. The call comes

to every citizen. It is an unending struggle to make
and keep government truly representative. Each
one should count it a patriotic duty to build at least
a part of his life into the life of his country, to do
his share in the making of America according to the
plan of the fathers.
Introduction to "The Making of America," 1905.

The People and Private Monopoly

The American people believe private monopoly
intolerable. Within the last dozen years trusts and
combinations have been organized in nearly every
branch of industry. Competition has been ruthlessly crushed, extortionate prices have been exacted
from consumers, independent business development
has been arrested, invention stifled, and the door of
opportunity has been closed, except to large aggregations of capital. The public has not, as a rule,
received any of the resultant economies and benefits of combination which have been so abundantly
promised. But ordinarily the combinations have
demonstrated that the hand of monopoly is deadening, and that business may as easily become too
large to be efficient, as remain too small. And as
related to government, it is everywhere recognized
that trusts and combinations are today the gravest
danger menacing our free institutions.

Autobiography, 1913.

Crime of Guarantee of Profits.

Private ownership and operation of the railroads
was a demonstrated failure soon after we entered
the European war. By December, 1917, the paraly-
sis of the system was so extreme that the govern-

ment took possession and conducted operation to avert complete collapse of transportation and total disaster in the war.

Shortly before the president seized the roads, England, France and Italy had notified him that by December first, owing to our failure to supply food to the allies, the Italian and French armies were short-rationed and would certainly revolt if further reduction in rations were made.

Throughout our own country there was great suffering because of the failure of the railroads to move the traffic. Transportation was stalled. People could not obtain fuel and yet the railroad yards in all the great cities were literally jammed with loaded coal cars. Train loads of grain, provisions and general supplies blockaded the side tracks from the Atlantic seaboard to the Rocky mountains. There was a shortage of engines and cars on every road in the country.

The end was in sight. The transportation of food and war munitions to sustain our own and the allied armies could not be longer delayed and escape utter disaster. The government was forced to act and to act at once.

The failure of private ownership and operation had plainly been inevitable for years. It only required the increased demands of war traffic to reveal the inherent weakness and hasten the failure of the entire transportation system under private ownership and operation.

The primary cause of it all is as plain as a pikestaff: You cannot successfully yoke private monopoly with an honest, impartial public service. The whole railroad transportation system has from the beginning carried the enormous burden of a double capitalization. No business can overload itself with a fictitious capital account and maintain its property in a sound healthy condition.

The railroads would have broken down and gone into receiverships decades ago but for the fact that they have been permitted to force from the public a return in exorbitant rates, sufficient to float their watered capitalization.

And now it is proposed by the pending measures dealing with this vital problem—the Cummins Bill and the Esch Bill,—to perpetuate all the wrongs and oppression of this private monopoly under a scheme of guarantees to watered capital, that must inevitably burden the traffic of the country with increased rates, running into untold billions.

This is the price which the public must pay to "re-establish railroad credit."

Before we joined in a crusade with Great Britain to make Egypt and India and China and Ireland and the good old United States unsafe for democracy, before senators and representatives acquired the habit of voting the people's money out of their treasury like drunken sailors, these same public officials would have regarded support of the Cummins or the Esch Bills as a bargain with political suicide. But woe unto him who today dares question the merit or the magnitude of any raid on the treasury at the behest of the masters of private monopoly!

La Follette's Magazine, January, 1920.

Trusts and Monopolies

The Only Way Out

Are the trusts and combinations stronger than the government itself? That is the supreme issue. Can the people free themselves from this power? Can the unjust burden of fraudulent capitalization be lifted from them? The trusts and combinations, the railroads, the steel trust, the coal trust, all are scheming to secure some action by the government which will legalize their proceedings and sanction their fictitious capitalization. The situation is critical. It may be expected from the attitude of the supreme court as shown in the Standard Oil and Tobacco cases, that any act on the part of the executive or the legislative branch of government, giving countenance to a trust or combination will be construed as an approval of the thousands of millions of watered stocks and bonds issued, and will fasten upon the people for all time the speculative capitalization of our public service and business corporations.

The time is at hand to declare for a statute which shall make it everlastingly impossible for any president, or any congress, or any court, to legalize spurious capitalization as a basis of extortionate prices.

The progressive republican platform must take advance ground upon this question.

La Follette's Magazine, March 16, 1912.

Against Court of Commerce

This bill, Mr. President, is the boldest raid upon public rights, in the form of legislation on this great subject, that the system has ever succeeded in forcing upon the serious consideration of congress.

Never before has it attempted, with the support of the national administration and of the party in congress, to legislate for special privilege and against the public interest, and to foster irrevocably upon the commerce of the country the public burden of transportation charges to pay interest and dividends upon all the watered stocks and bonds which unrestrained corporate greed has set afloat in the financial channels of this country.

If the consolidation, combination, and merger, to which I shall invite the attention of the senate, was not a violation of the anti-trust law, and the attorney general has, in effect, so decided, then we might well strike from this bill the provisions which profess to save the anti-trust law from repeal as to interstate railroads, and openly confess the real purpose of this proposed legislation.

Mr. President, if the federal anti-trust law can be repealed by a state legislature, if the department of justice at Washington will hold conferences with and lend countenance to the agents of law-breaking corporations while they are engaged in lobbying through state legislatures, a pretended sanction of their violation of the criminal statutes of the federal government, and then by official edict make such state statutes a shield and cover under which the criminal corporations may go unwhipped of justice, if the door of the federal court may thus be closed in the face of a wronged and outraged public by the attorney general of the United States, then, sir, the law becomes a black art and justice a mere juggler's pawn.

Speech in U. S. Senate, April 12, 1910.

(Note—The extracts given above are from a notable speech by Senator La Follette against the bill to create a court of commerce. It is sometimes called the New Haven railroad speech from the fact that he drew his arguments from the exploitation of this road.)

The Non-Partisan League

So, I have faith that this new movement up here known as the non-partisan organization, born on the farms of this old northwest territory, contains within it the seeds of a great social and political advancement. And, Mr. President, and fellow-citizens, ladies and gentlemen, I know you will pardon me for harking back to the old granger movement— I am constrained to believe that this new movement is another crop of the seed of that time. Now, fellow-citizens, there would not be the slightest occasion in the world for the organization of a non-partisan league; and you would not be able to enlist the farmers of a dozen or fifteen or twenty states in this union unless there was something fundamentally wrong with our government. There is something fundamentally wrong with it. Of course, I know the fellows who are waving the flags today most frantically, the bloated representatives of wealth who are shouting loudest for democracy today, are trying to invest this particular time with a new form of democracy; a democracy that has attached to it as a cardinal principle, not liberty, not equality, but profit.

Now, I do not take the political dope of any papers that serve interests hostile to representative government. Fellow-citizens, I come before you here tonight to talk to you particularly about this great movement you have adopted up here, and to give you a word of encouragement, to bid you to be brave, not to be intimidated because there may chance to be sneaking about here and there men who will pull back their coats and show a secret service badge. Until Bunker Hill is destroyed, until Little Round Top and the Hornet's Nest at Gettysburg shall have been obliterated and relegated to oblivion, there shall be free speech in this country. Mr. President, I have stood all my life for law and order. Twenty years ago this very season at a little farmers' gathering in Fern Dell, Wisconsin, I opened the fight against corporate power in that state. I was denounced then as the non-partisan league has been denounced now. I was denounced then as an iconoclast and a destroyer of conditions that ought to be preserved just as some of the advanced thinkers of today are denounced for proclaiming not a new doctrine, but the doctrine of Franklin and Madison and Adams and Thomas Jefferson. What was the central thought of the little speech I delivered on that day? It was only this, that the corporations in Wisconsin were not paying their fair share of the taxes, and that they ought to be made to pay them, just as the farmers and owners of lands did; that was all, but that was considered treason, just as the same things are denounced as disloyal today; but, fellow-citizens, I did not stop then, and I won't stop now. And then, twenty years ago, I was asking for justice and equality in government, in taxation, and, fellow-citizens, I came from Washington directly here, and on the floor of the house of representatives and in the committee on finance, the greatest committee in the senate, I have been struggling for this same thing that I struggled for down at the Fern Dell picnic in Wisconsin twenty years ago. There is not a shade of difference in principle. The only difference lies in the fact that where we in Wisconsin were considering thousands and hundreds of thousands, in this great government of ours and in the times in which we find ourselves now, we are considering billions upon billions beyond the power of the human mind to grasp; that is the only difference. A little handful of men in Washington have been demanding—only a little handful of men—have been demanding that the taxation should be laid according to the principles that prevail wherever justice prevails, that taxation shall be laid according to the ability of the property to meet the taxes. We have been contending for that principle in the first speech made on the 27th of August, 1897, to a farmers' picnic in Fern Dell, Wisconsin, which opened the campaign that lasted through a decade or a decade and a half of time.

Speech Before Minnesota Non-Partisan
League, Sept. 20, 1917.

How Monopoly's Grip Could be Broken

MR. KING. I was very much interested in the statement of the Senator. * * * I was glad to hear the Senator say—and I wish to see if I understand his position in that respect—that the Government cannot by attempting to fix prices effectuate the objects so many people are seeking now to bring about; that if we would enforce the laws against trusts and monopolies and allow the free play of the law of supply and demand and the economic forces of the country, we should have nothing to fear with respect to the industrial freedom of the American people or the progress and growth and development of our country. Have I interpreted generally the attitude of the Senator?

MR. LA FOLLETTE. Mr. President, of course, right out of hand on the moment one would hardly be expected, I suppose, more than to suggest remedies to restore to our people their industrial freedom.

I want to see broken, first of all, this artificial power which controls prices and production by agreement and which, in violation of law, is able to dictate the market prices of raw materials and finished products for practically all of the products of this country. I would break that power.

I would enforce the law firmly and relentlessly as to the wrongdoers.

I would press for the freedom of all business from unlawful control as rapidly as the business of the country could be readjusted to the natural laws of trade.

I do not underestimate the magnitude of the task. The failure of every President to keep faith with the people and enforce the law has aided to intrench lawless monopoly in business throughout the land.

It has so long ruled in business and government that it scoffs at authority.

It has had its way alike with Republican and Democratic administrations.

It has its "rough-neck" daily press to manhandle any troublesome public official. It has its "high-brow" weekly and monthly publications which criticize in choice diction any suggestion of curing existing evils by "putting a few gentlemen in jail" and then vaguely prescribe "a better adjustment of distribution."

But it is high time for us to realize that the public will not submit longer to be juggled with. The Government must soon make its choice. It must destroy private monopoly wherever it exists in this country or monopoly will destroy government.

It will not be possible to restore industrial and commercial freedom at once.

Unrestrained lawless wealth in combination has run amuck for a score of years, until it has so involved our entire industrial and commercial structure that to attempt to effect a radical and immediate cure would endanger the whole structure.

But we must make a beginning. We must make that beginning at once if we would avert disaster.

If I had the power, I would start with the United States Steel Corporation. I would begin there, because iron is the basis of everything in the industrial life of any people on the face of the earth.

It is really staggering to think what iron means. There is not a great architectural structure in the world that would be standing tomorrow morning if iron turned to dust overnight. * * * There would not be a railroad line anywhere, there would not be a wheel turning, there would not be a blacksmith shop stand, there would not be an agricultural implement in existence, if iron in all its forms were destroyed. Did you ever stop to think of the extent to which the price of iron and its products controls the price of everything?

So I would begin with iron. I would take the actual valuation of all of the property of the United States Steel Trust. I would ascertain the actual investment in the business. I would not give them credit for a dollar of value which is the result of their monopoly control, but only that which they had actually invested in the business, together with a fair return upon the investment.

Then, Mr. President, taking their actual investment in their manufacturing plant and allowing them a reasonable return on the investment, I would make public a fair and reasonable price list on their manufactures—pig iron, billets, merchantable iron and steel rails, structural shapes—all their manufactures of iron and steel, and would allow a reasonable measure of time for public opinion to enforce an observance of such fair and reasonable price list.

Their failure to adjust the selling prices of their manufactures of steel and iron to the fair-price list published by the Government would invite to more

Trusts and Monopolies

drastic action by the Government in dealing with them.

But, sir, I would proceed in a much more radical way as to their raw material.

I would condemn and take away from them such of their holdings as would be called raw material—or natural resources. I would have the Government take back the title to its iron ore and coal and copper and timber and the other natural products. Then I would maintain such an absolute control of the production and the prices of those basic products, either by a strict leasing system or by actual Government operation, or both, that every manufacturer, small as well as large, should have an equal opportunity to get the raw material at the same price. I would do that for the purpose of restoring competitive conditions at the very foundation of all manufactured production.

I would apply the same method to all others who own the great primary products that may be called, in a general way, the resources of nature. I would have the Government hold the title to and maintain the absolute control of all these primary products. I would try, perhaps, operating them under a strong leasing system, under which the Government should control prices.

But I would introduce a limited amount of Government operation in various lines of production, to the end that we might have a measure, a standard of fair production cost and fair selling price. I would try that as an initial proceeding for the ultimate achievement of industrial freedom.

That may be temporizing, but I would try that to give the old theory of individual initiative its fair chance, and if that experiment failed, then I would go after Government operation of all those basic essentials, absolutely; and in the meantime I would not hesitate at all about Government control and ownership of all transportation and all lines of communication—everything of that character.

I expect to stand here and make a fight alone for Government ownership and control of the railroads. I am for Government ownership of railroads and every other public utility—every one—and I propose to show on this floor that where it has ever been given a fair chance in any part of the world that it has been successful. I am going to show that the "cards were stacked" on Government operation here in this country during the war period by those who were interested and that it was not possible for Government operation to make a fair showing.

I do not know whether I have answered the question of the Senator from Utah (Mr. King) or not, but I have at least tried to do so frankly.

Speech in U. S. Senate, Aug. 29, 1919.

Monopoly Cause of High Prices

Do you not understand that * * * down to 20 years ago the price of every manufactured commodity that any body of organized society bought gradually declined? Why? Because methods of production were improved and there was competition between the producers that kept profits at a reasonable level. About 1897 they began to combine

Trusts and Monopolies 125

to suppress competition and to control the markets, and from that hour, if you will consult the statistics for 20 years you will find that the price of everything you have had to buy has increased in this country. Why? Because combinations and trusts were formed to control the prices; to take the benefits of the improvements for those who owned the factories and parasitical middlemen and to give none to the laborers, and to give none to the consumers.

That is what this thing means; that is the meaning of this great struggle. That is the biggest problem that confronts you. It is not Shantung; it is not the League of Nations; it is not the treaty made at Versailles; but it is whether you can save democracy in the United States. That is the fundamental problem of the American people. The power that is trying to take the Naval Reserves is only one of the many that is encroaching upon the rights of the American people and upon their democracy.

Mr. President, I say that it lies with the people of this country to settle this great problem and to settle it under the Constitution without violence.

Speech in U. S. Senate, Aug. 29, 1919.

Strikes and Monopoly

We have strikes on every hand. Senators have attempted here by resolutions and by speeches on the floor to intimidate and to restrain labor and to restrict free speech in this country not only in time of war, but after. The American people are patient people, but it is possible to push things too far. Is it not worth while for enlightened, conservative statesmanship to stop and consider this situation so that effective steps can be taken to meet these issues? We must curb this mighty monopoly power and give to the people of this country a free, open, competitive market, and free, open, competitive conditions under which they may buy the products of all manufacturing and producing organizations in this country at reasonable prices regulated by competition.

Speech in U. S. Senate, Aug. 29, 1919.

Monopoly and Radicalism

I have said on the floor of the Senate again and again that there is not any way of accounting for the increase in the cost of living excepting that we are in the grip of monopoly. You have built up, in the first place, a protective system and shut off foreign competition, and you have left it to the fellows inside of the tariff wall to fix the prices and, by combination, they have fixed the prices as high as they pleased, and they have destroyed competition, and as a result of that they have taken out of the American public just what profits they pleased, and Congress has sat by and permitted that thing to be done

There is no justification for it. It is a betrayal of everything that goes to the heart of representative government. It has builded up the conditions that have led a committee of this Senate to put into this bill a proposition to appropriate $2,000,000 to suppress radicalism in this country. Do you think you could have a government, representing just simply those who have an opportunity to take out of the

Trusts and Monopolies

people of this country whatever prices they please for the things they produce, and not have criticism of your government?

I say, Mr. President, right now that in 20 years this Government has not been representative of the public interests. I think that this Government has been representing the interests of combinations and trusts and great aggregations of capital and no man can successfully deny that. * * * I have said it a good many times on the floor of the Senate, and I am going to keep on saying it as long as I live, as long as I am a member of this body.

Speech in U. S. Senate, June 28, 1919.

Prices and Cost of Production

From 1897 down to the time that the war began, prices advanced every year on the products consumed in this country. Now, I say that is unjust, that is wrong, and this is so only because the Government did not serve the people. * * *

Senators draw their salaries, and sit behind these desks, and let this thing go on, and then pile law on law to repress criticism because it is so! * * *

I am not talking of the war period, but before the war, from 1897, down to the war period. * * * Study Dun's and Bradstreet's and you will find that it increased every year. Why should it increase? It increased because the Congress of the United States and the executive departments did not serve the public interests. * * * It increased because the aggregations of capital were permitted to defy the law of competition and fix prices as they pleased. Why? Why did not prices fall? Did you ever know of a period of invention that was comparable to it? There never was. From 1897 down to the year 1914 Yankee ingenuity and invention revolutionized the cost of production, and yet the prices increased upon the people of this country. Tell me if you were doing your duty and the executive department was doing its duty, when you had a law on the statute books that said that there should be no control of prices against public interest; why were these combinations permitted to ignore and defy the law? You cannot name to me a single industry in the United States that has not cut the cost of production in two again and again from 1897 down to 1914, and yet the cost to the consumer has mounted steadily every year.

Speech in U. S. Senate, June 28, 1919.

VII.
LABOR AND ITS RIGHTS

The Dignity of Manual Labor

I HAVE always had respect for the man who labors with his hands. My own life began that way. Manual labor, industry, the doing of a good day's work, was the thing that gave a man standing and credit in the country neighborhood where I grew up. We all worked hard at home, and the best people I ever knew worked with their hands. I have always had a feeling of kinship for the fellow who carries the load—the man on the under side. I understand the man who works, and I think he has always understood me.

Autobiography, 1913.

Protection to Railroad Employees

To your careful consideration I recommend the question of more efficient protection to employees of railroad companies who may be injured in the discharge of their duties, through carelessness or negligence of other employees or agents of the company. Of itself the employment is in most instances extremely hazardous to the employee. In the discharge of his duties he is frequently required not only to risk his life to save other lives, but he must jeopardize it to protect the property of the company and of the public. The duties of these men are quasi-public. The most efficient service that they can give is due to the public in the protection of life and property, the safety of which depends upon their fidelity and courage. No man should be called to the discharge of such duties without assured compensation for injuries which he may receive through no fault of his own, or without reasonable provision for the support and maintenance of wife, children, or other dependents, if his life be destroyed in the performance of his duty.

Message to Legislature, Jan. 15, 1903.

The Courts and Labor Combinations

There is one class of so-called restraints of trade that was not intended, or at least not understood, to come under the prohibitions of the Sherman antitrust law. These are labor organizations. It is a curious fact about the enforcement of the law that, while the courts have carefully protected investors in trusts against loss of values, the only instance where the extreme penalty of three-fold damages has been imposed is in the case of a labor organization. The court has gone to the extent of seizing upon the savings of members of a labor organization and has ordered that these little investments should be paid over, as far as they go, toward giving the employers three times the damages that the union had caused to them. Certainly it is very strange that when the court goes to its furthest limit in imposing penalties on combinations of capital, all of the capitalist owners get away with the full value of their property, even though the court explicitly says that the biggest ones committed crimes in getting it; but when the court goes to the same limit in enforcing penalties on combinations of labor, it takes away the homes and small savings of the guilty members. A law which treats investors as innocent if they form a trust, and guilty if they form a labor union, does not command the respect, nor appeal to the sense of justice of the American people. The fact is, the law was not understood by the people to apply to labor organizations, and it is a mistaken judicial construction that has made it so apply. The law should be amended, so as to get back to its original intent, by taking out from under its operation all labor organizations and all employers' associations. These are combinations which do not regulate the prices of commodities, but they regulate the wages and conditions of labor.

Speech in U. S. Senate, 1910.

The Taylor System

Mr. President, it behooves us not to stand for any of the exactions upon labor which would grind the last ounce of work out of the toilers of this country by any process of sweating. I care not what may be used, whether the stop watch be held over the operative or whether men who have the co-ordination of mental, nervous, and muscular organization to enable them to win are tempted by a bonus system to strive for the prizes and drive their competitors, their fellow workmen to the breaking-down point.

Mr. President, it is nothing but a "sweating system." It drives men to perform a given number of motions within a fixed time. It offers a premium to men who can do that thing; it subjects men who are by nature differently organized mentally, physically, and nervously to a strain under which they are broken down.

I remember well, Mr. President, when I stood some years ago upon this floor appealing to members of this body to pass a bill fixing 16 hours as the limit of time that men engaged in conducting the train service of the country should be permitted to work without interruption, there were engineers and conductors and other trainmen who objected to having any limitation put upon the number of hours that they might be permitted to operate a train, because there were a compartively few who could run a train 36 hours, 40 hours, perhaps 72 hours, and keep awake, keep their faculties concentrated upon their work, and earn a larger sum each month. They did not want any limitation upon the number of hours that they should be permitted to operate trains; but, Mr. President, the public has some rights in these matters; it has some rights in every question which involves labor generally.

It had in that particular case some rights in addition to that; it had some rights as to the safety of interstate transportation. Against the wishes of some of the engineers and conductors and trainmen of the country, I remember I, with some others upon this floor, stood here and fought for a limitation upon the hours of service of the men operating the trains of the country. The great body of the trainmen were in favor of a limitation. The great body of the trainmen today are in favor of a much greater limitation than the 16-hour limitation which, after a long struggle, we succeeded in putting upon the hours of train service men.

Mr. President, I understand the author of the Taylor system, in his book, says that he takes no account of the 80 per cent. who cannot come up to the high standards. Those who install this system say to a manufacturer or business man, "Permit us to install our system. For $100 a day our experts will teach it to your operatives and to your managers. By adopting this system, which takes account of every movement a man makes and exacts of him the highest possible speed, you will be able to reduce the unit cost of the output of your product 20 per cent." Capital seizes upon that, sir. Capital takes no account of what may happen to the men who are thrown out of employment because they cannot make the given number of motions within the limited period.

Mr. President, let us, as we did on yesterday, by a decisive vote hold to the position taken and say to the House of Representatives, "We agree with you. There shall be nothing left in disagreement between the Senate and the House on this proposition."

We will not permit to be put into this bill a line, or word, or a syllable that will give the conferees the opportunity to work out some legislation that shall be framed up by six men and shall come in here in the conference report in a form that has to be accepted by the Senate.

Speech in U. S. Senate, July 26, 1916.

The Eight-Hour Law

The eight-hour law for railway trainmen has been much misrepresented. During the many months of negotiations between the trainmen and the railroad managers, the railroad companies conducted a tremendous campaign in an effort to influence public sentiment against the granting of an eight-hour day to their men. Their agents worked through chambers of commerce, manufacturers' associations and other organizations of business men, inducing them to pass resolutions condemning the demand of the trainmen, and memorializing congress to enact legislation to empower the interstate commerce commission to fix the hours and wages of men employed on railroads engaged in interstate commerce. All of the big newspapers, and some of the small newspapers, of the country were flooded with advertisements putting before the public the railroads' side of this controversy. Millions of dollars must have been expended in this campaign. And these millions did not come from the pockets of the railroad managers or the railroad owners. This campaign was conducted with money that really belonged to the people. The shippers and the passengers were made, in the last analysis, to finance a publicity campaign to influence their own judgment upon one side of this great question.

The railroad trainmen had no such resources to enable them to carry on a publicity campaign to shape public opinion in favor of their own demands. Nor did they have the additional advantage, enjoyed by the railroad companies, of placing huge, flam-buoyant placards upon the walls of waiting rooms at railway stations setting forth the case for the railroads before the traveling public.

This eight-hour law has been called a "force bill" enacted under the demands of organized railroad workmen. This is not true. The railroad employees demanded the eight-hour day from the railroads, not from Congress. They made no demand whatever upon Congress. They said if the railroads did not grant the eight-hour day they would quit work. This was their right—a right long judicially declared to be theirs. They set a day to quit work in case the railroad managers refused them the eight-hour day. Then the railroads inaugurated a strike against the public. They refused to accept freight for shipment, especially perishable goods. In many parts of the country this meant appalling disaster to farmers and particularly to fruit growers. It meant great damage to all business—even to the railroads themselves.

The president stepped in and sought to adjust the trouble and avoid the disaster about to be thrust upon the country. He was not successful. The railway managers were particularly obstinate and refused to concede the principle of the eight-hour day. At this point the president put the matter up to Congress for its consideration. Congress, disinterested, under law bound to consider only the public good, was forced to act in the public interest. It was not forced to act because of any demands upon congress by the workingmen or by the railroad managers, but because the public interest demanded immediate action.

Congress acted. It passed what is known as the eight-hour day law for men in the employment of railroads in interstate commerce, engaged in moving trains. Every Wisconsin representative present voted for the bill which became a law and averted the strike.

I believe they did right. I believe in the eight-hour day. It is claimed that congress acted "without due consideration." Did it? The question of the eight-hour day for skilled employees was not new. Every congressman who was alive to the issues of the day must have been fairly familiar with the arguments pro and con on the subject of the eight-hour day. I had given this matter consideration years ago when I secured the sixteen hour limitation for railroad employees—the best I could get at that time.

At that time I was met with the same arguments which are now being made against the eight-hour day. The railroads and some other large employers are slow to learn, but abundant experience has shown that for the trades, professions and crafts where skill, courage, caution and close attention to business are required the eight-hour day is the maximum for efficiency. Had the railroads accepted this principle there would have been no trouble.

However, railroads generally yield to no principle of progress that is not forced upon them by legislation.

The dawn of a better day would never brighten the path of workmen were it left to the railroad managers.

The railroad employees have been patient and long-suffering. Theirs is a hazardous business. Their calling takes them away from their homes at all times of the day and night, in all kinds of weather. Their labor is performed under dangerous conditions. Their span of life is short and full of grief. They have seen their brothers in other less hazardous callings secure the eight-hour day without a struggle, but they have been held to a day of indefinite hours so long as it did not exceed sixteen, and in cases of unforeseen trouble their day might exceed sixteen hours. I wonder that their just demands were not sooner made.

Shorter Work Day Spells Efficiency

All practical experience shows that shorter hours means better health and higher efficiency of employees, the quality of the work and the character of the output more than offsetting any loss from cutting down the working hours of the day. In other words, shorter hours means stronger bodies, greater physical efficiency, a higher degree of mental alertness, keener and more intelligent concentration on the machinery and material handled by the wage-earner, fewer accidents, added time for home life, rest, recreation, and reading, all making for moral, mental, and physical improvement.

Congress has given men employed by the government or by contractors employed on government work, the eight-hour day. Wisconsin provides by law for the eight-hour day for state work. Twelve states limit the working day of minors to eight hours in one day.

The courts have held again and again that rest from labor one day in seven is "essential for health, morals, and general welfare."

The courts will ultimately hold that it is vital to the health and well-being of the toiler, and for that vital to the general welfare, that the state should limit the hours of labor for the day as it limits the days of labor for the week.

Let the wage-earner take heart. The eight-hour day will come, and come soon, to all of the skilled workers of every state in the nation.

La Follette's Magazine, 1915.

Limiting Hours of Service of Trainmen

The Railroad Brotherhood of Engineers, Firemen and Trainmen, a remarkably intelligent body of men, had long maintained a very efficient and faithful legislative representative, Mr. Hugh Fuller, here at the national capital, but they had found it impossible even to get a record vote on important measures in which they were interested. No bill in their interests relating to hours of service or liability of the employer for negligence was permitted to get out of the committee. I took up the matter of an Employers' Liability Law and attempted, in 1906 to have it adopted as an amendment to the interstate commerce act. Failing in this, by an unexpected move I got a bill before the Senate where I could force a record vote. Now, no Senator wanted to put himself wrong with the railway employees, and so after fencing for delay I finally got it passed without a roll call. This law, having been held unconstitutional by the supreme court

Labor and Its Rights 139

(by vote of five to four), I introduced another Employers' Liability bill in the next session, and had it referred to the Committee on Education and Labor (of which Dolliver was chairman) instead of to the committee on interstate commerce. This bill was reported out by Dolliver, was passed and is now the law.

I also secured the passage in 1907, after much opposition and filibustering, of a law to limit the hours of continuous service of railroad employees. This law has been of great use in preventing those accidents which formerly arose from the continuous employment of men for twenty-four or even thirty-six hours without sleep or rest.

Autobiography, 1913.

(Note—Senator La Follette scored two victories in the senate session of 1907. One resulted from his fight for the passage of the bill limiting the hours of service of railroad employees. Until 1907 there had been no limit to the number of hours a railroad man might be kept on duty.

To La Follette sixteen consecutive hours seemed a longer day than men who have in their keeping the lives and limbs of hundreds of thousands of people daily should be permitted to work, but to limit the hours of labor at all was a big step in the right direction. All manner of testimony was presented to show that many wrecks had been caused because men in charge of trains or some part of the railroad service had been on duty so long that they could no longer keep wide awake. Sixteen hours, La Follette thought was considerable of a concession to the railroads. But the railroads fought the bill with all the pressure and influence they could wield. After days of fighting La Follette succeeded in forcing through the senate, only after the railroads had exhausted every trick of parliamentary practice, the bill limiting the hours of service of railroad men to sixteen.

La Follette's second victory in the senate session of 1907 was the passage of a new employers' liability law which established as a principle of federal law the doctrine of comparative negligence. Heretofore when an employee was injured the employer had but to show that the employee was guilty of slight negligence in order to set up a complete defense in a suit for personal injuries. Under this law the fact that the employee may have been guilty of contributory negligence is no longer a bar to recovery, if it can be shown that the employee's negligence was slight and the employer's negligence was gross in comparison.)

On Children's Bureau

I am loath to believe that any member of the Senate would favor the reduction of the appropriation of any reasonable sum of money which could be expended by the children's bureau in the work which it was commissioned to do by the statute which created that bureau. I do not know of any way in which we can build so strongly into our national life as by an intelligent and scientific study of the child from birth.

Twenty-five years ago you could bring an audience of laboring men to their feet—cheering for Old

Glory and what it did for liberty, for freedom, for emancipation; but, Mr. President, when you grind the faces of the poor, when you force the parents to put children into the factories in order that they may exist, when you have little care for the death rate in the homes where the children of the poor are born, you are sowing the seed of resentment against this Government of professed equality.

There seems to be a fatal blindness upon the part of all of us, and when the little opportunity is afforded by the expenditure of $72,000 to carry forward an investigation here that will tell the story of this awful mortality among the children of those who work for wages, we find it opposed. When there is a little opportunity here to let the light into the homes of the toilers to know why it is that one out of every four babies of those who earn $450 a year must die before they are 12 months old, it is to be blocked in the interests of economy.

It may be, Mr. President, that I am expressing undue feeling upon this matter. I am not entirely a novice in public affairs. I have spent almost my whole life in dealing with these questions, and I am constrained to believe that it behooves the statesmanship of this country to give consideration to these things that concern the millions of the toilers of this country.

Speech in U. S. Senate, January 22, 1917.

The La Follette Seaman's Act

The act to promote the welfare of American seamen and safety of life at sea, approved by President Wilson March fourth, makes America sacred soil and the thirteenth amendment finally becomes a covenant of refuge for the seamen of the world. It has taken a twenty-one year struggle to accomplish this result.

The law makes the sailor a free man.

It standardizes his skill.

It limits the number of hours of continuous service.

It provides better conditions of living for him on shipboard,—more food, more water, more light, and air, larger and more sanitary sleeping and living space, and a hospital section separate and apart from that portion of the vessel in which the sailors must sleep and eat.

While the law does not completely safeguard the public interest, it is a great advance in the right direction. Furthermore it substitutes enforceable statutes for the rules and regulations of an inspection service which are more often disregarded than observed.

It requires every vessel leaving an American port for a foreign country to carry lifeboats sufficient to accommodate at least seventy-five per cent of all on board, and to carry life rafts for the remaining twenty-five per cent. Formerly the number of lifeboats required to be carried by ocean liners was committed to the discretion of the inspection service, which has had less consideration for public safety than for the interests of steamship companies. It was my contention from the beginning that there should be lifeboats for all, and the Senate adopted the amendment I offered to that end. But the influence of the ship owners was strong enough in the House to reduce the number of lifeboats to seventy-

Labor and Its Rights

five per cent. Twenty-five per cent of the passengers must resort to life rafts in the event of disaster. Life rafts in mid-ocean would only serve temporarily to keep afloat the people so unfortunate as to be dependent upon them; and with a high sea running and in chill weather they would inevitably drown or die from exposure.

Aside from the sections of the law primarily for the benefit of the passengers, the public has a direct interest in many of the provisions intended especially to benefit the seamen.

Safety Demands Sailor's Contentment

Making the sailor a free man will make his calling equal under the law with that of every wage-earner. It will remove the stigma of involuntary servitude which has driven tens of thousands of the bravest and best men to abandon the sea. Sailors of intelligence and character and courage on the deck of every ship means immeasurably greater security for passengers in a time of peril.

The public safety is conserved by limiting the number of hours of consecutive service which can be required of seamen, precisely as it is conserved in limiting the number of railway employees who may be required to work in running railroad trains. Whether serving in the cab of an engine or serving on watch or at the wheel on the deck of an ocean liner, safety for human life demands that the engineer or the seaman shall be keen, vigilant, alert, every faculty concentrated on the duty of the hour. No man exhausted in mind or body is fit for the great responsibility which such a position imposes. Just as the public interest required a law restraining railroads from overworking trainmen, so the public interest demands a limitation on the hours of continuous service at sea.

The law provides that in every port where a vessel of the United States, after the voyage has commenced, shall load or deliver cargo, before the voyage is ended, a seaman is entitled to receive on demand from the master of the vessel to which he belongs, one-half of the wages which he shall then have earned.

The old law conferred upon the seaman the right to demand half pay as above, provided there were "no stipulation to the contrary in the shipping agreement." But this provision in the old law was uniformly defeated by "stipulating to the contrary" in the articles of shipment. This has enabled the ship owner to hold seamen in the service against their will, by depriving them of pay in port. This authority over the seamen was made absolute through the right of the master to imprison any seaman who quit service, even though the vessel were in safe port. No other laboring man in the United States can be compelled on pain of imprisonment to serve out his term according to the letter of his agreement. He can forfeit his wages and quit if he finds the conditions of the service intolerable. Not so the sailor. Under the old law, fair or foul, his body was bound to the master of the ship. He was compelled to continue in the service of the ship owner even though willing to forfeit all his earnings in order to free himself from the terms of his contract of service whenever he found them too harsh or severe to be endured.

The American sailor in his bondage has been forgotten for generations. At last his appeal has been heard. It was reserved for President Wilson in the closing hours of the Sixty-third congress to approve a measure which blots out the last vestige of slavery under the American flag. The seaman's bill is the second proclamation of freedom. The fourth of March, 1915, is the sailor's emancipation day.
La Follette's Magazine, March, 1915.

Seaman's Law Has Made Good

(Note—The following extract is from the New Republic, 1919):

"Furuseth's prophecy has in fact come true. In 1911, the last year for which official statistics were available, British wages for seamen and firemen ranged from $20 to $25 a month, while American wages ranged from $30 to $50 for the same employment. Wages of other European maritime nations were even lower than the British. By the end of 1918, the American rate had risen to $75 a month for both seamen and firemen.

"The result has been to place American seamen and American ship owners in a better position than any they have occupied since the civil war. Wages have increased, not only absolutely, but in relation to purchasing power—for seamen in the trans-Atlantic trade the increase in wages since 1914 has been 164 per cent, and for firemen 89 per cent. This means, according to Governor Bass' report, an increase in purchasing power of 38 per cent for seamen and 5.4 per cent for firemen. Wages are high enough now to attract the best type of American labor. Yet as compared with foreign vessels, the cost of operating American ships is relatively cheaper than before the war."

One Issue in History

Ah, Mr. President, let me say here in this connection that there has, in my opinion, been only one great issue in all the history of the world. That issue has been between labor and those who would control, through slavery in one form or another, the laborers. That is history. Read it. Study it. Nations have gone down in ruin from the first dawn of history that have sought to make slaves of the great masses of men. That is the destiny of nations, for the God of justice and humanity is over all, and when one privileged powerful class of the human race seeks to benefit itself unjustly from the great masses of people, they run counter and bring down upon themselves ultimately the judgment, the justice of God Almighty. We are on the road, I fear, that other nations have traveled. I do not know that it is possible, sir, to arrest that progress. It may be that it is a disease that must afflict all nations and all peoples. It may be that it is an inexorable law of evolution.

Here in this country we have been led to hope for something better than that. I have inherited, as it were, the belief and the hope that this was the place for the consummation and the working out of the most perfect Government attainable.

We had in this country a splendid opportunity, better, I think, than any other nation in the world.

If the human race is gradually to be lifted to higher and higher levels, if civilization is to be truly democratic and progressive, and if we are ultimately to come to as high a degree of perfection in government in this world as finite human beings can attain, it ought to be here in America, above all other places in the world, for we had here the best opportunity. We had virgin soil in which to lay our foundations. We had the new material that came from the Old World. Every immigrant wanted more liberty and democracy, wanted freedom, and hoped to realize the ideals to which the human heart aspires. It is the only place, as I see it, for the human race to attain it.

I see forces carrying us in the other direction: The Standard Oil, the Copper Trust, the Beef Trust, and all the great organizations of power and capital that have been built up here in violation of the law of the land; that have thriven and controlled and defied the Government.

Speech in U. S. Senate, Aug. 29, 1919.

VIII.

BIG BUSINESS AND GOVERNMENT

The Legislative Lobby

HE legislature of 1899 enacted chapter 243 of the laws of 1899, designed to control and somewhat restrict the operations of what is commonly termed "the lobby" in relation to legislation. The principle involved in that enactment has my unqualified approval. It is of course neither possible nor desirable to isolate the members of the legislature from the people of the state. All public officers are but the servants of the people, and in discharging their various duties the more closely they keep in touch with, and learn the wishes and interests of, the people, the better. But when either individuals or corporations keep at the seat of government, a body of salaried agents, or counsel, whose duty it is to bring about or prevent legislation, as their employers may desire, who accomplish such results not so much by open and public argument before the legislature and legislative committees as by personal influence exerted in various ways upon individual members of the legislature, it becomes an evil which ought to be controlled and checked as a menace to the welfare of the state.

In my judgment the fullest opportunity ought to be given for free and fair discussion of all subjects

Big Business and Government

of legislation before the two houses and their various committees by all who are interested in these subjects; but, in my opinion, that ought to be the extent of the services permitted to be performed by legislative agents or lobby counsel. Any argument which cannot bear the light of publicity ought not to be permitted to influence legislation or to be permitted to be made.

Message to Legislature, 1901.

For Effective Corrupt Practices Act

We are opposed to the excessive use of money in political campaigns. It is the weapon of special interests. It is an instrument of evil. It debauches manhood and corrupts the electorate. It serves every bad cause and embarrasses every good one.

We favor the enactment of a law which will authorize the publication by the state of necessary information concerning the qualifications of candidates at all primary and general elections.

No candidate for office should disburse money for the purpose of promoting his nomination or election, except—

First, for his own personal traveling expenses;

Second, payments required to be made to the state for information published;

Third, contributions to his personal campaign committee;

Fourth, contributions to his party campaign committee.

Except for these purposes no money should be expended or disbursed by any person to nominate or elect any candidate for office unless by and through a publicly registered campaign committee to be appointed by the candidate himself or through the regular party committee of his party. Such committees should be required to keep accurate books of account and file sworn statements with public authority at regular intervals during the progress of the campaign, showing all moneys contributed to and disbursed by it, the amount thereof, from whom received, to whom paid, and for what purposes. Within thirty days after every primary and general election a complete statement, in detail, of all financial transactions of such committees should be filed in like manner.

The total expenditure by or on behalf of any candidate should be limited by law and restricted to the following purposes: Hall rent, traveling expenses of speakers, clerical assistants, printing of literature and distribution thereof by mail or public messenger, and newspaper advertising. All campaign literature and advertising should bear the name of the author and of the person causing a publication thereof. No political activity should be permitted on either primary or general election day.

Compliance should be compelled by rigorous penalties, including imprisonment and disqualification of the candidate for public office.

We pledge legislation embodying these principles.
Republican State Platform, 1910.

Respect for, and Obedience to the Law

I remember a few days ago in the discussion here that the senator from Ohio (Mr. Foraker) rose in his place and said that the railroad officials of this country are not criminals. I say to the senator that the records, so far as they have been exposed, show that the railroad officials of this country arc, with rare exceptions, criminals under the statute.

Now, I mean what I say. I see senators on that side smile; but let me say to you, gentlemen, that when in Wisconsin we summoned the railroad companies into court to answer for having juggled the reports of their annual earnings, which they were required by law to make under oath to the state officials, when they appeared before the court and the testimony of the state was but partly offered, when the arguments over certain law propositions had been concluded, those officials—and they are just as honorable as the officials of any railroad companies in the United States—came into court and stipulated that they had violated the law, and went to the supreme court on a question of the statute, as to whether or not, to state it specifically, their report to the state officer and its acceptance by that officer, even if the report was a violation of the statute, had not bound the state. That is what they did. They confessed a violation of the statute; they confessed having under oath reported their gross earnings short of the true amount as required by the statute; and they are just as honorable as the railroad officials of any state in this union.

Speech in U. S. Senate, April 19-21, 1906.

The Half-Loaf in Legislation

In legislation no bread is often better than half a loaf. I believe it is usually better to be beaten and come right back at the next session and make a fight for a thoroughgoing law than to have written on the books a weak and indefinite statute.

I believe that half a loaf is fatal whenever it is accepted at the sacrifice of the basic principle sought to be attained. Half a loaf, as a rule, dulls the appetite, and destroys the keenness of interest in attaining the full loaf. A halfway measure never fairly tests the principle and may utterly discredit it. It is certain to weaken, disappoint, and dissipate public interest. Concession and compromise are almost always necessary in legislation, but they call for the most thorough and complete mastery of the principles involved, in order to fix the limit beyond which not one hair's breadth can be yielded.

Autobiography, 1913.

On Compromise

In every contest situations may arise, or be created, inviting to a compromise on candidate or principle. The temptation to yield is strong. Yet in my whole course I have always insisted on driving straight ahead. To do otherwise not only weakens the cause for which you are contending but destroys confidence in your constancy of purpose.

I have always believed that anything that was worth fighting for involved a principle, and I insist on going far enough to establish that principle and to give it a fair trial. I believe in going forward a step at a time, but it must be a full step. When I went into the primary fight, and afterward into the railroad fight—and it has been my settled policy ever since—I marked off a certain area in which I would not compromise, within which compromise would have done more harm to progress than waiting and fighting would have done.

Autobiography, 1913.

Placing the Responsibility

It is true that men everywhere who dare to show that they are my friends are being intimidated and punished in innumerable ways. I wish that it might be otherwise. I wish that I might either receive the blows aimed at them on my account, or else that I could be more conciliatory in matters of public interest by which I am deeply moved. But I can no more compromise or seem to compromise where what I regard as an important matter is involved than I could by wishing it add twenty years to my span of life. My friends must accept me with this limitation, if such it is, or not at all.

From Unpublished Letter to a Supporter, 1918.

The Packers

No more infamous organization ever existed in the United States than the packers' combination. It has defied the criminal law. It has defied the Congress of the United States. It has defied the President. It has defied the executive and legislative authority. It has done what it pleased; it has ridden down the Sherman anti-trust law. It has not confined itself to meat products alone but it has reached out into almost every field of food products and is seeking to control and dominate the prices of food of the people of this country. * * *

Mr. President and Senators, some man will some day gather together the testimony that has been submitted to the Committee on Agriculture of the Senate, and when he throws it upon the screen so that the people of this country may see it as it is, a leash will be needed to hold the people in this country in restraint. * * *

* * * As we read from day to day the work of this organization * * * we know that at a time when the people of the country were sending their boys away and were giving and giving to the purchase of Liberty bonds, when the old men and the old women were trying to do the work upon the farms, when everyone was giving, giving, giving, we find that this packers' organization was grinding the life out of the people by continually and unnecessarily increasing the cost of the necessaries of life.

Speech in U. S. Senate, June 28, 1919.

Must Not Surrender Rights

The gravest danger menacing republican institutions today is the overbalancing control of city, state, and national legislatures by the wealth and power of public-service corporations. This is not more marked with one political party when in power than with another. It deals with public officials. It makes no political distinctions. It cannot be cured by denunciation. It cannot be defended by the cry of "purist" or "populist" or "demagogue." It goes directly to the root of government. It threatens to sap the life of American citizenship. The voter elects the candidate; the corporation controls the official. It leaves the citizen the semblance of power which is actually exercised against him.

The problem presented is a momentous one. It calls for no appeal to passion or prejudice or fear. It calls for courage and patriotism and self-sacrifice. It calls for solution. Shall the American people become servants instead of masters of their boasted material progress and prosperity—victims of the colossal wealth this free land has fostered and protected? Surely our great cities, our great states, our great nation, will not helplessly surrender to this most insidious enemy which is everywhere undermining official integrity and American institutions. Surely the party of Abraham Lincoln which abolished slavery, which kept the United States undivided, upon the map of the world, will not abandon its traditions, its memories, its hopes, and become the instrument of injustice and oppression. It will do its plain duty now, as it did in that greatest epoch of the country's history. It will meet the issues with rectitude and unfaltering devotion, strong in the faith of ultimate triumph.

Gentlemen of the convention, the contest for equal and just taxation and nominations by direct vote is not yet completely won. The nomination which you have just tendered me is the unmistakable, the emphatic demand of the republican party for the prompt enactment of these laws. But between that expressed will and the ripening of these measures into law, there are caucuses and conventions for the nomination of candidates for the senate and assembly. When the legislature convenes there are the same forces to be met and contended with that led to the undoing of the last legislature. I appeal to you, and through you to the people of the state, to be vigilant to the last hour. Do not relax your efforts until this good work is finished. Let no man be named for the legislature who is not fully in accord with the republican platform. Name only men who are willing to go on record for this legislation, who are free from all entanglements or complications that may force them to vote contrary to desire and conscience. Wherever senators or assemblymen already have been nominated, let them openly and publicly proclaim their position with respect to these issues. This is equally the right of the party and the public.

Gentlemen, the contest through which we have just passed strengthens the pillars of government by the people and for the people. It teaches the sacredness of public obligation. It elevates moral standards in public life.

Fight Is for Principle Only

These are lessons which we should cherish. Let all else of this contest be forgotten. It does not signify who began it, or why it was begun. It has been decided. Let that suffice. I do not treasure one personal injury or lodge in memory one personal insult. With individuals I have no quarrel and will have none. The span of my life is too short for that. But so much as it pleases God to spare unto me I shall give, whether in the public service or out of it, to the contest for good government.

Every pledge of the platform which you have adopted here today has my unqualified approval, and, if elected, I shall, in so far as the direction of public affairs is committed to me, faithfully strive to carry out those pledges.

I accept a renomination firm in the resolution to discharge every duty that devolves upon me conscientiously, sustained by the abiding conviction that the republican party will redeem its pledges and press on to other victories.

If again chosen chief executive of this commonwealth, it will be my highest endeavor personally, and with the aid of my associates in office and the co-operation of the legislative department, to give to the people of Wisconsin an efficient and economical state government, honestly administered in a spirit of justice to all men and to all interests.

Speech Accepting Nomination for Governor,
July 16, 1902.

The Iniquity of the "Conference" System

Mr. President, one of the iniquities of our legislative system is that we turn over to conferees almost, if not quite, the absolute power to make legislation.

I hope that we shall early adopt a rule that conference reports shall be open to consideration in their items and be open to amendment on the floor.

Mr. President, a system of rules giving into the hands of a conference the power to make legislation is destructive of democracy.

Why, sir, the Senate is practically powerless when considering a conference report. It has to consider and to accept or reject the report as a whole. Legislation about which there is a wide difference of opinion between this legislative body and the one at the other end of the Capitol goes to conference. Out of the Conference committee will come a proposition that has almost no relation to the opinion expressed by the other House or the opinion expressed by the Senate when the original measure was under consideration.

This new proposition may be embodied in a report covering scores of pages. Every senator knows that when a conference report comes in, particularly in the latter days of a session, its details receive no consideration. It is passed without discussion of each of the many subjects it may cover. Maybe one single item in a conference report will be taken up and discussed; but, Mr. President, the senate knows from long experience that when such a report comes in, it is a hopeless proposition to undertake to deal with it in detail. And so, I say, it lies with the conferees to make our legislation.

I hope that as a member of this body I shall live to see the rules with respect to conference reports so changed that it will not be possible for two or three men to dictate and put through legislation. This is a democracy. We are supposed to be the representatives of the people.

Our work upon this floor and the work of our associates at the other end of the Capitol is supposed to represent public opinion and the interests of the great masses of this country. But I need not say to the Senators what everybody knows, that very often the public will is defeated, that public interest is perverted, and democracy is shackled in legislation as we enact it.

La Follette's Magazine, September, 1916.

Big Business and Government 159

(Note—There are many tricks in the making of laws. Perhaps the most familiar trick is known as the "joker." A "joker" in legislation is a well-known device by which bad provisions may be slipped into an otherwise acceptable bill. A "joker" is thoroughly dishonest. It is resorted to on every possible occasion by privileged interests that wish to destroy the effect of a good law demanded by public opinion.

But there is another legislative trick employed in congress quite as effectively as the "joker." This trick is in the system by which "conferees" from both the house and senate are appointed to adjust differences between the two houses on any measure of legislation. In actual practice it is possible in these conferences, for a handful of representatives to shape legislation.

This system should be thoroughly understood by every voter. It was explained by Senator La Follette in his speech on the floor of the United States Senate July 26, 1916, when he exposed Gallinger's attempt to have the Taylor "sweating plan" for working men slipped into the army appropriation bill—in conference—after it had been rejected by both the House and the Senate. See La Follette's Magazine for August, 1916.)

IX

THE TARIFF

What Tariff Should Be

HE passage of the Payne-Aldrich bill was the most outrageous assault of private interests upon the people recorded in tariff history.

In order to place the tariff on a scientific basis it is necessary to know:

What is the nature and use of a given commodity under consideration; what are the raw materials used in its production and manufacture; what is the amount of its production and consumption in this country; how many concerns are engaged in its manufacture; who are the principal producers; what are the ruling markets in this country. Then we must know the ruling market prices of this commodity in competing countries, what is the cost per unit of production in this and competing countries, what is the percentage of labor cost to the total cost of a unit of product, in this and in competing foreign countries; what is the cost of transportation to the principal markets from the points of production in this and competing foreign countries; what part of the proposed duty represents the difference in cost of production between this and foreign competing countries; what part of the proposed duty represents the reasonable profits of the American manufacturer, if he is to be given a reasonable profit.

La Follette's Magazine, 1912.

Tariff—For Amendment to Canadian Pact

Mr. President, shall we incur the risk of letting this chance of at least a partial tariff revision go by? How shall we answer to the public if we then fail of tariff reduction altogether?

Sir, the President has declared Schedule K an "indefensible outrage." Further, he made a campaign and was elected upon a declaration that the revision of the tariff should be downward and not upward. I believe he will think it unwise to withhold approval of a bill that enacts into law his particular measure—this Canadian pact, which is not reciprocity in any sense—because we have amended it, even though not to his liking. This will be especially true when our amendments actually reduce taxation upon the people of this country by revising downward that same Schedule K and some others nearly, if not quite, so intolerable.

Mr. President, what I shall offer to the senate as an amendment to the Canadian administration bill, as a revision of Schedule K and of the cotton schedule, will be shown to be easily and safely within the line of the difference in production cost. It will be offered with the expectation that when the Tariff Board shall have completed its expert work upon any one of these schedules that schedule can be taken up by Congress for thorough and scientific revision. I have no doubt that when that work shall have been done it will be found that upon the difference in the cost of production between this and the competing countries we can cut far below the duties which I shall propose in the amendments I offer.

Speech in U. S. Senate, June 21, 1911.

Tariff—Great Industries Over-Protected

I anticipate, Mr. President, that whenever we attempt tariff revision or seek to enact legislation interfering with the trust control of business a panic will be foreshadowed, that prices will be depressed for the products of the farmer, that labor will be thrown out of employment. and that all of the threats which will serve to frighten the farmer and the wage-earner will be heard on the hustings and seen on the printed page. But I shall do what I can to persuade the business men of small means and the wage-earners of this country to discredit those warnings as having any logical relation to wholesome legislation.

The predictions of panic resulting from tariff reductions may come true. They can be brought to pass. They need not come true. These great industries are overprotected. Their duties could be reduced in most cases much below the point fixed in this conference report and not disturb in the slightest degree a single industry in the country. Of that I am confident. These duties will be reduced, Mr. President, if not at this session, of the congress then in the very near future; and defeat at this time, whether it be here or whether it be interposed by executive veto, as threatened, will not long delay the lifting of these great burdens from the backs of the American people.

Speech in U. S. Senate, August 15, 1911.

The Farmer and the Tariff

The voters should not be misled and vote to increase the cost of living by high tariffs without any benefits in return. For years and years the farmers of this country, particularly in the northern states, have stood solidly for protective principles. They have gone to the polls election after election and returned to power the party pledged to this doctrine. It was not directly for their advantage that the tariff walls were raised higher and higher. But in the belief that they were ultimately to come into their own through the upbuilding of a great home market, for many years they consented to the maintenance of these high duties. They were not unmindful of the fact that they were thereby compelled to pay more for manufactured products they purchased than otherwise would be the case if these products came to them untaxed. But strong in the faith that they would be rewarded in the price paid for their products in the American market, they were content to go on paying more to the manufacturers who made their clothes, their machinery, manufactured their lumber, furniture and all supplies which they were required to purchase. They believed that by fostering our manufacturing industries the general prosperity of the nation would be enhanced, that a great and well paid manufacturing population was the best guarantee of a great and well patronized farming population.

Thus the farmer was persuaded to support the protective system. With patience and good cheer he gave long years of toil to the hardship of opening up new lands and creating new agricultural empires to afford a wider and firmer foundation for the nation's prosperity.

What was his reward?

The home market was then created, but it was not just the home market which had been the farmer's dream, and for which he sacrificed so much. Behind the protective tariff wall which he had helped to rear, the industries of the country sheltered from foreign competition had grown rich and powerful. They had become allied with other great and powerful interests, engaged in transportation, and those in turn had formed monster organizations for the control of stock yards, packing houses, and grain elevators. In short, these interests owned and controlled the home market. They fixed the farmer's prices arbitrarily. They took the profit of his toil. Added to this, the manufacturers protected against competitors and compelled the farmer and other consumers to pay higher and higher prices for manufactured products.

The result of these conditions may be said to be somewhat reflected in the recent census report, which shows a steady increase in the proportion of farms mortgaged over those which are free from incumbrance. In 1890, the number was 28.2 per cent; in 1900 it was 31.1 per cent; in 1910, the percentage of farms mortgaged had increased to 33.6 per cent!

With the market in which he must buy all his manufactured products controlled largely, if not wholly, by combinations, which has steadily increased the price of everything he buys, and with the market in which he must sell everything he produces controlled by combinations which arbitrarily fix the price that he receives, the farmer's support of the protective system will be a constantly diminishing factor as long as these conditions exist.

Speech at Sun Prairie, Wis., August 14, 1916.

Tariff Commission

I believe in protection to American industries and American labor. I believe that reasonable protection is measured by the difference in cost between the manufacture of the article in this country and the cost of manufacture abroad. A tariff based on this principle can be made only upon scientific study and research. I have favored, together with other progressive Republicans, a tariff commission whose duty it will be to ascertain the cost of production in this country and other countries of the world. A tariff bill deals with thousands of products. Reliable data for determining the cost of production has been worked out with accuracy on several of the most important schedules covered by the tariff. As to the products the cost of producing which is not known, we must make the best estimates possible with the material at hand. With a tariff commission to gather accurate data it will not be difficult to pass a tariff bill that will protect the American manufacturers who are dealing fairly with the American people.

La Follette's Magazine, October, 1916.

X
MONEY AND BANKING

On Amending the National Banking Law

T is quite generally admitted that our currency and banking laws need revision. In my reading I have found no authority to the contrary. Throughout this debate there has run a note of apology and excuse for this bill; that it is, granting all that its author and friends claim for it, but an expedient for extreme and perilous situations. It is admitted to be a makeshift.

A review of the debates of recent years touching our banking laws shows that necessity for revision has long been recognized. The subject has recurred from time to time whenever forced upon the attention of the Senate by some financial or commercial disturbance, but not otherwise. Propositions are always forthcoming, timed to fit some particular trouble, calling for some specific action, and usually resulting in benefit to the Special Interests. It would appear that we might learn much from European countries in regard to bank management and currency legislation.

For my own part, Mr. President, I believe this subject one of supreme importance, requiring study and research, such as no committee of this body will bestow upon it. I do not believe that any other great nation in the world situated as we are would fail to create a suitable commission for investigation and report. Such a commission should be composed of men representing not the banking interests of the country alone, representing not the banking interests engaged in speculative banking at all, but representing commercial banking interests, representing transportation interests, representing producers and consumers, to which should be added a Government expert who has served in the office of the Comptroller of the Currency, and one or more eminent economists who have made a special study of Government finance.

Mr. President, I have talked in vain if I have not made plain the thought that there is just one issue before the country today. It is not currency. It is not tariff. It is not railroad legislation. These and other important questions are but phases of one great conflict.

Let no man think he is not concerned; that his state or his constituency is not interested. There is no remote corner of this country where the power of special interests is not encroaching on public rights.

Let no man think this is a question of party politics. It strikes down to the very foundation of our free institutions. The System knows no party. It is supplanting government.

Mr. President, I think I may say without risk of being misunderstood, at least by those of whom I speak, that I know something of the sentiment of the people of this country.

I have found no difference of opinion among them as to existing conditions and the causes underlying it all. In Wisconsin, and from New York to the Pacific states, the people I have met hold one opinion, have one conviction.

They are deeply concerned. They understand. Men back of the system seem to know not what they do.

In their strife for more money, more power—more power, more money—there is no time for thought, for reflection. They look neither forward nor backward. Government, society, and the individual are swallowed up in the struggle for greater control. The plain man living the wholesome life of peace and contentment has a better perspective, a saner judgment. He has ideals and conscience and human emotions. Home, children, neighbors, friends, church, schools, country, constitute life. He knows very definitely, the conditions affecting the rights guaranteed him by the constitution, but he longs for expression, he longs for leadership. Blind indeed is he who does not see what the time portends. He who would remain in public service must serve the public, not the system. He must serve his country, not special interests. I believe this bill will strengthen the power that grows every day a greater menace to the industrial and commercial liberty of the American people. I believe this will strengthen the very element that is undermining the commercial banking of the country.

Speech in U. S. Senate, '1908.

Private Control of Legislation

Do you know that something over forty years ago patriotic independent postmasters-general began to appeal through their reports to congress for postal savings banks? I was a member of the house of representatives in 1886. I was the youngest member of the house then. I want to say right now so as not to have any misunderstanding about my age. William F. Vilas was postmaster-general. William F. Vilas figured it out that we were paying to the railroad companies for the use of the car which you see in every train marked "Railway Postal Car," or something like that, to indicate that it is a post office on wheels—that we were paying for the rent of those post offices (that is all they are, just as your post office here is a federal building, so are these cars our post offices) annually on these cars $500,000 more than enough to build them and take care of them every twelve months.

An old Wisconsin boy then in the house of representatives, Henry Clay Evans, a car manufacturer at Chattanooga, Tennessee, came over to my desk to talk to me about that. "Why," he says, "that is an awful thing." He was a member of the committee on post offices and post roads. He said, "I am going to have that amended in committee, and I am going to put through an amendment to have the government as Postmaster General Vilas recommends, build those cars and own them just as the government owns its other post offices, and merely hire the railroad company to pull them around."

"Well, Clay," I said, "I think that is a splendid thing; now you let me know how you get along with that down in the committee." I had been there one term longer than he had, you know. He came up one day after a committee meeting, a square-jawed fellow, you know, and he looked positively frightful, he was so angry. He said: "Do you know I offered that resolution in the committee and I got one, just one vote for it—my vote." "But," he said, "I will fix it on the floor. I am going to offer it on the floor, I gave notice to the committee that I would." I said, "All right Clay, now you just go in; I will do what I can to help you." He offered it on the floor and you know what happened to it. We got four or five votes out of 325—that was the membership of the house at that time.

We go on today paying that same exorbitant rent for the use of those cars. I have tried since I have been back in the senate to get some action, to get an investigation of the subject, to do something. You know the same men who own these great group banks own the railroads of this country They do. That is just a suggestion, you know. I could stand here all night long, so could your own senator here, and detail to you the history, piece after piece of legislation the last ten or fifteen years just like that, just like that.

Currency Reform Is Long Battle

Take the banking and currency laws of the country. We have got a currency commission now. Senator Aldrich is at the head of it. He named the other members. They are going to help him out. They are going to report out a measure this coming congress. I suspect it is going to be for a central bank. But I suspect the control of that bank will be here. Fight, as you would fight for your lives against that legislation. I don't care who backs it up or who endorses it. I don't care what sanction it may have from high places; fight it as you would fight for your lives, because the control of the currency is the last ditch.

Money and Banking 171

Do you know what the acting comptroller of the currency said in an interview while the Aldrich emergency currency bill was pending in the United States senate? He said that for forty years, and he named the number of comptrollers of the currency that had been in office during that period of time, they had, in their annual reports to congress, made recommendations in the interests of the depositors of banks and of the public generally, not one of which had been adopted in all that time by congress.

Acting Commissioner Kane, who has been in office for many years, is assistant comptroller of the currency. He is a man whose knowledge and whose information and whose character and standing are high enough and important enough to be retained there to do the real work while nominal heads come and go over him. He said boldly in an interview over his own name, while that so-called emergency bill was pending in the United States senate, that no legislation recommended in the public interest had received any attention from congress and that the only legislation on the currency question which did get attention from congress was legislation which served some financial power. He was driven so by his sense of what was right and just and due to the American people, during the pendency of that gigantic fraud as a financial proposition that was perpetrated on the American people merely for the purpose of finding a market among the banks of this country for the securities of these over-capitalized organizations that were made and legitimatized by that measure as a proper basis for emergency currency in time of distress. He felt so

outraged by that legislation that on Sunday morning in the Washington Post he gave that interview which was a challenge to and a denunciation of congress on its record through all those years.
Speech at St. Paul, Oct. 9, 1909.

High Finance—Interlocking Directorates—Backbone of the Money Power

The most effective invention for the centralized control of capital and credit which the ingenuity of high finance has contrived, is the interlocking directorates.

The scheme is simple. To establish a common interest and bind together great banking concerns the necessary stock is acquired by purchase or exchange in the various banks of an extended chain of such institutions, which it is desired to combine. This carries with it the right of representation on the several boards of directors and unifies the organization. It establishes a stable working connection which mere commercial exchanges in the ordinary course of banking transactions cannot begin to approach. In short, it enables a few men to exercise wide control over all who must deal with these allied banks. It is the backbone of the money power.
La Follette's Magazine, September 27, 1913.

XI

INITIATIVE, REFERENDUM AND RECALL

Instruments of Democracy

FOR years the American people have been engaged in a terrific struggle with the allied forces of organized wealth and political corruption. Battles have been won and lost. The unequal contest goes on. The lesson is obvious. The people must have in reserve new weapons for every emergency, if they are to regain and preserve control of their government.

The forces of special privilege are deeply entrenched. Their resources are inexhaustible. Their efforts never relax. Their political methods are insidious. It is impossible for the people to maintain perfect organization in mass. They are often taken unawares and are liable to lose at one stroke the achievements of years of effort. In such a crisis nothing but the united power of the people expressed directly through the ballot can overthrow the enemy.

Through the initiative, referendum and recall the people in any emergency can absolutely control. The initiative and referendum make it possible for them to demand a direct vote and repeal bad laws which have been enacted, or to enact by direct vote good measures which their representatives refuse to consider. The recall enables the people to dismiss from public service those representatives who dishonor their commissions by betraying the public interest. These measures will prove so effective a check against unworthy representatives that it will rarely be found necessary to invoke them.

People Have Last Word

Constitutions and statutes and all the complex details of government are but instruments created by the citizen for the orderly execution of his will. Whenever and wherever they fail, they will be so changed as to make them effective to execute and express the well-considered judgment of the citizen.

For over and above constitutions and statutes, and greater than all, is the supreme sovereignty of the people!

We need not fear, Mr. President. This is the people's government. They will not destroy it. They will not permit organized privilege to destroy its vital principle. They will restore and forever preserve it as a government that shall be truly representative of the will of the people.

They know that the initiative and referendum will place in the hands of the people the power to protect themselves against the mistakes or indifference of their representatives in the legislature. Then it will always be possible for the people to demand a direct vote and to repeal a bad law which the legislature has enacted, or to enact by direct vote a good measure which the legislature has refused to consider.

The recall will enable the people to dismiss from public service a representative whenever he shall cease to serve the public interest. Then no jackpot politician can hold his office in defiance of the will of a constituency whose commission he has dishonored.

Wherever representative government fails, it fails because the representative proves incompetent or false to his trust. Intrenched in office for his full term, his constituency is powerless and must submit to misrepresentation. There is no way to correct his blunders or to protect against his betrayal. At the expiration of his service he may be replaced by another who will prove equally unworthy. The citizen is entitled to some check, some appeal, some relief, some method of halting and correcting the evils of misrepresentation and betrayal.

La Follette's Magazine, October 17, 1914.

To the Voters of Wisconsin

I believe in the intelligence and patriotism of the people of Wisconsin. I believe they are capable of self-government. The common, average judgment of the community is always wise, rational and trustworthy. I would see them clothed with the largest power to say the final word as to the laws under which they are to live and the government they maintain.

The republican platform of Wisconsin is the strongest guarantee yet given for perpetuating self-government. If the pledges of the republican platform become the law of this state, government of the people, by the people, will be forever safe in Wisconsin.

A perfected primary law will insure majority nomination. Then the will of the majority can no longer suffer defeat through division of votes among several candidates representing the same principles.

A strong corrupt practices law will limit the use of money in elections. Then no man can buy political office and power in Wisconsin and the public service will be equally within the reach of all men.

Fellow citizens, if you would insure faithful and efficient administration of progressive legislation enacted in recent years,—the regulation of railway rates and services, the regulation of the rates and services of all public utilities, the collection of a just and reasonable tax upon all public-service corporations in this state, the rigid enforcement of the pure food and dairy statutes, the thorough inspection of factories, the strict enforcement of laws for the protection of the public health, the vigilant supervision of insurance, the advancement and support of our educational system, the proper care and management of our charitable and penal institutions—if you would secure the conservation and control of waterpowers by the state for the benefit of all the people, the enactment of a graduated income tax law, home rule for cities, the benefits of a workmen's compensation statute, a thorough investigation of co-operative buying and selling, storage and warehousing as affecting the farmer and the consumer, co-operative credit and collective bargaining and arbitration between employers and employees,—if you approve of the course of the progressive representatives of Wisconsin in congress, their fight against a tariff bill that violated platform pledges and imposed ever increasing burdens upon the consumer, their struggle to frame

a just and efficient postal savings bank law to serve
the interests of the people rather than promote the
interests of Wall Street, their successful labors in
so reconstructing the railway rate bill as to make
it a public benefit instead of a positive public
injury—if you would maintain Wisconsin as the
leader of this great progressive movement to
restore government to the people, then make the
majority for the principles declared in this platform
and for the candidates who really and truly represent those principles, the largest and most decisive
ever recorded in the history of the state.

Voter Wields Supreme Power

At no time in the last half century has there been
such imperative reason for patriotic independence
on the part of the American voter. The ballot is his
weapon. He should use it everywhere independently, fearlessly. Teach both political parties that they
can no longer play the voter for a fool. Strike down
as an enemy of the republic any candidate of any
party whose past record or present connection
marks him as the agent of special interests. To
seek to invoke in this hour of the life of American
democracy the party spirit to maintain party solidarity, and to assure a party victory regardless of the
relative merits of opposing candidates, regardless
of a record of subserviency to privilege, is a surrender of every principle that has made the progressive movement the hope of millions. Let it go to
the country on November eighth that Wisconsin
places service to the public interest above service
to any political party, and that her progressive
leaders never betrayed their cause. Sometimes,

mistaken in men, they have suffered humiliation and temporary reverses, but the leaders of the progressive movement and the great mass of the voters in Wisconsin, have kept the faith alike, and regardless of party, have fought a good fight, a successful fight to make state government in Wisconsin a real representative democracy.

Letter to Wisconsin Voters, November 3, 1910.

The Recall

* * * I do not believe you will ever get any true representative government in the United States, until there is in the hands of the people the power to recall the representative who betrays them.

Every business institution in America has that right in the case of an unfaithful employee,—be he a cashier in a bank, the manager of a big trust concern, the president of a railroad. It does not make any difference how long the term of office or the term of contract of such a man, if it be found that the man failed to serve faithfully under the terms of his contract and had betrayed the party to whom he has made obligations in his contract of faithful service, he can be thrown out of his position.

But the United States Senator and Member of the House of Representatives and the other gentlemen who may get in under false pretenses, pretending to represent the public interest, and who then betray the public interest, cannot be driven from power for six years or four years or two years. I think that is unfair to the public

Speech in U. S. Senate, June 28, 1919.

XII

FEDERAL JUDGES AND INJUNCTIONS

The Election of Federal Judges

THIS is a democracy. The people shall rule.

The ballot should be the safeguard against bloodshed and anarchy. Wise men will look to the future through the history of the past. They will desire to avoid the throes of revolution by force by peaceful change through the ballot and we will win. We shall not, we must not, let this thing go on to bloody tragedy.

Government must be made more responsible to the people. Life terms of office should be abolished. The appointing power should be limited to administrative officers. Federal judges with powers greater than the Congress should be subject to election by the people, as judges are in the state courts. Upon their records as judges they should be required to go to the people.

From "Sanctified Crime," La Follette's
Magazine, March, 1920.

The Sacred Rights of Property

Why should we temporize? Why should we approach this subject on tiptoe, with apology to special interests and apostrophe to property rights? Honest wealth needs no guaranty of security in this country. Property rightfully acquired does not beget fear—it fosters independence, confidence, courage. Property which is the fruit of plunder feels insecure. It is timid. It is quick to cry for help. It is ever proclaiming the sacredness of vested rights. The thief can have no vested rights in stolen property. I resent the assumption that the great wealth of this country is safe only when the millionaires are on guard. Property rights are not the special charge of the owners of great fortunes. Even the poor may be relied upon to protect property. They have so little—the little they have is so precious—that they are easily enlisted to defend the rights of property.

Speech, U. S. Senate, April 19–21, 1906, *on
"Regulation of Railway Rates and Services."*

A Judicial Oligarchy

The judiciary has grown to be the most powerful institution in our government. It, more than any other, may advance or retard human progress. Evidence abounds that, as constituted today, the courts pervert justice almost as often as they administer it. Precedent and procedure have combined to make one law for the rich and another for the poor. The regard of the courts for fossilized precedent, their absorption in technicalities, their detachment from the vital, living facts of the present day, their constant thinking on the side of the rich and powerful and privileged classes have brought our courts into conflict with the democratic spirit and purposes of this generation. Moreover, by usurping the power to declare laws unconstitutional and by presuming to read their own views into statutes without regard to the plain intention of the legislators, they have become in reality the supreme law-making institution of our government. They have taken to themselves a power it was never intended they should exercise; a power greater than that entrusted to the courts of any other enlightened nation. And because this tremendous power has been so generally exercised on the side of the wealthy and powerful few, the courts have become at last the strongest bulwark of special privilege. They have come to constitute what may indeed be termed a "judicial oligarchy."

Sensing this, the people have become distrustful. In various ways they have shown their dissatisfaction with the work of the courts. Severe attacks have been made recently upon the integrity and ability of certain judges. Everywhere there is a growing public demand for a change that will bring the judiciary again into its proper sphere and into closer communion with the progressive ideals of this generation.

La Follette's Magazine, June 22, 1912.

XIII

THE PROGRESSIVE MOVEMENT

What is the Progressive Movement?

FTER all it is a simple matter to define the progressive movement. It can be expressed in a single sentence. It comprehends the aspirations of the human race in its struggle from the beginning down to the present time.

The will of the people shall be the law of the land. Constitutions, statutes and all of the complex details of government are but instruments to carry out the will of the people, and when they fail —when constitutions and statutes and all of the agencies employed to execute constitutions and statutes fail—they must be changed so as to carry out and express the well formulated judgment and the will of the people. For over all and above all, and greater than all, and expressing the supreme sovereignty of all, are the people.

Address at Republican Platform Convention, 1910.

Origin of the Movement

The essence of the progressive movement, as I see it, lies in its purpose to uphold the fundamental principles of representative government. It expresses the hopes and desires of millions of common

The Progressive Movement 183

men and women who are willing to fight for their ideals, to take defeat if necessary, and still go on fighting.

In the state of Wisconsin the progressive movement expressed itself in the rise to power of the Patrons of Husbandry. The Grange movement swept four or five middle western states, expressing vigorously the first powerful revolt against the rise of monopolies, the arrogance of railroads and the waste and robbery of the public lands.

In Wisconsin the granger movement went so far as to cause a political revolution and the election in 1874 of a democratic governor. A just and comprehensive law for regulating the railroads was passed and a strong railroad commission was instituted. It was then, indeed, that the railroads began to dominate politics for the first time in this country. They saw that they must either accept control by the state or control the state. They adopted the latter course; they began right there to corrupt Wisconsin—indeed to corrupt all the states of the middle west. And as usual they were served by the cleverest lawyers and writers that money could hire.

Introduction to Autobiography, 1913.

Wisconsin's Progressive Laws

Wisconsin stands in the forefront of states by reason of the progressive legislation enacted under Republican administration during the last ten years, including laws for direct nominations; for an untrammeled vote at the election; for the ad valorem system of taxing railroads; to remove the pernicious influence of the lobby in legislation; to promote education and particularly agricultural and industrial training; to provide adequate regulation through the railroad commission of rates and services of railroads and public utilities; to conserve the state domain through the forestry commission; to regulate insurance; to protect employees in hazardous occupations; to regulate child labor; to prevent adulteration in foods; and to protect public health by sanitary regulations.

Republican State Platform, 1910.

Keeping Faith with the People

I am informed by your committee that you have elected me to represent Wisconsin as United States senator. Assembled in joint session under organic and statutory law you are empowered to speak for all the people of this commonwealth. Any man, at any time in his life, may well regard an election to the United States senate as the highest honor to which he can attain in the public service. That you should have chosen me at this time, and in this way, and in the spirit manifested, fills me with a sense of gratitude I can in no wise express. You have bestowed upon me, unsought, the greatest distinction which any state can confer upon any citizen. This mark of your confidence I shall cherish in grateful memory while I live.

Whenever I have believed that I could be helpful in the public service, I have frankly and openly declared my candidacy. It has seemed to me the more honorable way. Months ago, had I been free to become a candidate for the office of United States senator, I should have so declared at that time. But for many years, issues in which I feel a profound interest have been pending in this state. Believing that I could best serve the public by so doing, I offered myself as a candidate for governor in support of these issues. I was twice elected, and, as God gave me to see the right, served the state as best I could. Great progress was made, but the work was unfinished. To assist in that unfinished work, I was, for the third time, elected governor.

I am sure that none of you, who have borne with me the bitterness and fury of campaigns for a decade of time, would, for any consideration, endanger the consummation and protection of that work in which we have been engaged.

We have seen it grow from the assertion of principle to the enactment of broad and comprehensive statutes which bulwark and fortify the foundations of representative government. We have seen it grow in interest until it passed the boundaries of the state and fixed the attention of the nation, and we have seen it expand upon the national side into the dominant issue in national legislation, where it has slumbered for many years.

I would not have any member of the legislature, nor any citizen of the commonwealth, believe that I do not comprehend the wide scope of the duties of the high office of United States senator, nor of the obligation it carried to serve impartially the whole state and the whole nation, and all the people, and all the people's interests.

Feels Solemn Responsibility

But I believe I am not blinded by any feeling of prejudice, nor warped by any hard experience, in regarding the past decade in political history in

Wisconsin and the next decade in the political history of the United States, as epochmaking years in state and national government. There are important patriotic duties of this generation of men to perform in both of these great fields. Mindful as I must always be and you must always be—for the most of you carry wounds and scars of this long civic strife—of the profound significance of the last ten years of political history in Wisconsin for the principles which underlie government by the people, your action in electing me United States senator seems to come as a commission from you, and the people of the state through you, to carry a message, out of our service here, into the wider field of national legislation. Your call invites me to participate in that great work, which was to deal immediately with the problems President Roosevelt has courageously pressed upon congress for solution.

I appreciate that you have the same sense of obligation to the people of Wisconsin which I have. I fully realize that if you did not believe I could serve the people's interests better as senator than as governor, you would not have taken this action today.

It would, indeed, be presumptuous for me to assume that you have not fully considered every phase of every question that can be raised by the action which you have taken. It would be doubly presumptuous in me to assume that my presence here is vital. I do not indulge that presumption, but I cannot at this time wholly divest myself of a sense of duty to the people of Wisconsin that, however difficult to define in specific terms, nevertheless exists, and is a valid reason for the course I am impelled to take, and which I trust your deliberate judgment will commend. For all of us must recognize the common obligation. We are commissioned by the same sovereign authority. We have accepted from them the same trust. The obligation is binding and the trust is sacred. They must be kept inviolate and fulfilled according to their intent and spirit. To achieve this we must each, in his own sphere, give to the state all that an important official duty, once assumed, may demand.

Pledges Faithfulness to People

We are at the very beginning of the session, and while at the present time there would seem to be no reason for any conflict of obligation, and while I do not believe that any one can arise in state and national affairs to make that which today seems plain and simple appear complex and difficult, nevertheless, I desire to exercise every possible precaution against future contingencies.

I wish to be entirely frank with you and the people of the state, as I have always tried to be. There shall be no concealments nor any misunderstanding through any fault of mine. If a public office is a public trust, there should be no deception on the part of the official in the relation to those for whom he holds the trust.

I cannot but feel I was elected governor of this state because the people believed I stood for certain things in government, and that I would not relax my efforts until I had done all in my power legitimately as governor to accomplish certain results.

If, at the very beginning of the session, before any legislation has been enacted, before there is any certainty that there will not be a conflict in duty as United States senator-elect and as governor of the state, I accept without qualification or explanation the honor you have tendered me, I fear my action would be misinterpreted by the people of Wisconsin. It might lessen their faith in official obligation, it might undermine their confidence, and weaken their interest in the final fulfillment of the pledges made to them. I cannot believe that we can even partially fail in the faithful performance of every duty. I cannot at present see what I could do as governor for this legislation after this session should terminate, if there were failure, either in whole or in part, which I might not do equally well, and, perhaps, more effectively, as a United States senator, in co-operation with the people of this commonwealth for a people's government. But, recognizing, as I must, the present obligations which rest upon me, I am compelled to be in readiness to meet any unforeseen issue which may develop.

For these reasons, then, I say, in accepting your high commission, that, if there should appear any conflict in the obligation I entered into when I took the oath of office as governor, and that of United States senator-elect, then I shall ask you to receive it from me and place it in other hands of your own choosing. The selection of United States senator is your prerogative and will, of course, be preserved to you.

Huge Task Seen Ahead

That it would call for any great personal sacrifice on my part to be compelled for any reason to decline the office of United States senator, I need scarcely say. The opportunity which you offer to me to serve the state is the greatest which could come to any man in this generation. At no time, since the close of the war, have the essential principles of popular government been in greater peril. The government is seeking to control public-service, corporations and industrial combinations are seeking to control government. The next few years will test the vital principles of democracy in this country as never before.

Gentlemen, I thank you from a full heart for this great opportunity, this great honor, this great trust. I feel that the close relationship and mutual confidence which have heretofore existed between my self and the people of Wisconsin are equally vital as between the people and one elected to serve as United States senator. If that relation continues, it shall ever be my care to strengthen and preserve that intimacy and confidence. State government and national government are inseparably associated and constantly react upon each other. The interdependence in the spirit is closer than in the letter of the law.

If I enter this service, it will be in the hope that friendships and associations with the people will strengthen and increase. That the republican party will find me in sympathy with and enlisted in the support of issues which deeply concern state government, and that in so far as I have ability and power, I shall represent all the interests of the state and sacredly keep faith with the people in all things.

Speech on Election as U. S. Senator, Jan. 25, 1905.

XIV

MILITARISM

Preparedness Should be for Defense

THE present congress will pass a military program that will impose upon the people of the United States the greatest tax burden for an alleged preparedness against an alleged danger that has ever been known in any country at peace with all the world.

The appropriations by the present congress for all military purposes, that is to say for army and navy and coast defense, military academies, naval academies and pensions, will approximate the sum of $840,000,000.

For the same purpose a year ago congress appropriated in round numbers $429,000,000. The appropriation for this year is nearly double that of a year ago.

This appropriation is so colossal as to stagger the imagination. Applying the figures to Wisconsin we find that Wisconsin's share of this military and naval appropriation will be approximately $20,000,000.

This is equivalent to $8 per capita, that is $8 each for every man, woman and child in the state. Counting five persons to the family it is equivalent to $40 for each family.

Militarism

You understand that government revenues are largely raised by tariffs or taxes on the things we eat and wear, and use in our daily life. As a general rule it is not a direct tax and you do not appreciate the day of reckoning, but it is a constant drain on the resources of the American people. There is something to pay today and every day. It goes into the cost of living and adds to the burdens of the poor.

What do we want of an increased navy and an increased army such as this great military program provides? What changed conditions warrant doubling the appropriation of a year ago? There is absolutely nothing in the situation, nothing in the conditions that can be made to justify placing this extortionate tax burden upon the people of the United States. There is not one substantial reason why this congress should double the appropriation for military purposes at this time.

They claim that we are preparing for defense, not for aggression. Logically we should inquire first of all as to our coast defenses, should we not? What about our coast defenses?

The highest authority on this subject is Gen. Erasmus Weaver. He testified before the house committee on military affairs that "We have the best coast defenses in the world. The guns now mounted and those contemplated will give us an entirely satisfactory defense."

Speech at Menomonee Falls, Wisconsin, 1916.

Prepare for Peaceful Industry not War

According to the statement of Gen. Nelson A. Miles, we have expended $200,000,000 upon our

coast defenses. I do not disparage expenditures for
this purpose. I give them my cordial support.
Coast fortifications, coast artillery and a sufficient
mobile force of soldiers for coast and harbor defense, I will as strongly support as any other man.
They are for defense. They cannot be used for
overseas conquest; they cannot be used to coerce
weaker nations in the interest of speculative investors in foreign countries. They offer little or no
inducement for powerful war traders to lobby congress for extravagant appropriations. They constitute one class of expenditures for preparedness
which makes for peace instead of war.

Just in the proportion that they destroy the soldiery of Europe, just as they feed the men between
18 and 45 years of age to the cannons, wiping out
ten to twelve millions of the virile manhood of the
world, just by so much the reasons diminish why
we should begin an extravagant, extortionate program of taxation upon the people of this country
for what we call preparedness.

I want you to understand that for the past 15
years our naval appropriations have exceeded those
of Germany by 50 per cent., they have exceeded
those of Japan by 300 per cent., and now in this
last year of our Lord 1916, we double the appropriation of the preceding year, and the appropriation of 1915 was $55,000,000 more than Great Britain had expended on her navy during any year of
peace. Compare the preparations for peace with the
preparations for war. The Panama canal, the greatest and most extensive piece of engineering the
world has ever seen, cost the United States $400,-

Militarism

000,000. But one appropriation for war preparation cost the United States more than twice the vast sum, or nearly $800,000,000.

We have better uses for our money.

Beneficent Use of Money

Let us prepare the manhood and the womanhood of our country for the struggles of peace; more compensation for the industrial soldiers who fall by the wayside by reason of the hazards of their occupations; more compensation to their widows and children; pensions for the aged and infirm who have failed in the struggle of life to gain a pittance against old age or misfortune; more wages; more education; more money for the common good; more money to fight contagious diseases. This is the preparedness toward which we should turn. We should spend less to prepare to kill and more to prepare to live.

I stand for adequate defense of our country against any aggressor, but when our capitalists draw their money from this country to stake it on the turn of fortune's wheel in some foreign land, let them take the gambler's chance. If money is to be spent to make their foreign risks secure, let it be their own money. If lives are to be risked, men sacrificed to protect their possessions in foreign lands, let it be their own lives that take the hazard. Believing in democracy, the right of self-government—ready to defend the precious heritage of our own sovereignty—let us here and now resolve and declare that we will never permit the armed force of the United States to be used to despoil our sister republics of their property, nor to interfere with their right to govern themselves according to their own standard, nor violate their sovereignty—as sacred to them as our sovereignty is to us.

Mr. President, the interests that are behind this preparedness program in the United States do not fear Germany, do not fear England, do not fear any nation on this earth; but they do want a large army, they do want a large navy. It fits into the commercial, industrial, and imperialistic schemes of the great financial masters of this country.

Senators may think it expedient to vote for this increased appropriation at this time. The people may be under a certain vague fear and in doubt now, but when they see that their fears have been played upon, when the tax burden comes, when the weight begins to press down, when you double on every member of the family the cost of sustaining this military program, then you will be called to account, then you will have to answer their stern, deliberate, second judgment.

The danger of an attack upon our country has been made to appear very real and very imminent. It has been painted in lurid colors—motion pictures showing New York's splendid edifices toppling to destruction under the shots of enemy guns, the enemy garbed to convey the idea that they are Germans; volumes written to show New York and New Orleans and San Francisco already captured; that the foreign hordes are sweeping across the country—have these volumes been sent to you, Senators? I have received them. Who do you suppose pays for all this? Why, the Du Pont Powder Co. had a hand in it; the Bethlehem Steel Co. doubt-

Militarism

less made its contribution of millions of money. It was paid for out of the bloody profits made from shipping arms and ammunition abroad within the last year.

True, the American people may be influenced by the advertisements of the Bethlehem Steel Co., may be swayed by the headlines and editorials of the great metropolitan press. They may be deeply moved, the blood may tingle and the pulse quickened to the strains of hundreds of bands playing as hundreds of thousands of men and women march in parade; but when it is known that many American citizens felt impelled to march in fear of a penalty—the loss of wages or of being discharged—it alters folks' attitude as to the impressiveness of such demonstrations.

Speech in U. S. Senate, July 19-20, 1916.

Mexico and Financial Imperialism

Back of all modern war is practically one policy. It is financial imperialism. It is the scheme of using the surplus wealth wrung unlawfully from the people of a country by the financial interests that dominate that country, and the use of that surplus wealth through investments in the weaker, undeveloped governments of the world.

The Boer war which lasted three years cost Great Britain $1,250,000,000.

And it did not accomplish anything!

Keep that in mind when some of the gentlemen who are speaking for American investments in Mexico clamor for war with Mexico. There is a momentous lesson in the efforts of the representatives of two nations to arrive at an understanding and avert the consequences of war. But if there should come some flaming up of passions, if there should come some opportunity for the representatives of those who have bought Mexico with American money and want to rule it—want intervention—then let us all remember what happened to England in an effort to subjugate the Boers.

If we ever enter upon the conquest of Mexico—and the office of prophecy is a somewhat hazardous one—let me say that in a hundred years we will not conquer Mexico; we will maintain for a hundred years a standing army of a million men in Mexico; we will place the burden of that on the American people.

If the time ever comes when we shall attempt to invade Mexico, it will be because American capital has gone down there and invested. They who own Mexico are the ones who want war.

Now, Mr. President, it may be a new doctrine to the senate of the United States, but I think it is pretty nearly time to have the issue made. It may not win in the first struggle here. It will win ultimately, because it is everlastingly right. That is the reason for the amendment I have offered.

I believe every dollar that goes into a foreign country and every man who goes into a foreign country with his money looking for profits should accept the laws of the country as the arbiter to which he will appeal for justice if he feels at any time that he is required to protect his rights in that country.

The thing that attracts capital to Mexico is its rich natural resources. They have an unstable gov-

Militarism

ernment there. That unstable government lowers the value of property. American money there can buy for $100,000 because of the government conditions, property that is worth a million dollars. Now, if this new doctrine that the flag shall follow the investment of the citizen is to prevail, then our government is to be called upon to guarantee the speculative investments of its citizens in the countries where the governments are weak, and so to make those speculative investments worth face value.

The people of the United States do not want war with Mexico. The Mexican people do not want war with us. And both President Wilson and Carranza have manifestly done everything in their power to avert war.

What is it, then, that menaces the peace of these neighboring countries?

The Game of Foreign Investors

It dates far back of the Columbus raid. That outrage upon the residents of one of our border towns was the logical outcome of conditions for which the Mexican people were in nowise responsible. Worse than that! Both Governments were the victims of traitors in our midst. For it is charged upon the highest authority that the raid was inspired and arranged for in our own country.

There you have it! The gentlemen who want war with Mexico are the gentlemen who "have Mexican properties." They are a very powerful lot. They own most of the United States and a good big slice of Mexico. They are our captains of industry; our masters of finance. They own or control our great newspapers. They are for a "strong Mexican policy," a "strong foreign policy," a big army, a big navy.

There is just one risk, and that is a large risk. The governments are most of them weak. Revolutions in many of them are frequent; property rights are insecure.

But a scheme has been worked out by the masters of finance to make foreign investments as good as a government bond. Just put the stars and stripes back of them.

The interests of this country are confronted with the alternative of loaning their surplus wealth to the farmer, to the merchant, to the small enterprise at a constantly lowering interest rate or of withdrawing the surplus capital from this country, keeping interest rates high here and going down into the weak governments of Mexico, Central and South America, which are rich in natural resources, minerals, oil, timber, coal, and iron, surpassing all imagination, we are told, and acquiring control there.

As a protest against the use of our navy to enforce the claims of these interests, I have offered the following amendment:

Provided, That no battleship, cruiser, scout cruiser, torpedo-boat, destroyer, or submarine herein appropriated for shall be employed in any manner to coerce or compel the collection of any pecuniary claim of any kind, class, or nature, or to enforce any claim or right to any grant or concession for or on behalf of any private citizen, copartnership, or corporation of the United States against the government of Mexico or of any Central or South American government.

When our capitalists withdraw their money from this country to stake it on the turn of fortune's wheel in some foreign land, let them take the gambler's chance.

If money is to be spent to make their foreign risks secure, let it be their own money. If lives are to be risked to protect their Mexican mines—their Central and South American concessions—let it be their own lives that take the hazard.

Believing in democracy, in the right of self-government—ready to defend the precious heritage of our own sovereignty—let us here and now resolve and declare that we will never permit the armed forces of the United States to be used to despoil our sister republics of their property, interfere with their right to govern themselves according to their own standards or violate their sovereignty—as sacred to them as American sovereignty is to us.

Speech in U. S. Senate, July 19-20, 1916.

XV
WAR

The Meaning of War

IT is well for us to remember that war is always cruel; that its iron tread means destruction and devastation, whether its march is across Europe or from Atlanta to the sea; that war arouses all the fiercest human passions; that there are always cases of brutality and outrage—and that usually there is quite as much of it on one side as upon the other.

La Follette's Magazine, Oct. 17, 1914.

Resolution for Conference of Neutral Nations

WHEREAS the most powerful nations of Europe have been engaged for over half a year in a terrible war of cumulative intensity and increasing destruction of human life; and whereas, recent inventions have revolutionized methods of warfare giving rise to unprecedented situations and conditions; and whereas the ever widening field of hostile operations in the war zone encroaches more and more day by day upon the common highways of commerce, inviting to complications which may at any moment entagle one or more of the neutral nations in situations of the gravest peril; and

WHEREAS it becomes of the utmost importance that at the earliest moment a conference of the neu-

Robert M. La Follette

tral nations should be called to consider the rights of neutrals under existing conditions, to work out a policy for the preservation of their own peace, and to tender their best offices of mediation to the belligerent nations; and

WHEREAS we, the people of the United States, are bound to each of the warring nations by ties of blood and country, compelling in us a profound interest in the cessation of hostilities and the restoration of peace, and by inheritance are best fitted to make initial appeal to each nation; now, therefore, be it

RESOLVED, ETC., that the president be authorized to convey to all neutral nations the desire of this government that an international conference be held for the purpose of promoting by co-operation and through its friendly offices:

First. The early cessation of hostilities and the establishment of peace among the warring nations of Europe;

Second. The consideration of uniform rules and regulations for the general limitation of armaments and the nationalization of the manufacture of all equipment and supplies used exclusively for military and naval purposes;

Third. The consideration of rules and regulations for the prohibition of the export of arms, ammunitions, artillery, vessels of war, armor plate, torpedoes, or any other thing designed exclusively for military and naval purposes from one country to another;

Fourth. The ultimate establishment of an international tribunal where any nation may be heard on any issue involving rights vital to its peace and the development of its national life, a tribunal whose decrees shall be enforced by the enlightened judgment of the world.

Fifth. The consideration of plans for the federation of the neutral nations in the adoption of rules and regulations which will provide for the neutralization of certain waters and maritime trade routes, and such other and further action as shall insure if possible, the peaceful maintenance and preservation of the sovereign rights of neutral commerce against dangers to which it is exposed through the extraordinary conditions developed by the world's greatest war; and

Sixth. For such other and further action as may tend, however remotely, to establish permanent world peace.

RESOLVED FURTHER, that the president be authorized to appoint commissioners to represent the United States at any conference whether called by the United States or by any other nation.

Introduced in the U. S. Senate, by Senator La Follette, Feb. 8, 1915.

Appeal for Conference of Neutral Powers

The neutrality of the United States cannot and should not be that of selfish indifference. It is based on sympathetic love and understanding. As a people we are intensely interested in the cessation of a war that is slaying our kindred, bringing indescribable desolation to the lands we love and to the homes of our fathers.

We do not want to see the map of Europe changed by might of conquest. We cannot believe that it is in the interest of human progress that any one of the nations should be wiped off the face of the earth. It is our inherent desire that each should preserve its natural autonomy; that each should have the largest opportunity for self-development, the largest share in the world's progress; and that each should be given, as of right, access to the highways of the sea.

It is a mistaken policy that assumes a community of nations can prosper any more than can a community of individuals by one or more tyrannizing over the others and monopolizing the world's markets. The world's greatest progress must be best served by the largest possible development of the national life of each country. We believe there is still room for all in the vast and undeveloped areas of the earth.

Mr. President, I have not attempted to discuss in any comprehensive way the vital questions with which the proposed conference would deal. These problems the nations themselves must solve.

What stands out in bold relief is the unmistakable duty of the American congress to authorize the president to convey to neutral nations the desire of this government for an international conference for the purpose of promoting by co-operation and through its friendly offices the early cessation of hostilities, the establishment of peace among the warring nations of Europe, the clear definition of the rights of neutral nations, and for the other purposes to which I have briefly adverted.

Speech, "Conference of Neutral Powers to Secure World Peace," U. S. Senate, February 12, 1915.

Congress Should Prescribe Foreign Policies

As I understand the pending controversy, the president assumes it to be the exclusive prerogative of the executive to pursue any foreign policy, whatever the issue, independent of any suggestion from either or both branches of congress.

The peremptory manner in which the administration forced action upon the resolution in the senate, the extraordinary proceedings by which the resolution was changed and tabled, without opportunity for debate or explanation, warrants the belief that the president denies congress the right to express its opinion upon a matter which lies within its constitutional authority quite as much as that of the executive.

I believe it to be vital to the safety and perpetuity of this government that congress should assert and maintain its right to a voice in declaring and prescribing the foreign policy of the United States.

And, sir, there is a larger international aspect of this question, with its accompanying responsibility, that cannot be shirked or ignored. Across the water the nations of Europe are giving their life-blood in a fratricidal struggle, which in its inception the people neither desired nor sanctioned.

And now the plain people, the saner people of the warring countries are organizing. For what? Why, to make sure that never again after this conflict has ceased shall the autocratic heads of European governments have it in their power, through secret diplomacy, to bring on such another world catastrophe.

Democratic control of foreign policies is a basic principle of all organized effort looking for the future establishment of permanent world peace. To this end, throughout the world, leagues of earnest, determined men and women, animated by a common purpose, are formulating plans, based on the provisions by which, in this country, one or both of the legislative branches of government have a share in the control of international affairs.

Shall we in this crisis of the world's history fail to assert our constitutional rights and by our negligence and default permit the establishment in this country of that exclusive executive control over foreign affairs that the people of Europe are now repenting amid the agonies of war?

Speech, "Congress has a Right to an Authoritative Voice in Declaring and Prescribing the Foreign Policy of the United States," U. S. Senate, March 10, 1916.

Consult the People

War is the most ghastly experience that can come to any country. And always it is the people—not the handful of men in positions of power—who must pay the full price. The price in dollars and cents. The price in dismembered families. The price in heart agonies. The price in bodily suffering. The price in numbed minds. The price in precious human lives. The price in putting together the nation's pieces, afterwards. Always it is the masses who pay.

Why not let those who must pay have something to say? Why not let the people themselves, on whom the burden of war falls, have a voice,—some direct expression,—along with finance and diplomacy, in determining whether there shall be war, or whether there shall not be war?

I believe that on a question like this, the gravest that can possibly come before the people of a nation, more than on any other problem of national policy or well-being, the people should be consulted.

The day is coming when the people, who always pay the full price, are going to have the final say over their own destinies. They themselves are going to decide whether they shall spill their blood out upon murderous battle fields. They themselves shall decide what questions of "defense," of "aggression," or of "national honor" may be involved, compelling enough to make them desire to kill and be killed. They who do the fighting and the dying will do the deciding.

The day is not yet here. We should all strive to hasten its coming. Meanwhile we should make it possible for the people to give voice to their deep convictions in a way that will register. Let us have an advisory vote upon this matter of war that will serve as a dictaphone within the chambers of congress, through which the voice of the people—the people who pay and who suffer—shall indeed reach the ears of those who represent them and who have, under the constitution, the sole power to declare war.

La Follette's Magazine, May, 1916.

Armed Ship Bill Gave War-Making Power to President

I was opposed to the armed ship bill. Under my oath as a senator it was my duty to do everything legitimately within my power to defeat it, and I exercised my constitutional rights and discharged my constitutional obligation to defeat the measure, in so far as permitted by the tyrannical action of a majority. This majority as I believe, and as I think the record plainly shows, resorted to a perversion of the rules and to the very filibustering methods which it so violently condemned, in order to prevent me from obtaining the floor to speak against the bill.

The armed ship bill provided that the president be authorized to supply our merchant vessels "with arms and also the necessary ammunition and means of making use of them," also that the president be "authorized and empowered to employ such other instrumentalities and methods as may in his judgment and discretion seem necessary and adequate to protect such vessels." It appropriated $100,000,000 to be expended by the president "for the purpose of carrying into effect the foregoing provisions."

The bill attempted to confer upon the executive not only the authority to place guns and gunners upon merchant ships and send them to sea with orders to fire on German submarines at sight, but sought to empower the president to use any other method and any other instrumentalities in his judgment necessary to protect such merchant ships.

Give validity and effect to such provisions and it removes every limitation upon his acts.

He might do whatever it pleased him to do and there could be no check or halt upon him.

He might decide to order our navy out to convoy merchantmen loaded with arms and ammunition, or with food and clothing and shoes for the allied armies.

He might decide that our navy should patrol the trans-Atlantic lanes through the German war zone hunting submarines in the interest of the owners of our munition ships.

He might decide that the best way to protect our merchant ships would be to land an army in Germany and destroy the Krupp works and any other manufacturing plants where Germany is constructing submarines.

Nowhere would there be lodged any power to prevent any president from doing anything his judgment dictated with the army and navy to protect the merchant ships of our war traders.

If the language of this bill does not seek to confer authority which would leave it in his discretion to make war, then there is no power in human language which could accomplish that result.

The armed ship bill is therefore contrary to the letter and spirit of the constitution, which expressly vests the war power in congress—without which provision the constitution could not have been adopted.

La Follette's Magazine, March, 1917.

People Opposed to Entering the War

For my own part, I look upon Europe as cursed with a contagious, a deadly plague, whose spread threatens to devastate the civilized world. If it were indeed the Black Death that was mowing down its millions of victims, instead of this more ghastly war, we should not hesitate to quarantine against it; we should keep our ships in their ports and our people at home without any hesitation whatsoever; all personal consideration, all thought of material loss, or commercial inconvenience would fall before the necessity of protecting our people from being stricken with the dread disease.

I am not an extremist, I do not say there may not be supreme principles for which men must fight to the death as a last resort. But I do believe that as organized society in its slow evolution has developed more rational means of settling individual differences than brute force, so must the nations of the world ultimately find other ways of deciding their disagreements than war.

So far as the masses of men who are killing each other are concerned, the European war is a bootless conflict. The multitudes who are dying in the trenches and the millions who are suffering more agonizing pain at home, do not know what it is all about. They are doing their patriotic duty as they have been told to do it.

It is unthinkable that with this awful object lesson before them, the American people are nevertheless today being stampeded into war in blind thoughtlessness of its awful consequences. Thirty-seven million men are now under arms in Europe. The peace strength of the standing armies of Europe, before the war began, was less than five millions. It follows that more than thirty-two millions have been drawn from the farms and industrial pursuits, and placed in the trenches to be mowed down at the rate of five thousand a day. The United States once in, will stay in to the end. Who can foretell what it means?

The United Press, from the casualty lists of the belligerent nations, estimates that more than 21,-000,000 men have been killed, wounded or reported missing, to date, affecting a hundred million non-combatants. And these brutal facts of death and mutilation only suggest the horrors of the insane conflict—women and children homeless, desecrated, starving. Already $70,000,000,000 of debt piled up. For unnumbered years to come, generations of helpless people must bow their bended backs under the tax burdens entailed by this war of destruction. For long years to come, all the resources that should go to the world's betterment, mortgaged beyond redemption to pay for this awful holocaust. Think of it! Any economical loss because of the interruption of commerce, is but a grain of sand, compared to the colossal costs of war.

Ask any plain citizen if he wants war. The involuntary answer is "we ought to know better from the lesson in Europe." How can we justify the insistence of our right to push through the mines and submarines of the war zone when that right is compared with the obligation to protect all our people here at home from the terrible effect of war?

If the silent masses who found opportunity for expression at the November election, could today make themselves heard above this clamor for war, instigated and sustained by the money power and subjugated press, they would with even a stronger voice, pray God that this country be kept out of war.
La Follette's Magazine, March, 1917.

War With Germany

Mr. President, I had supposed until recently that it was the duty of senators and representatives in congress to vote and act according to their convictions on all public matters that came before them for consideration and decision.

Quite another doctrine has recently been promulgated by certain newspapers, which unfortunately seems to have found considerable support elsewhere, and that is the doctrine of "standing back of the president," without inquiring whether the president is right or wrong. For myself I have never subscribed to that doctrine and never shall. I shall support the president in the measures he proposes when I believe them to be right. I shall oppose measures proposed by the president when I believe them to be wrong. The fact that the matter which the president submits for consideration is of the greatest importance is only an additional reason why we should be sure that we are right and not be swerved from that conviction or intimidated in its expression by any influence of power whatsoever. If it is important for us to speak and vote our convictions in matters of internal policy, though we may unfortunately be in disagreement with the president, it is infinitely more important for us to speak and vote our convictions when the question is one of peace or war, certain to involve the lives and fortunes of many of our people and, it may be, the destiny of all of them and of the civilized world as well. If, unhappily, on such momentous questions the most patient research and conscientious consideration we could give to them leave us in disagreement with the president, I know of no course to take except to oppose, regretfully but not the less firmly, the demands of the executive.

Speech, "War With Germany,"
U. S. Senate, April 4, 1917.

The Sovereign Power of the People

We need not disturb ourselves because of what a minority may do. There is always lodged, and always will be, thank the God above us, power in the people supreme. Sometimes it sleeps, sometimes it seems the sleep of death; but, sir, the sovereign power of the people never dies. It may be suppressed for a time, it may be misled, befooled, silenced. I think, Mr. President, that it is being denied expression now. I think there will come a day when it will have expression.

The poor, sir, who are the ones called upon to rot in the trenches, have no organized power, have no press to voice their will upon this question of peace or war; but, oh, Mr. President, at sometime they will be heard. I hope and I believe they will be heard in an orderly and a peaceful way. I think they may be heard from before long. I think, sir, if we take this step, when the people today who are staggering under the burden of supporting families at the present prices of the necessaries of life find those prices multiplied, when they are raised a hundred per cent, or 200 per cent, as they will be quickly, ayé, sir, when beyond that those who pay taxes come to have their taxes doubled and again doubled to pay the interest on the nontaxable bonds held by Morgan and his combinations, which have been issued to meet this war, there will come an awakening; they will have their day and they will be heard. It will be as certain and as inevitable as the return of the tides, and as resistless, too.

Speech, "War With Germany,"
U. S. Senate, April 4, 1917.

True Course of Neutrality

Had the plain principle of international law announced by Jefferson been followed by us, we would not be called on today to declare war upon any of the belligerents. The failure to treat the belligerent nations of Europe alike, the failure to reject the unlawful "war zones" of both Germany and Great Britain, is wholly accountable for our present dilemma. We should not seek to hide our blunder behind the smoke of battle, to inflame the mind of our people by half truths into the frenzy of war, in order that they may never appreciate the real cause of it until it is too late. I do not believe that our national honor is served by such a course. The right way is the honorable way.

One alternative is to admit our initial blunder to enforce our rights against Great Britain as we have enforced our rights against Germany; demand that both those nations shall respect our neutral rights upon the high seas to the letter! and give notice that we will enforce those rights from time forth against both belligerents and then live up to that notice.

The other alternative is to withdraw our commerce from both. The mere suggestion that food supplies would be withheld from both sides impartially would compel belligerents to observe the principle of freedom of the seas for neutral commerce.

Speech, "War With Germany,"
U. S. Senate, April 4, 1917.

XVI
DRAFT AND CONSCRIPTION

The Purpose of the Draft

HOWEVER uncertain the meaning of some portions of this bill may be, its main purpose is clear. About that there is no dispute. The main purpose is to clothe one man with power, acting through agents appointed by him, to enter at will every home in our country, at any hour of the day or night, using all the force necessary to effect the entry, and violently lay hold of 1,000,000 of our finest and healthiest and strongest boys and against their will, and against the will and wishes of their parents or family, deport them across the seas to a foreign land, and to require them, under penalty of death if they refuse, to wound and kill other young boys just like themselves and toward whom they feel no hostility and have cause to feel none.

That is what the draft means. I have not overstated—indeed, no one can overstate—the horror it is proposed to perpetuate, or the insult which it conveys to the intelligence and patriotism of the people of this country. Anyone who would have prophesied one short month ago that this body would seriously consider, under existing circumstances, such a measure as this would have raised a question as to his sanity.

For such action as it is proposed to take by this bill under present conditions there is no precedent in all our history, and, I believe, there is none in the history of any people making the slightest claim to freedom.

The draft is the corollary of militarism and militarism spells death to democracy. No war can be successfully prosecuted that has not the spontaneous support of the men who do the fighting. There is not the shadow of an excuse for pressing men into involuntary military servitude for the conduct of this war.

But if we must have an army of such magnitude for an overseas expedition let it be a volunteer army on the Canadian and Australian basis. Let its ranks be made up of free, willing men who desire to go. This will not raise any constitutional question nor be in such flagrant violation of our traditions, nor will it necessitate any such upheaval of our economic life as this draft proposition seems to call for.

Speech, "The Draft," U. S. Senate, April 27, 1917.

Let Voters Decide

I come now to the amendment I have proposed providing for an advisory vote on the part of the qualified electors upon the following question:

"The government of the United States having declared war against the government of Germany, shall the United States government at this time raise an army by draft to send to Europe to prosecute the war?"

Draft and Conscription

The methods by which the advisory vote can be obtained are very simple. This vote could be secured while registration was going forward under the bill, which,'according to my amendment, strikes out the draft features and provides for raising the required number of men by voluntary enlistment. Practically no expense would be involved in obtaining the vote, and every voter would be given the opportunity of expressing his opinion upon this most vital question. If the people vote in favor of the draft and of sending the Army to Europe, that closes the discussion.

If the friends of this bill are sure that it has the support of the people, they should be the first to agree to this amendment. If the principle of the bill has not support of the people, it should be abandoned.

Speech, "The Draft," U. S. Senate, April 27, 1917.

Cost of War to the Republic

I do not mean to speak of the horrors of war. Were I to do so I should dwell most upon the anguish of those at home, of families broken up, hopes blasted, bodies crippled, insanity and disease, debt and poverty, and want and famine, which are only a few of the results of every great war. I would speak of liberties lost, constitutions destroyed, of peoples exterminated by the immediate savagery of war or languishing in bondage for generations under the tyranny, foreign or domestic, military or economic, that always rides in the wake of war. I will not let my mind dwell upon the distress and disaster this war is bound to bring us in the future, but we cannot forget what has happened in the few days that have elapsed since it began.

What a transformation has been wrought during the first few hours of this war! Only a few days ago we were at peace with all the world and cherished nothing but the kindliest feeling toward the peoples of every land. We were engaged in peaceful occupations. Our youth were in the schools and colleges of the country fitting themselves for the useful and helpful work that they were to do in the world. As a nation we were the one great power that was almost free from debt and in position to help bring peace to a distracted world. As a people we were prosperous. Our taxes were relatively light and cheerfully borne because they were expended largely for objects calculated to promote our material and social welfare. We were apparently secure in our liberties, and, slowly it may be but none the less surely, we were winning peaceful victories for democracy and self-government, not only for ourselves but for our children and the generations to come, which we fondly hoped would bring a little nearer the day of peace on earth and good will to men.

But in a moment all this has been changed. We have declared war against a government and a people with whom we have always previously lived in perfect friendship. We have made ourselves distrusted or feared by other governments and lost the power we had as a neutral nation to promote the cause of peace. Already our most cherished constitutional rights have been invaded and will soon be destroyed. The agent provocateur is in our midst. Men are being daily cast into prison in violation of the law, and in many cases without even regarding the forms of law.

Within a few months, under a pretext of carrying democracy to the rest of the world, we have done more to undermine and destroy democracy in the United States than it will be possible for us as a nation to repair in a generation of time.

By a single act the people have been saddled with a burden of debt amounting to an average of four or five hundred dollars for each responsible head of a family in our country, and we have scarcely made a beginning.

Never in all my many years of experience in the house and in the senate have I heard so much democracy preached and so little practiced as during the last few months.

Speech, "The Draft," U. S. Senate, April 27, 1917.

XVII

WAR TAXES AND PROFITEERING

Wealth and War

WEALTH has never yet sacrificed itself on the altar of patriotism in any war. On the contrary, it has ever shown itself eager to take advantage of the misfortunes which war always brings to the masses of the people. That has been true of every war we have had in this country and of every war in Europe of which I have any knowledge, and it is certainly true of the present war. Every bond that is issued must some time be redeemed with interest out of the taxes that the people must pay. Nothing is gained by borrowing except that money for immediate use is obtained from those who have it to loan, to be repaid to them in the future with interest, out of the taxes largely exacted from those who can ill afford to pay them.

Mr. President, to what extent the recent "liberty loan" campaign succeeded in selling these bonds to the small investor I do not know but we all do know that these bonds were a poor investment to the man of small means, in comparison with the advantages which the owners of large incomes could secure from investing millions of their taxable incomes in these nontaxable bonds. It is shown in the minority report on this bill that by exempting these bonds from taxation, the Government has made them the equivalent of an investment paying from 5 to 9 per cent and more to persons with large incomes who will escape the income tax on every dollar thus invested; while to the wage-earner and the man with a salary so small as not to be reached by the income tax, who pinched and saved and sacrificed in order to purchase them, they return but a meager 3½ per cent.

But this is not all, Mr. President. Paying for a war mainly by selling bonds inevitably forces inflation. Inflation raises prices, greatly increasing the cost of living to the masses. There is no escape from this result. As the Senator from Oklahoma (Mr. Gore) suggests, with sacrifice to the Government also, reason and experience warn us that the policy of financing a war by borrowing the larger part of the money required is in itself one of the severest financial burdens which war brings to the average man.

The borrowing system gives an impression of false prosperity. Where heavy taxation would induce economy, borrowing induces extravagance. The government must bid against the citizen for supplies. Prices soar, but wages and income do not increase correspondingly. The result is that the ordinary citizen whose income only exceeds his normal expenses by a small margin finds his expenses doubled; his income insufficient to meet his needs, even before the Government has laid a single dollar of taxation upon his necessaries.

Mr. President, blind is the man, dull, indeed, the brain that does not read from the war histories of the world the fact that accumulated wealth has been behind the wars and has been potential enough with all the cabinets and all the war ministers who planned the financing to make the prosecution of the war a financial harvest. Sir, that is why the world has had so many wars.

Taxation Need not Cripple

The rule to determine what is the largest possible amount to tax is plain, though its application may not always be easy. We should not tax high enough to cripple industry or impede production. Everyone must accept that. The reason that we should stop at that point is not because of any rights that an individual or corporation may have to a certain income or return on investment but simply because it is wisdom on the part of the government to leave enough so that the processes of production may continue uninterrupted in order that new taxes for the government may be produced. This is the iron law of necessity in war time. It is the law that is applied to me; let it also be applied to money.

We are counseled by the highest economic authority, we are admonished by all history, we are commanded by every consideration of justice to the American boys who are marked for slaughter, to the American homes already in the shadow of death, to declare here and now by our votes on this record that the wealth of this country will be taken as mercilessly through the power of taxation as men are taken by force of the draft.

It behooves this congress, Mr. President, to deal in these times with even-handed justice by the poor and the rich. How the rich shirk and grind not only in times of peace but in times of war, while they prate of patriotism and national honor and democracy! Do not forget that. They are now the loudest advocates of democracy between the two oceans. They who have been serving special interests for from 18 to 20 years, undermining and destroying the democracy of this country, have become the apostles of democracy.

It is pretty rare indeed to find Senators standing on this floor uttering one word of criticism of these long-existing wrongs. A little outbreak here and there on the part of labor seeking to get just a bit more for the family will inspire the introduction of a bill or an amendment to jail the strikers or to authorize resort to armed soldiers to deal with them, but down through the centuries the wrongs that wealth and power have imposed upon the great masses of humanity have too often passed unchallenged in any legislative body.

Taxes upon the necessaries of life are wrong in principle. Many of the articles taxed in this bill already pay a tax in the form of a tariff duty. They are largely articles the consumption of which is necessary to maintain the health and the well being of the mass of people. Why stop with taxing tea, coffee, sugar, and medicines of the poor man? Why not levy a tax upon every pound of flour and upon every peck of potatoes and upon every ounce of butter that he buys for his family? The principle is the same. I am aware that taxes of this sort have been resorted to in previous wars. They may have been resorted to in all wars, so far as I know. I am aware also that it has been the history of all wars that the burdens imposed both on life and property have been borne by the masses of the people, while the few have used them as a means of acquiring great fortunes, through which they have dominated the life of the country when peace was restored.

You have but to call the roll of American millionaires to remember how many of them laid the foundation for their fortunes in the Civil War. Jay Gould and Black Friday, Morgan and his unsavory munition contracts, which were the subject of a congressional investigation; Vanderbilt, the ship-purchasing agent of the Government, who purchased and sold to the government condemned and worthless vessels, as the result of which he made unnumbered millions of dollars—all will be readily recalled upon mere mention. Rockefeller, Carnegie, and many others laid the foundations of their great wealth in the necessities of the Government in the civil war. That was not the patriotism we are commending so highly today, which leads a man to shoulder a gun and die in the front rank of battle. But they had cunning and sagacity, and the determination to grow rich out of the opportunities for profit which the war offered, while the great mass of the people were giving their property and their lives to defend and perpetuate our Government.

Remember that the rule to be applied alike to taxation for war purposes and to the conscription of men for the same purpose is simply what is best for the state. If a widow has two sons upon whom she

War Taxes and Profiteering

is dependent for support and the draft takes one and leaves the other, it is not, as we have been repeatedly advised by the rules promulgated by the war department, because of any tenderness for the widow and mother that one son is left. It is merely because to draft both into the army would mean that the widow would be left without support and become a public charge to the injury and detriment of the state. The same rule applied to incomes would take all the surplus income. Suppose all incomes were taken and it became necessary for our citizens of great wealth to use a little of their capital to live on, it would do no harm to the state. It might even result in forcing the members of this class to a little wholesome industry whereby the state would greatly benefit.

Speech, "War Profits Tax," Senate, September 1 and 10, 1917.

Eighty Per Cent Is Fair

Tax the War Profits.

The policy of raising money to pay the expense of this war by borrowing and issuing bonds is vicious in principle and as rankly unjust to the present generation as it is to the next.

It is impossible to issue bonds without inflating the currency, depreciating the value of the dollar, and increasing prices. The public suffers, the government, which is a large buyer of war material at these inflated prices, also suffers as a purchaser. It then borrows more money, issues more bonds, and still further inflates the currency and raises prices each time it repeats the vicious practice.

Suppose that 80 per cent of the war profits and excess profits had been taken in taxation, the government would have had $3,280,000,000 more in revenue, and all of these great war-profiting corporations would have been left net profits—that is profits after all expenses had been paid, equal to 10 per cent of their capital and 20 per cent war profits added to that.

La Follette's Magazine, September, 1917.

Taxation of War Profits and Surplus Incomes

And so it has become the policy in this country, and I regret to say that that policy has to some extent been practiced in this body, of condemning as disloyal and unpatriotic any man who has dared stand for principles of sound finance and just taxation as a means of meeting the expenses of this war, and who has ventured to oppose the shifty and evasive methods being applied to this greatest of all problems of war finance.

If they (the railroads) are never allowed to make another dollar out of this war, they have already made fortunes out of it that should satisfy the wildest dreams of avarice and greed.

The railroads of the country made last year $200,000,000 net above all expenses, more than during any preceding year in the history of the country.

Two-thirds of all the traffic in the United States was handled last year by railroads earning more than 7½ per cent on all their capital stock outstanding in the hands of the public, and by stock I mean not only the stock legitimately issued but the watered stock as well.

Two-thirds of the traffic in the eastern district was handled by railroads making an average of over 15 per cent on their outstanding capital stock.

Two-thirds of the traffic in the western district was handled by railroads that made an average of over 12 per cent on all their capital stock.

Two-thirds of the traffic in the southern district is handled by railroads that last year made an average of more than 13 per cent on all their capital stock.

Twenty-seven railroad systems handled two-thirds of the traffic in the United States.

They have an accumulated unappropriated surplus of over one thousand million dollars.

We conscripted men almost as soon as war was declared, and in doing so overturned our traditions as a nation and, as I believe, violated our constitution. We immediately invested the Executive upon his demand with the most searching and arbitrary power over the lives and property and welfare of the people of this country that has ever been exercised by potentate or ruler in any country since civilized government was established among men. We have done all this, sir, whether wisely or unwisely is not now the question; but we have done it because of the plea that the necessities of war demanded it.

It is only when we come to the proposition that some of the surplus wealth of the country shall be wrested from those who control it, though they do not need it, nor sometimes wisely use it, that a halt is called.

Speech, "War Profits Tax," U. S. Senate, September 1 and 10, 1917.

Profiteers Should Pay Cost of War

The ardor and war spirit of wealth and the wealthy will be destroyed if you reduce their profits down to a beggarly 33⅓ per cent on their investments. This is too "onerous a burden," to quote the language of the Senator from North Dakota (Mr. McCumber), for their patriotism to bear.

Mr. President, upon this proposition I fundamentally disagree with senators who have taken that attitude. I tell them one and all that by their refusal to justly tax war profits and excessive incomes they are destroying the war spirit among the hundred million people of this country which is absolutely necessary if we are to acquit ourselves even creditably in this great war. Mr. President, the two or three hundred thousand people in this country—for there are no more—who are the possessors of large incomes, and the few thousand corporations who are making these war profits, are not the people of this country. Why, Mr. President, there is a strange misunderstanding on the part of the Senator as to who are the people of this country. The Senator says that high taxes on large incomes and high taxes on war profits will "create dissatisfaction." Where?

He says "among the people;" that will "lessen their ardor"—and I quote his words—"among the people;" that it will "lessen their ardor for the conflict which is before them, and thereby cripple and hinder our war efforts." Who does the senator think are the people of this country? Is it the 2 per cent, owners of two-thirds of the wealth, or is it the 98 per cent of the population who have to divide among themselves the meager balance of this country's wealth, which, apportioned among them per capita, is a little over $800 apiece? Will the latter be dissatisfied because the swollen and unnecessary incomes of the former are taxed to pay a little of the frightful cost of this war? Does the word which you are getting from the country indicate that the people—the 98 per cent, the people upon whom this Nation must depend in this and every other crisis—are dissatisfied with the suggestion that excessive incomes and war profits should pay a high rate of taxation? No, Mr. President; the senator may think that the people of this country are composed of the fortunate possessors of large incomes and the happy recipients of the bloody profits of this war; he may think that the success of this war depends upon the ardor with which these profiteering patriots support it.

I know not what associations or habits of thought incline him to that opinion, but I declare, Mr. President, in that view he is mistaken; and all persons who entertain like views are mistaken. And, Mr. President, if that view is written by this bill into the law of this country, by that very act you are liable to create, if it does not already exist in the public mind, the belief that the war is a profiteering enterprise. The sound of military preparations may continue to fill the land, drums may beat, soldiers march, patriotic organizations financed by war profits may acclaim the glory of a war for democracy, but in every humble home in this country where manhood counts more than dollars, where patriotism is not associated with profits, will have entered the conviction, and rightfully so, that a monstrous injustice has been done to the mass of the people. With the war spirit tainted with mercenary interests, in those homes you will render the prosecution of this war more and more difficult.

No man can justify the refusal of the senate to impose the highest rate of taxation on war profits and incomes which has been demanded here. The senators who have attempted to justify that course in this body have failed. The country knows that they have failed. They have failed for no lack of ability in themselves, but for the lack of justice in their cause. A popular war could hardly survive the spirit of resentment the injustice of this bill will arouse; and if it be a fact that this is already an unpopular war, then such a course will but intensify that feeling.

Speech, "War Profits Tax," U. S. Senate,
September 1 and 10, 1917.

XVIII

FREEDOM OF SPEECH AND PRESS

La Follette Peace Resolution

UGUST 11, I introduced in the United States senate a concurrent resolution declaring that the constitution vests in congress the right to determine and announce the objects and purposes for which this government shall continue to participate in the European war; and that the United States will not contribute to the efforts of any European government to annex new territory or to enforce indemnities and favoring the creation of a common fund to be provided by all belligerents out of which to assist in the restoration of portions of countries most seriously devastated by war. It also provided that congress shall declare for a public restatement of the allies' peace terms disavowing any advantages in the way of indemnities, territorial acquisitions or commercial privileges by which one nation shall strengthen its power abroad at the expense of another nation.

That resolution has been misrepresented both as to its terms and purpose. It is here printed in full:

Whereas the provisional government of Russia did, on the 19th day of May, 1917, declare in favor of "peace without annexation or indemnities on the basis of the rights of nations to decide their own destiny;" and

Whereas the imperial reichstag, representing the great majority of the German people did on the 19th day of July, 1917, by a vote of 214 to 116, pass resolutions in favor of peace, "without forced acquisition of territory and without political, economic, and financial violations" and declaring for "a mutual understanding and lasting reconciliation among the nations and the creation of international judicial organizations;" and

Whereas the German chancellor, speaking for the Imperial German government on the 17th day of May, 1917, made the following official declaration in the reichstag:

"We did not go to war, and we are not fighting now against almost the whole world, in order to make conquests, but only to secure our existence, and firmly to establish the future of the nation;" and

Whereas on behalf of Great Britain on the 23rd day of May, 1917, Lord Robert Cecil, as one of the ministers of the present government, replying in the house of commons, declared that—

"Our aims and aspirations are dictated solely by our determination to secure a peace founded on national liberty and international amity, and that all imperialistic aims based on force and conquest are completely absent from our program;" and

Whereas duly organized bodies of loyal citizens of Great Britain representing millions of other citizens, many of whom are eminent in official life and exert a wide influence upon public opinion, have declared that—

"A stage in the war has been reached when the democracies of all the belligerent countries are beginning to work toward a peace based on the same general principles;" and

Whereas the above principles are those by which the respective warring governments of Europe profess common willingness to be bound and are principles to which the United States subscribes; and

Whereas one and all of these declarations bespeak a willingness to adopt the doctrine of "a peace without victory," proclaimed by President Wilson on the 22d day of January, 1917, as the only possible peace that can be enduring; and

Whereas there have recently emanated from official and unofficial sources, both in this country and abroad, statements indicating that we are to continue in the war until a peace is obtained which gives to the entente allies, or some of them, punitive damages and territorial advantages as a result of the war; and

Facts of Treaty Withheld

Whereas the people of this country do not know the terms of the secret treaties or agreements existing among the entente allies, defining the advantages, if any, either in the way of indemnities or territorial acquisitions or commercial privileges, which each is expected to receive as a result of the war; and

Whereas there is naturally a widely expressed demand coming from the people of our own country for some declaration of the purpose and object for which the United States is expending, in the first year of the war, from thirteen to seventeen billions of money, and raising by draft and otherwise an army of 2,000,000 men ostensibly for service in foreign countries; and

Whereas the people have a right to know with certainty for what end their blood is shed and their treasure expended; and

Whereas in this free government congress, in whom the war-making power resides under the constitution, is charged primarily with the responsibility of deciding upon the objects of the war at its commencement or at any time during its existence: Now, therefore, be it

Resolved, by the senate (the house of representatives concurring),

That the constitution vests in the congress as the accredited and lawful representatives of the people full authority to determine and to declare definitely the objects and purposes for which this government shall continue to participate in the European war.

Resolved, further, That the congress hereby declares that this government will not contribute to the efforts of any belligerent for the purpose of prolonging the war to annex new territory, either in Europe or outside of Europe, nor to enforce the payment of indemnities to recover the expenses of the war; but the congress does hereby declare in favor of the creation of a common fund to be provided by all the belligerent nations to assist in the restoration of the portions of territory in any of the countries most seriously devastated by the war, and for the establishment of an international commission to decide the allotment of the common fund.

Resolved, further, That congress declares that there should be a public restatement of the allies' peace terms, based on a disavowal of any advantages, either in the way of indemnities, territorial acquisitions, commercial privileges, or economic prerogatives, by means of which one nation shall strengthen its power abroad at the expense of another nation, as wholly incompatible with the establishment of a durable peace in the world.

La Follette's Magazine, August, 1917.

Right of Congress to Declare Objects of War

It is no answer to say that when the war is over the citizen may once more resume his rights and feel some security in his liberty and his person. As I have already tried to point out, now is precisely the time when the country needs the counsel of all its citizens. In time of war even more than in time of peace, whether citizens happen to agree with the ruling administration or not, these precious fundamental personal rights—free speech, free press, and right of assemblage so explicitly and emphatically guaranteed by the Constitution should be maintained inviolable. There is no rebellion in the land, no martial law, no courts are closed, no legal processes suspended, and there is no threat even of invasion.

But more than this, if every preparation for war can be made the excuse for destroying free speech and a free press and the right of the people to assemble together for peaceful discussion, then we may well despair of ever again finding ourselves for a long period in a state of peace. With the possessions we already have in remote parts of the world, with the obligations we seem almost certain to assume as a result of the present war, a war can be made any time overnight and the destruction of personal rights now occurring will be pointed to then as precedents for a still further invasion of the rights of the citizen. This is the road which all free governments have heretofore traveled to their destruction, and how far we have progressed along it is shown when we compare the standard of liberty of Lincoln, Clay and Webster with the standard of the present day.

This leads me, Mr. President, to the next thought, to which I desire to invite the attention of the Senate, and that is the power of Congress to declare the purpose and objects of the war, and the failure of Congress to exercise that power in the present crisis.

For the mere assertion of that right, in the form of a resolution to be considered and discussed, which I introduced August 11, 1917, I have been denounced throughout this broad land as a traitor to my country.

Speech, "Right of Congress to Declare the Objects of the War," U. S. Senate, Oct. 6, 1917.

Reply to Critics of Attitude on War

I am aware, Mr. President, that in pursuance of this general campaign of villification and attempted intimidation, requests from various individuals and certain organizations have been submitted to the senate for my expulsion from this body, and that such requests have been referred to and considered by one of the committees of the senate.

If I alone had been made the victim of these attacks, I should not take one moment of the senate's time for their consideration, and I believe that other senators who have been unjustly and unfairly assailed, as I have been, hold the same attitude upon this that I do. Neither the clamor of the mob nor the voice of power will ever turn me by the breadth of a hair from the course I mark out for myself, guided by such knowledge as I can obtain and controlled and directed by a solemn conviction of right and duty.

Speech, "Right of Congress to Declare the Objects of War," U. S. Senate, Oct. 6, 1917.

People Retain Right to Control Government

But, sir, it is not alone members of congress that the war party in this country has sought to intimidate. The mandate seems to have gone forth to the sovereign people of this country that they must be silent while those things are being done by their government which most vitally concern their wellbeing, their happiness, and their lives. To-day and for weeks past honest and law-abiding citizens of this country are being terrorized and outraged in their rights by those sworn to uphold the laws and protect the rights of the people. I have in my possession numerous affidavits establishing the fact that people are being unlawfully arrested, thrown into jail, held incommunicado for days, only to be eventually discharged without ever having been taken into court, because they committed no crime. Private residences are being invaded, loyal citizens of undoubted integrity and probity arrested, cross-examined, and the most sacred constitutional rights guaranteed to every American citizen are being violated.

It appears to be the purpose of those conducting this campaign to throw the country into a state of terror, to coerce public opinion, to stifle criticism, and suppress discussion of the great issues involved in this war.

I think all men recognize that in time of war the citizen must surrender some rights for the common good which he is entitled to enjoy in time of peace. But, sir, the right to control their own government according to constitutional forms is not one of the rights that the citizens of this country are called upon to surrender in time of war.

Rather in time of war the citizen must be more alert to the preservation of his right to control his government. He must be most watchful of the encroachment of the military upon the civil power. He must beware of those precedents in support of arbitrary action by administrative officials, which excused on the plea of necessity in war time, become the fixed rule when the necessity has passed and normal conditions have been restored.

More than all, the citizen and his representative in congress in time of war must maintain his right of free speech. More than in times of peace it is necessary that the channels for free public discussion of government policies shall be open and unclogged. I believe, Mr. President, that I am now touching upon the most important question in this country to-day—and that is the right of the citizens of this country and their representatives in congress

to discuss in an orderly way frankly and publicly and without fear, from the platform and through the press, every important phase of this war; its causes, the manner in which it should be conducted, and the terms upon which peace should be made.
Speech in U. S. Senate, October 6, 1917.

Free Discussion Essential

I am contending for this right because the exercise of it is necessary to the welfare, to the existence, of this government, to the successful conduct of this war, and to a peace which shall be enduring and for the best interest of this country.

Suppose success attends the attempt to stifle all discussion of the issues of this war, all discussion of the terms upon which it should be concluded, all discussion of the objects and purposes to be accomplished by it, and concede the demand of the war-mad press and war extremists that they monopolize the right of public utterance upon these questions unchallenged, what think you would be the consequences to this country not only during the war but after the war?
Speech in U. S. Senate, October 6, 1917.

How War Might Have Been Avoided

Mr. President, we are in a war the awful consequences of which no man can foresee, which, in my judgment, could have been avoided if the congress had exercised its constitutional power to influence and direct the foreign policy of this country.

On the 8th day of February, 1915, I introduced in the senate a resolution authorizing the president to invite the representatives of the neutral nations of the world to assemble and consider, among other things, whether it would not be possible to lay out lanes of travel upon the high seas and through proper negotiation with the belligerent powers have those lanes recognized as neutral territory, through which the commerce of neutral nations might pass. This, together with other provisions, constituted a resolution, as I shall always regard it, of most vital and supreme importance in the world crisis, and one that should have been considered and acted upon by congress.

I believe, sir, that had some such action been taken the history of the world would not be written at this hour in the blood of more than one-half of the nations of the earth, with the remaining nations in danger of becoming involved.

I believe that had congress exercised the power in this respect, which I contend it possesses, we could and probably would have avoided the present war.

Mr. President, I believe that if we are to extricate ourselves from this war and restore this country to an honorable and lasting peace, the congress must exercise in full the war powers intrusted to it by the constitution.

Speech in U. S. Senate, October 6, 1917.

The Citizen's Right to Oppose War Policies

Lincoln, Webster, Clay, Sumner—what a galaxy of names in American history! They all believed and asserted and advocated in the midst of war that it was the right—the constitutional right—and the patriotic duty of American citizens, after the declaration of war and while the war was in progress, to discuss the issues of the war and to criticize the policies employed in its prosecution and to work for the election of representatives opposed to prolonging war.

The right of Lincoln, Webster, Clay, Sumner to oppose the Mexican War, criticize its conduct, advocate its conclusion on a just basis, is exactly the same right and privilege as that possessed by every representative in congress and by each and every American citizen in our land to-day in respect to the war in which we are now engaged. Their arguments as to the power of congress to shape the war policy and their opposition to what they believed to be the usurpation of power on the part of the executive are potent so long as the constitution remains the law of the land.

Speech in U. S. Senate, October 6, 1917.

Cruelties of the War

The first chill winds of autumn remind us that another winter is at hand. The imagination is paralyzed at the thought of the human misery, the indescribable suffering, which the winter months, with their cold and sleet and ice and snow, must bring to the war-swept lands, not alone to the soldiers at the front but to the non-combatants at home.

To such excesses of cruelty has this war descended that each nation is now, as a part of its strategy, planning to starve the women and children of the enemy countries. Each warring nation is carrying out the unspeakable plan of starving noncombatants. Each nurses the hope that it may break the spirit of the men of the enemy country at the front by starving the wives and babes at home, and woe be it that we have become partners in this awful business and are even cutting off food shipments from neutral countries in order to force them to help starve women and children of the country against whom we have declared war.

There may be some necessity overpowering enough to justify these things, but the people of America should demand to know what results are expected to satisfy the sacrifice of all that civilization holds dear upon the bloody altar of a conflict which employs such desperate methods of warfare.

The question is: Are we to sacrifice millions of our young men—the very promise of the land— and spend billions and more billions, and pile up the cost of living until we starve—and for what? Shall the fearfully overburdened people of this country continue to bear the brunt of a prolonged war for any objects not openly stated and defined?

The answer, sir, rests, in my judgment, with the congress, whose duty it is to declare our specific purposes in the present war and to state the objects upon the attainment of which we will make peace.

Speech in U. S. Senate, October 6, 1917.

People Should Discuss the Objects of War.

And, sir, this is the ground on which I stand: I maintain that Congress has the right and the duty to declare the objects of the war and the people have the right and the obligation to discuss it.

American citizens may hold all shades of opinion as to the war; one citizen may glory in it, another may deplore it, each has the same right to voice his judgment. An American citizen may think and say that we are not justified in prosecuting this war for the purpose of dictating the form of government which shall be maintained by our enemy or our ally, and not be subject to punishment of law. He may pray aloud that our boys shall not be sent to fight and die on European battlefields for the annexation of territory or the maintenance of trade agreements and be within his legal rights. He may express the hope that an early peace may be secured on the terms set forth by the New Russia and by President Wilson in his speech of January 22, 1917, and he cannot lawfully be sent to jail for the expression of his convictions.

It is the citizen's duty to obey the law until it is repealed or declared unconstitutional. But he has the inalienable right to fight what he deems an obnoxious law or a wrong policy in the courts and at the ballot box.

It is the suppressed emotion of the masses that breeds revolution.

If the American people are to carry on this great war, if public opinion is to be enlightened and intelligent, there must be free discussion.

Congress, as well as the people of the United States, entered the war in great confusion of mind and under feverish excitement. The president's leadership was followed in the faith that he had some big, unrevealed plan by which a peace that would exalt him before all the world would soon be achieved.

Gradually, reluctantly, congress and the country are beginning to perceive that we are in this terrific world conflict, not only to right .our wrongs, not only to aid the allies, not only to share its awful death toll and its fearful tax burden, but, perhaps, to bear the brunt of the war.

And so I say, if we are to forestall the danger of being drawn into years of war, perhaps finally to maintain imperialism and exploitation, the people must unite in a campaign along constitutional lines for free discussion of the policy of the war and its conclusion on a just basis.

Permit me, sir, this word in conclusion. It is said by many persons for whose opinions I have profound respect and whose motives I know to be sincere that "we are in this war and must go through to the end." That is true. But it is not true that we must go through to the end to accomplish an undisclosed purpose, or to reach an unknown goal.

Speech in U. S. Senate, October 6, 1917.

The Surest Way to Win the War

But it is said that Germany will fight with greater determination if her people believe that we are not in perfect agreement. Mr. President, that is the same worn-out pretext which has been used for three years to keep the plain people of Europe engaged in killing each other in this war. And, sir, as applied to this country, at least, it is a pretext with nothing to support it.

The way to paralyze the German arm, to weaken the German military force, in my opinion, is to declare our objects in this war, and show by that declaration to the German people that we are not seeking to dictate a form of government to Germany or to render more secure England's domination of the seas.

A declaration of our purposes in this war, so far from strengthening our enemy, I believe would immeasurably weaken her, for it would no longer be possible to misrepresent our purposes to the German people. Such a course on our part, so far from endangering the life of a single one of our boys, I believe would result in saving the lives of hundreds of thousands of them by bringing about an earlier and more lasting peace by intelligent negotiation, instead of securing a peace by the complete exhaustion of one or the other of the belligerents.

Such a course would also immeasurably, I believe, strengthen our military force in this country, because when the objects of this war are clearly stated and the people approve of those objects they will give to the war a popular support it will never otherwise receive,

Speech in U. S. Senate, October 6, 1917.

Honest Dealing With the Allies

Then again, honest dealing with the entente allies, as well as with our own people, requires a clear statement of our objects in this war. If we do not expect to support the entente allies in the dreams of conquest we know some of them entertain, then in all fairness to them that fact should be

stated now. If we do expect to support them in
their plans for conquest and aggrandizement, then
our people are entitled to know that vitally important fact before this war proceeds further. Common honesty and fair dealing with the people of this country and with the nations by whose side we are fighting, as well as a sound military policy at home, requires the fullest and freest discussion before the people of every issue involved in this great war and that a plain and specific declaration of our purposes in the war be speedily made by the Congress of the United States.

Speech in U. S. Senate, October 6, 1917.

(Note: The following is a summary of Senator La Follette's voting record on war measures. It is taken from a speech in the Wisconsin senate February 23, 1918, by Hon. Henry A. Huber, state senator from Dane county. This speech was published in La Follette's Magazine in February, 1918.)

From April 7, 1917, when war on Germany was declared to January 12, 1918, sixty different war measures were passed by Congress. La Follette supported and voted for 55 of these.

He voted for the various bond issues.

He voted for the various appropriation bills to equip the army and provide for the best supplies and the highest pay for our soldiers. He repeatedly urged that the boys who go to the trenches must have the best of everything in arms, ammunition, and equipment.

He helped to perfect the bill for soldiers' insurance and voted for it.

Freedom of Speech and Press 247

He voted for every measure to provide enormous appropriations for building ships.

After war was declared he recognized in every act and word the existence of a state of war as a fact, and stood for those measures which were calculated to bring that war to a speedy, successful and honorable conclusion.

He opposed the armed ship bill BEFORE WE WENT INTO THE WAR. He did not speak upon this measure although he was accused of filibustering it to death.

He opposed the declaration of war.

He opposed the draft provisions of the bill to provide an army, but voted to raise that army by the volunteer system.

He opposed the draft provision of the Aviation bill because of his general objections to the draft as undemocratic and un-American. But he made it clear that he endorsed the six hundred million dollars appropriation for aviation.

He opposed the espionage bill because it contained a provision giving the postmaster-general power with the stroke of the pen to suppress any newspaper and destroy the property of any publisher.

He voted for the food control bill when it passed the senate but later voted against the conference report on the bill because the conference radically changed the bill to the great injury of the farmer and because the inevitable effect of the change would be to curtail agricultural production.

He voted against the war tax bill because it did not justly tax wealth and especially war profits and would therefore force the raising of war revenues by excessive bond issues, resulting in all the evils of inflation, among others increasing the cost of the necessaries of life.

General Amnesty Is Demanded

Do the American people know that in this Christianized country, under a government dedicated to political and religious liberty, there are hundreds of men imprisoned because of their opinions?

Do they know that many of these brave souls have been starved and beaten and scourged and tortured until some of them have been driven insane and others have died for their religious and moral convictions?

At the beginning of the war the liberals, to whom both Mr. Wilson and Mr. Baker owe their political power, expected this problem to be met with the tact, firmness and honesty which it required. On the other hand, certain jingo elements who looked upon our armed forces as an instrument for protection in their future machinations for extending investments and gaining control of world markets, at whatever cost to our own or the world's population, saw in this group of dissenters a menace to their program.

It was not a question of whether the conscientious objectors were right or wrong. They were there, and they presented a problem which called for a very definite disposition. Should they be shot without trial, as was done in Germany? Should they be imprisoned at hard labor for short terms, which could be renewed from time to time, as England

Freedom of Speech and Press 249

had done? Or was there a third and more satisfactory solution? Our war department preferred not to make the decision. It issued a series of vague "orders" to the camps—orders which on the surface appeared to be a highly satisfactory solution, but which were, in fact, open to any interpretation which officials in the various camps wished to place upon them. These officials, in many instances, newly endowed with a degree of power which their experience in no way warranted, proceeded to execute the orders, and court martial trials were held for those who violated them.

The sentences imposed ranged from 1, 5, 10, 20, 45 years and life terms, to the death penalty. One man, for instance, was given thirty years because he refused a second vaccination; one a life term because his religion forbade him to wear a military uniform; one the death penalty for refusing to peel potatoes. All of these extreme sentences were commuted to shorter terms before their absurdity became too apparent to the public.

The war is over. Demobilization is almost complete. England and Canada have released all of their conscientious objectors. But our war department is still floundering between the possible opposition of two hostile political forces. As a concession to the liberal it occasionally releases a group of religious objectors, or surreptitiously drops an individual objector here and there. For the pacification of the jingoes it continues to hold hundreds of others, whom it labels "riotous and unruly" but whose real offense is that they have given the public facts about the unspeakable conditions of our military prisons. It would, no doubt, be embarrassing to the war department to make public its records and let the people know that five objectors have died from exposure and cruelty, that not a few have gone insane, that the health of scores has been permanently impaired—that, in fact, everything has been done to break them both in body and spirit.

The charge now lodged against the administration is not that it sent these men to prison,—that is passed over,—but that it has never met the issue with a clear and definite policy; that it constantly concealed facts which the public had a right to know; that it never let its right hand know what its left hand did.

What will the administration do now? Has it the courage to declare an amnesty as England and Canada have done? Or will it continue to play its double game to the end?

La Follette's Magazine, September, 1919.

XIX

THE PEACE TREATY AND THE LEAGUE OF NATIONS

The War Makers of Versailles

MR. PRESIDENT, the little group of men who sat in secret conclave for months at Versailles were not peacemakers. They were war makers. They cut and slashed the map of the old world in violation of the terms of the armistice. They patched up a new map of the old world in consummation of the terms of the secret treaties the existence of which they had denied because they feared to expose the sordid aims and purposes for which men were sent to death by the tens of thousands daily. They betrayed China. They locked the chains on the subject peoples of Ireland, Egypt, and India. They partitioned territory and traded off peoples in mockery of that sanctified formula of 14 points, and made it our Nation's shame. Then, fearing the wrath of outraged peoples, knowing that their new map would be torn to rags and tatters by the conflicting, warring elements which they had bound together in wanton disregard of racial animosities, they make a league of nations to stand guard over the swag!

The old world armies were exhausted. Their treasuries were empty. It was imperative that they should be able to draw upon the lusty man power and the rich material resources of the United States to build a military cordon around the new boundaries of the new States of the old world.

Senators, if we go into this thing it means a great standing army; it means conscription to fight in foreign wars, a blighting curse upon the family life of every American home every hour. It means higher taxes, higher prices, harder times for the poor. It means greater discontent, a deeper, more menacing unrest.

Mr. President, whatever course other senators may take, I shall never vote to bind my country to the monstrous undertaking which this covenant would impose.

Speech, "Secret Treaties—War Spoils Secured by Allies," U. S. Senate, Nov. 13, 1919.

Labor Betrayed in the Treaty

Mr. President, in our modern era of a highly organized industrial society, the movement for democracy in industry is tending to supersede at many points the old struggle for political democracy.

Competition between business men and manufacturers, which tended to lower prices and increase wages, has wholly disappeared. All the basic industries of the Nation and most of the subordinate industries have passed into the control of small groups of men. Their power is absolute, and they increase prices and lower actual wages at will.

The great mass of the working people, meanwhile, have become wage earners, employed in industry. With these fundamental changes, the battle line in the struggle runs through the industrial life of the entire nation.

By the labor section of this treaty we are giving to an international body—a superlegislature—an entering wedge through which it may intervene in the settlement of our industrial affairs.

At the very point where the fight for real democracy is most heated, where action is fraught with the most vital consequences to the mass of the American people, the treaty sets up an international body which has full authority and power to act.

Mr. President, I cannot consent to that grant of authority and power. Believing, as I do, in democratic principles; believing that the best results in legislation and government are obtained when those who legislate are in closest touch with, and elected directly by, the people; believing, in other words, in the wisdom of the principles written into the American constitution, which must be preserved if we are to save our free institutions; believing, finally, that America's best gift to the world and most effective aid to the cause of labor throughout the world would be the example of the perfection of our own democracy, unhampered and unrestrained by outside influences; believing, sir, these things, I shall move to strike out the labor articles of this treaty.

Speech, "Labor and the Treaty of Peace,"
U. S. Senate, October 29, 1919.

Effect of the Labor Articles

Mr. President, what is the broad significance of these labor provisions?

The practical effect of setting up international machinery of this kind is to crystallize the present industrial conditions and to perpetuate the wrong and injustice in the present relation existing between labor and capital.

As a substitute for natural evolution, which over a period of centuries has been bringing more and more recognition of the rights of labor, this treaty of peace sets up an arbitrary, artificial organization, clothed with definite powers and restricted by vague limitations, which has for its ultimate object the maintenance of the present system of a completely centralized control of industry. As stated in the preamble of the so-called "labor charter," varying conditions throughout the world make "strict uniformity in the conditions of labor difficult of immediate attainment"—but uniformity is the ultimate aim.

Speech, "Labor and the Treaty of Peace,"
U. S. Senate, October 29, 1919.

The Treaty and the Constitution.

It would be an insult to the memory of the wise and patriotic men who framed our constitution to suppose that they ever intended that the great treaty-making power with which they endowed the senate should be so prostituted as to become merely a means of registering the President's will. We know that nothing of the sort was intended by the framers of the constitution, and the language of the constitution permits no such construction. Nothing of the sort can happen if senators perform their sworn duty under the constitution, no matter what are the desires and ambitions which move the President.

I am not arguing that a good treaty should be rejected or amended merely because a president disregarded the constitution in refusing to advise with the senate concerning it; but I do say that any treaty which comes into the senate under such a cloud should be regarded with suspicion. The presumption is against it.

Speech, "Executive Usurpation—The Treaty and the Constitution," U. S. Senate, Nov. 6, 1919.

Great Britain's Territorial Gains from the War.

Mr. President, to sum up British territorial gains from the war: Great Britain has added to her empire, either by annexation or by protectorates and mandates, a territory of 3,972,000 square miles—larger than continental Europe—with a population of more than 51,725,000 people, 99 per cent of whom are natives.

Great Britain stands to-day the dominant power in Asia and Africa, and, in Canada, holds dominion over more territory along our northern boundary than is represented in the combined area of the United States and Alaska.

The aggregate area of the British Empire is one-fourth of the land surface of the globe, totaling 15,000,000 square miles, and her population of

475,000,000 souls represents one-fourth of the total population of the world.

The government of the British Empire is imposed upon 400,000,000 subject peoples, against their will, by 65,000,000 people of the English speaking race over a territory nine times larger in extent than the Roman empire at the height of its glory. It is the boundaries of this empire which the United States, under the league of nations, will be obligated to defend against the external aggression or internal disturbance which, in the opinion of the council, amounts even to a "threat of war" affecting the "peace of nations."

Speech in U. S. Senate, November 18, 1919.

Denial of Justice to Egypt

Mr. President, I shall not review here the sordid story of Egypt's betrayal at the peace conference.

How four men chosen by the Egyptian people to represent them at Paris were seized by the British authorities without warning, deported to Malta, and held in a military prison; how more than 1,000 unarmed natives were brutally shot down and killed by British machine guns on the streets of Alexandria and Cairo; how President Wilson refused to give the Egyptian envoys a hearing after they finally reached Paris, are facts too well known to all of us to require recital.

It is enough to say that the treaty of Versailles recognizes a permanent British protectorate over this unfortunate country. It makes Egypt, with her 13,000,000 inhabitants, all of one race, speaking the same language, and occupying 350,000 square miles of fertile territory, as much a part of the British Empire as India or her colonies in Africa. It gives to Great Britain, in addition, the immense area known as the Anglo-Egyptian Sudan, which is one-third as large as the United States. She acquired this domain, Mr. President, against the will of every one of its inhabitants, in violation of British pledges to Egypt and to the world, and in wanton disregard of the 14 points sponsored by the United States and specifically accepted and agreed to by Great Britain.

Speech, "Secret Treaties, and War Spoils Secured by Great Britain," U. S. Senate, November 18, 1919.

The War in Retrospect

President Wilson has again spoken on the League of Nations. He begins where he left off. He has forgotten nothing, neither has he learned anything. He repeats his cant phrases on the league compact and world peace.

He seems not to know that the American people have already passed judgment. God pity him when that time comes. He will find that judgment as harsh as truth, as unrelenting as justice.

From the first sentence to the last the league of nations is a sham and a fraud.

It pretends to be a league to preserve the peace of the world.

It is an alliance among the victorious nations of Europe to preserve for themselves the plunder and the power they gained by the war.

It bars the door of hope in the face of every people, embraced within its terms, now striving for freedom.

It betrays China and rivets the chains of bondage upon Egypt, India and Ireland.

It is an inseparable part of a treaty, conceived in fraud, in violation of the armistice, and written in a frenzy of hate to enslave the German people.

Woodrow Wilson and his three associates at Versailles were not peace makers. They were war makers.

If we should ever adopt the league of nations or ratify the treaty, we would stand convicted before the world as a nation without honor.

The American people are beginning to see the war in retrospect with clearer vision.

The dazzling rhetoric is now but shabby tinsel, much of the eloquence seems hollow and insincere, and the loudest appeals to patriotism smack of profiteering.

The great body of the American people were opposed to our entering into the European war.

The declaration that we were fighting for democracy was the baldest, most wicked lie ever imposed upon a people.

This country never before engaged in a war in which public opinion was so falsified and the convictions of a nation so stifled, and never before were the rights of the individual citizen so ruthlessly and brutally tramped under foot as during and after the war.

The Peace Treaty and the League   259

We sacrificed a quarter of a million precious American lives, incurred a war debt of ever growing billions, disorganized industry, engendered class hatreds in our social order, created a new crop of millionaires to further menace American democracy, —overturned a German autocracy and built up a British autocracy infinitely stronger to rule the world.

And what of the rights of men? You cannot name a single right that the common man has gained as a result of the late war,—either in our own country or in any one of the allied countries.

The common people of all the countries engaged in the war suffered and starved and died by the millions and what have they to show for it?

They must labor for generations to restore the ravages of the war. They and their children must bear for unnumbered years to come the fearful burden of the war debt, paying it over and over many times in vast interest charges and in the higher and higher living cost which the war debt with its depreciated dollar entails.

War Destroys Human Rights

The people of no country engaged in the war desired it, and the people of every country involved would have ended it quickly on just and honorable terms to all if left to their decision.

This was a war of big business for bigger business. It was a war for trade routes, and commercial advantages. It was a war for new territory and the right to exploit weaker peoples. It was a mean, sordid, mercenary war.

This was not so clear to some of us when the smoke of battle obscured our view. But it is written large in the terms of the treaty and the proposed alliance among the victorious governments.

It is the great commercial and exploiting interests in whose behalf this war was fought that are to be protected by the League of Nations and the Treaty, upon the ratification of which Woodrow Wilson still doggedly insists.

I challenge any man to name one new privilege, one added right which the common people of this or any one of the allied countries are to gain as the result of the war.

But pity the man so blind as not to see that the rights most cherished among free men in all ages and in all countries, were wickedly destroyed as a part of the war and the afterwar program.

Freedom of assembly, freedom of speech, and of the press, no arrests without warrant and without probable cause, no secret search and unlawful seizure of property, no trial except before impartial judges and juries, no forced military service especially in foreign lands—these are some of the rights which everyone knows have been wrested from the people of this country as a result of this war.

La Follette's Magazine, May, 1920.

League of Nations To Preserve Status Quo

Mr. President, there is one agency to which Great Britain may look for aid in holding her rebellious subjects in check, and that agency is the league of nations.

I care not what reservations or amendments we attach to this covenant. In the final analysis it is an instrument for the preservation of the status quo. Like the Holy Alliance of 1815, it is couched in the language of idealism and peace. But, like the Holy Alliance, it will be used for the suppression of nationalities and for the prosecution of oppressive warfare.

This covenant closes the door in the face of every people striving for freedom. Not one of the races now held in bondage had a voice in the making of this instrument. Not one was granted an opportunity to be heard at Paris. This covenant was so cunningly conceived that the first act of revolution in India, Korea, Egypt, or Ireland will be interpreted as a "threat of war" and a disturbance of the "peace of nations." Patriots of India, Egypt, Ireland, seeking external aid for their countries as Franklin sought aid in France for the struggling American colonies, and as Kossuth, Kosciuszko, DeValera, and many others have sought aid in the United States for the cause of human freedom, by the terms of this treaty become international outlaws. No ingenuity of interpretation of the articles of this document can remove from my mind the conviction that it destroys everywhere the right of asylum.

The White Man's Injustice to Asia

If we are to disregard every principle of our free institutions and every tradition of the past, there are yet other reasons why we should withhold our support from this new alliance.

We should not deceive ourselves into believing that there can be a permanent enforcement of the present system of exploitation in Asia. The civilization of these Asiatic countries is more venerable than our own. Asia's contribution to the world has been the principle of human brotherhood. Asia has produced the great moral teachers of history—Confucius, Buddha, Mohammed, Christ.

To these great teachers may be traced the non-resistance and pacifism of the Asiatic peoples.

The races of Asia have now suffered for three centuries under European exploitation. Off the east coast of China they see the smallest of the Asiatic nations—Japan—holding a place of power in the councils of the world. They know that Japan owes her present ascendancy to the military and naval strength which she built up in a decade. With this example before them, is it likely that the millions of Asia will continue long under foreign rule? China has already awakened under the stimulus of a revolution and the theft of Shantung. India is approaching revolt. Should the league of nations attempt to maintain indefinitely the status quo in Asia, the world will witness a more terrible war than the one from which we have emerged. It will be a continental war—a race war, in which the white races will be hopelessly outnumbered.

If we ratify the treaty with Germany we are leading this country farther into the shadow of that menace.

Mr. President, I do not speak of Great Britain's mighty empire in a spirit of covetousness.

The British Empire and the League

I do not covet for this country a position in the world which history has shown would make us the object of endless jealousies and hatreds, involve us in perpetual war, and lead to the extinction of our domestic liberty. I, for one, harbor no ambition to see this country start upon the path which has lured other nations to their ruin.

Mr. President, we cannot, without sacrificing this Republic, maintain world dominion for ourselves. And, sir, we should not pledge ourselves to maintain it for another.

Where are Great Britain's boundaries likely to be assailed? Certainly not in Australia, Canada, South Africa, or New Zealand. These self-governing dominions—colonized and peopled by Englishmen—have given ample proof of their loyalty to the motherland, and their Anglo-Saxon populations need no league of nations to guarantee the integrity of their territories.

It is the vast native populations, held in bondage for the enrichment of a small class of imperialist aliens—the millions of India, Egypt, and the Ottoman Empire—who are apt in the future to disturb the status quo created by this peace.

It is these peoples that the league of nations must hold in check. It is to maintain this part of her empire that Great Britain must keep her mighty navy and burden the English people with taxes.

It is my conviction that the English people residing in the dominions and the British Isles would benefit most if this illicit portion of the Empire should crumble and fall away.

If the British empire were limited to the dominions, with its government founded upon the consent of the governed, and hence requiring no guaranties from other nations, the peace of the world would rest upon a sounder basis.

Lincoln on the Subjugation of Weaker Peoples

Mr. President, I know the argument will be advanced here that the 400,000,000 unwilling subjects of the British empire enjoy better government than they would enjoy if left to govern themselves.

Senators, that is an argument which, even if it were based on truth, should have no place in the American congress. We owe our national existence to the courage of a handful of men who proclaimed to the world the self-evident truth that—

All men are created equal; that they are endowed by their Creator with certain inalienable rights; that among these are life, liberty, and the pursuit of happiness; that to secure these rights governments are instituted among men, deriving their just powers from the consent of the governed.

A controversy arose in this country 60 years ago as to the application of those great principles. In that contest, Abraham Lincoln contended that the Declaration of Independence applied not alone to white men, or to the descendants of the English settlers in the Colonies, but to all men, white and black, yellow and brown, and he declared that Declaration the "sheet anchor of American republicanism."

When the arguments were advanced in this country for the enslavement of the Negro which are now advanced for denying the natives of India and of Egypt self-government, Lincoln replied (Chicago, Ill., July 10, 1858):

"Those arguments that are made, that the inferior race are to be treated with as much allowance as they are capable of enjoying; that as much is to be done for them as their condition will allow—what are these arguments? They are these arguments that kings have made for enslaving the people in all ages of the world. You will find that all the arguments in favor of kingcraft were of this class; they always bestrode the necks of the people, not that they wanted to do it, but because the people were better off for being ridden. That is their argument, and this argument of the judge (Douglas) is the same old argument that says, you work, and I eat; you toil, and I will enjoy the fruits of it. Turn it whatever way you will, whether it come from the mouth of a king as an excuse for enslaving the people of his country, or from the mouth of men of one race as a reason for enslaving the men of another race; it is all the same old serpent."

Mr. President, when Abraham Lincoln contended for the right of self-government as the heritage of "all men in all lands, everywhere," who can say that he would have excluded the people of Egypt, of India and of Ireland?

These people do not ask that we send armies to Europe or Asia to aid them in gaining their freedom. They ask simply that we shall do nothing to hinder them in their struggle for independence from the power which once held sway over the American colonies.

The hope expressed here, that by entering the league of nations we can best serve these subject races, is, in my opinion, a forlorn hope.

If we were powerless to serve oppressed peoples at Paris, by what logic can it be argued that we shall be better able to serve them at Geneva?

At Paris our enemies, our allies, and the neutral nations of the world had accepted the 14 points which we were pledged to write into the peace.

How the representatives of the United States compromised those principles, how they set aside the doctrine of self-determination, how they abandoned "open covenants openly arrived at" for the secret treaties of the Allies are now matters of history. Can it be hoped that at Geneva, with the confidence of the world blasted in the stability of our purposes and ourselves bound to a covenant which pledges our support for the status quo, we shall be a powerful advocate for Korea, India, Egypt and Ireland?

The Terms of the Peace Treaty

Mr. President, when the American people were committed to this war the great mass of them were led to believe that they were suffering and fighting for the destruction of arbitrary power exercised by strong nations over weaker people—fighting to carry democracy to all parts of the world.

The war ended. We sacrificed a quarter of a million precious American lives, incurred a war debt of thirty billions, disorganized industry, engendered class hatred in our social order, created a new crop of profiteering millionaires, overturned a German autocracy and built up a British autocracy infinitely stronger to rule the world, and we are now engaged in creating a league of nations to perpetuate its power and bind this Government to respect and preserve its extended boundaries.

Look at the map of the world as Great Britain's boundaries were fixed before the war! British possessions—widely scattered, outlying, detached, isolated—waiting to be united, bound together, and made secure!

Look at the map to-day, with British boundaries reaching out over the earth to embrace her spoils of war.

The map of the world has become the map of Great Britain. It is not the work of chance. On its face it is the written confession of the guilt of British imperialists for their full share in the years of diplomatic intrigue which embroiled the world in war.

How puny appear the ambitions of Germany compared to the imperial power now actually attained by Great Britain!

In spite of the protestation of Lloyd George that England did not seek "one yard of territory," Great Britain has made capital of the sacrifices of the United States, of France and of the English people, to bring a vast new territory under her flag, and British bankers and traders are preparing for a new era of exploitation.

I do not believe that the British empire, in which the missing links were neatly fitted at the Paris conference, is an accident of events.

It is plainly the consummation of the long-considered and well-planned program of the imperialists who dominate the British Foreign Office, at the expense of the English people. To this source, in my opinion, may be traced many of the minor irritants which led up to the war.

It was this force which built up in the United States by subtle propaganda hatred of Germany. It is this power which now seeks American support for a treaty visiting upon the German republic a peace more crushing, more harsh and pitiless in its terms, than any peace threatened to be imposed upon the German empire under the rule of the kaiser and the junker.

That this venomous and unreasoning hatred of Germany still persists in some parts of our country will not restrain me from raising my voice in protest against the crushing of the German republic and the German people, who according to the president's own statement, were not responsible for the war.

If we ratify the treaty of Versailles, after pledging ourselves to a peace based upon the 14 points—which had been approved by the allies and accepted in good faith by the central powers—we shall stand convicted before the world as a nation without honor, and unworthy to be trusted to fulfill the pledges it has made.

Speech in U. S. Senate, Nov. 18, 1919.

Trying To Make It a Real League of Peace

(Note: On Nov. 10, 1919, Senator La Follette presented to the senate six reservations for adoption as part of the covenant of the league of nations. These reservations, all of which were voted down on the evening of Tuesday, Nov. 18, provided:

1. A guaranty to all nations of the right of self-determination.
2. Abolition of conscription.
3. A popular referendum.
4. Limitation of armaments.
5. Prevention of forcible annexations.
6. Prohibition against the use of mandates for the exploitation of the inhabitants and resources of weaker states.)

Independence of Nations

It is a mistaken policy that assumes a community of nations can prosper any more than a community of individuals by one or more tyrannizing over the others and monopolizing the world's markets. The world's greatest progress must be best served by the largest possible development of the national life of each country. We believe there is still room for all in the vast and undeveloped areas of the earth.

Speech in U. S. Senate, Feb. 12, 1915.

XX

INTERNATIONAL RELATIONS

An Illegal War in Siberia

PRESIDENT Wilson is conducting a war against Russia in open and notorious violation of the constitution.

Article I, Section 8 of the constitution provides as follows:

"The Congress shall have power,—

"To declare war, grant letters of marque and reprisal, and make rules concerning captures on land and water."

The framers of the constitution were unanimously opposed to vesting the president with power to make war upon any country or any people.

Congress has never declared war against Russia.

Congress has never raised an army or voted a dollar of money or made rules for the regulation of the land and naval forces in a war against the Russian people.

But the president is using an army raised for a wholly different purpose, and expending money appropriated by congress to a wholly different use, to prosecute a war against a people and a country, with whom under the constitution of the United States, we are at peace.

And called upon by senators and representatives, again and again, from the floors of congress, to ex-

plain why the lives of American soldier boys are being sacrificed in conducting an unconstitutional war on Russia, the president refuses and neglects to make an answer.
La Follette's Magazine, April, 1919.

Recognition of Russia

Why did the Wilson government refuse to recognize the soviet government of Russia? Was it because the soviet government, in order to maintain itself, executed a total of 3,200 people in Petrograd, Moscow and all other cities, most of whom had organized counter revolutions and were plotting the overthrow of the soviet government, and some of whom were spurious supporters of the soviet government who had been convicted of grafting and robbing that government?

If recognition of the soviet government was refused because of the execution of a total of 3,200 people in Petrograd, Moscow and all other cities, then why did Wilson's government recognize the Mannerheim white guard government in Finland, which had executed and murdered by starvation in its prisons more than 30,000 Finnish red prisoners?

In other words, if 3,200 soviet "atrocities" were sufficient to bar the Lenine government in Russia from recognition by the Wilson government, then why should not 30,000 white guard atrocities in Finland have constituted ten times as strong a bar against the recognition of the Mannerheim government in Finland by the Wilson government in Washington?

Or is it possible that the real reason for refusing recognition to the soviet government of Russia, and even denying to our merchants and manufacturers the right to buy and sell and trade with that government, is because it is a socialist government based upon the common ownership of all property?

And, did the Wilson government recognize the Kolchak "government" because Admiral Kolchak is a survivor of the despotic system of the czar. and will restore the "rights" of property, return the land to the select, aristocratic seven per cent, give the peasants black bread and the knout, and forever dispel the hope of an industrial democracy?

La Follette's Magazine, July, 1919.

The Rights of Neutrals

An Associated Press despatch cabled from Paris states that: "Norway has refused to join in a blockade of Germany, in case the German delegates refuse to sign the Peace Treaty."

Sweden, Holland and Switzerland have made like declarations.

Thus do these Christian nations rebuke the three men who control at Versailles, for applying the same savage policy of starvation of a people to force acceptance of "peace," which they employed in prosecuting the war.

The whole world will always owe a debt of gratitude to Norway, Sweden, Denmark, Holland, and Switzerland. With the menace of starvation hanging over them they preserved as best they could the integrity of their neutrality with Germany and refused to make an inhuman hunger-war upon innocent women and children.

For this brave, righteous stand in defense of the "right of self-determination," these independent little nations were terribly punished. Suffering horribly for food, compelled to eat in some sections bread made from the bark of trees, their death-rate rapidly increasing because short-rationed by Wilson's embargo, they heroically resisted to the bitter end the atrocious order—actual or implied—to "Fight or Starve."

And now Norway, Sweden, Holland, and Switzerland again refuse to be made a party to forcing the acceptance of a treaty on Germany through a policy of coercion by starvation.

Such a policy is a reproach to civilization.

These jugglers with the world's destiny at Versailles have for six months locked themselves away from the peoples they are supposed to represent.

Judged by the fragmentary data given out, they now seek to commit the world to peace terms which make a ghastly mockery of the Fourteen Points, and all of the other elocutionary frummery which preceded and followed their announcement by Mr. Wilson.

Aside from all question as to its terms—in so far as we are permitted to know anything about them—the method of compelling acceptance by the Germans and Austrians, cries to heaven for a protest from the Christianized world.

La Follette's Magazine, June, 1919.

"Martyred Ireland"

The domination of Ireland by England has been no less a tragedy than the domination of Poland by Russia, Germany and Austria. Racially and geographically, Ireland is as far separated from England as Poland is from Germany. Politically Ireland has been at war with England for 700 years. All the world knows the wonderful fertility of the Irish soil and that except for the cruel oppression of England, Ireland would today have many times its present population.

If President Wilson was seeking democracy for the world, he would have joined the cause of Ireland with that of Poland and the other small nations. Had the Emerald Isle been an enemy instead of an allied possession, the American representatives of the Irish cause would have been given a different kind of reception and the Irish republic might have been accorded recognition.

If the President had tried to secure self-determination for Ireland and had failed, he might have become the idol of Irish patriots. But he did not try. Under the cloak of professed friendship he left the Irish people to the mercy of their masters. The commercial interests of the British Empire overtopped the human rights of martyred Ireland.

La Follette's Magazine, June, 1919.

XXI

THE AMERICAN SOLDIER

Important Place of Militia

OUR forefathers wrote it in the constitution that states should have the right to maintain their militia. In every emergency of war this country has had to meet, the wisdom of its maintenance has been strongly demonstrated. As Shakespeare says of meeting death, so we may say of meeting war, "The readiness is all."

In times of profoundest peace, these military organizations serve a high and noble purpose. It is not alone that they uphold the law and create respect for it, but they preserve and inculcate the spirit of patriotism, of loyalty to state and country. They make social centers, where young men come together for self-government, where order, discipline and obedience are learned; where the spirit of disinterested comradeship is fostered; where united civic and military support of right and justice is stimulated.

The national guard of the state represents the health and vigor of its young manhood. Many of its members are sons and grandsons of the veterans of the civil war, who have learned from the spoken word—better than history can teach, what that war cost and what it was fought for. Back of that war was the one for independence, to establish this government of equal rights, equal opportunities, equal responsibilities and equal burdens—a government resting on the will of the people. Of this generation, it will never be forgotten that the flag of freedom was carried to a helpless people, an oppressed and suffering nation, under a despotism more cruel than human slavery. These gatherings and all the work of the guardsmen impress these lessons upon us over and over again and raise in each the highest standards of civic and military duty.

In these times of selfish commercialism and business absorption, whatever tends to loftier sentiment, purer patriotism, higher ideals of citizenship, should be fostered because it makes for the security of our most precious heritage.

Address to National Guard Officers,
January 31, 1902.

Back Up Our Boys

There is, and of course can be, no real difference of opinion concerning the duty of the citizen to discharge to the last limit whatever obligation the war lays upon him.

Our young men are being taken by the hundreds of thousands for the purpose of waging this war on the continent of Europe, possibly Asia or Africa, or anywhere else that they may be ordered. Nothing must be left undone for their protection. They must have the best army, ammunition, and equipment that money can buy. They must have the best training and the best officers which this great country can produce. The dependents and relatives they leave at home must be provided for, not meagerly, but generously so far as money can provide for them.

I have done some of the hardest work in my life during the last few weeks on the revenue bill to raise the largest possible amount of money from surplus incomes and war profits for this war and upon other measures to provide for the protection of the soldiers and their families. That I was not able to accomplish more along this line is a great disappointment to me. I did all that I could, and I shall continue to fight with all the power at my command until wealth is made to bear more of the burden of this war than has been laid upon it by the present congress.

Speech in U. S. Senate, Oct. 6, 1917.

Give Comfort to the Boys

The press dispatches inform us that our troops in France are occupying first line trenches in the fighting line. This means for them the supreme sacrifice for country. Their suffering will be unmeasured and unmeasurable. This country has appropriated immense sums for the war, but there are things money will not buy. The things that comfort the spirit of man come not only from the knowledge of great deeds well done but also from the feeling that our fellowmen are not unappreciative of such service. Even though the government is generous or even lavish in its official care of these men there will still be the need, the ever pressing need, of that spiritual comfort that comes from the gentle hand of woman; the home things that revive and sustain in the dark days of depression and pain; the little things that carry the thoughts of love and affection. These will be furnished, if at all, by those ministering angels of mercy, the Red Cross, the Woman's Relief Corps, the Y. M. C. A., and K. C., and kindred organizations. The fraternal orders can also be of great service to their members in the army.

There should be a generous outpouring from home people to sustain these organizations in the field. Everyone should make personal sacrifice to the end that our brave boys be remembered, not only for the day, but continuously and every day till their return.

War of today, as never before, brings suffering and horrors that we at home can never fully appreciate but which we can at least in some degree alleviate.

La Follette's Magazine, November, 1917.

On the American Fighting Man

American soldiers are now in France in large numbers. Over 800,000 men have already gone across. More are going every day.

American ship production is going on apace. A beginning has been made in production of aircraft. Machine guns will soon be manufactured in quantity.

The U-boats are still taking large toll, but relatively to shipments, destruction from submarines is growing less.

The struggle on the western front has been most desperate and critical since March 21. Undoubtedly the situation will continue to be critical for some time. But the force of this mighty nation is being felt more and more as the days go by. Eventually we must exercise a dominating influence in ending the war.

There have been serious and dangerous delays in equipping our armies. Happily the outlook is better for the future.

Our men at the front are giving a good account of themselves. They are preserving the best traditions of the American soldier. They are under no illusions. They know that war is hell. But they will meet the enemy on his own ground and uncomplainingly and cheerfully make every sacrifice demanded to win the fight.

We at home must make our sacrifices in the same spirit. Everyone must do his part. When each one of us has done his best he may with justice complain of him who has not done his share. The sacrifices of war are many. Least of these are the financial burdens.

La Follette's Magazine, June, 1918.

XXII

AGRICULTURE AND CO-OPERATION

The Farm Life of the Future

IT requires no gift of prophecy to foresee the changes which another generation will unfold.

The development of this new country, with its privations and hardships, made life upon the farm one of long hours, of exacting toil, anxious watching for results, and, often, the closest kind of living. There was little leisure, little opportunity for reading and study, almost no time for recreation or holiday. Yet, so wholesome was the life, so normal the education of hand and brain, so exacting the demands upon self-reliance and individual courage, so firm and secure the moral foundations made by habits of industry and thrift, that the farm has furnished not only the state and nation, but the professional and business world, with its leaders of men and captains of industry.

Only a few years ago one of the most vexing problems was how to keep the boys and girls upon the farm. But important and sweeping changes are taking place in the professional, the commercial, and industrial world. Consolidation and combination are rapidly narrowing the field of individual opportunity and effort, in the pursuits which a quarter of a century ago tempted ambition and rewarded talent and industry. Except for the few masters of finance, he who is now counted fortunate enough to find a place in the complex system of modern business life, must encounter an abnormal strain and tension, and from the very conditions of success, forego all opportunity for individual development and personal achievement.

With the increasing competition in the professions and the lessening opportunity for large profits and great fortunes for the average individual in business, contrasted with the advancement in agriculture and increasing advantages of country life, the conditions may soon be reversed and our problems be how to keep our sons and daughters away from the farm and with us in business and professional life.

Be that as it may, it is plain that agriculture in this country has a future heretofore unknown in the world. Farming is now the most distinctive American occupation. It is the source of our safest, most conservative citizenship and highest average of intelligence.

Put the farm in direct communication with the world by the rural delivery, the telephone, the electric railway, the traveling library, the township school, the improved highway, and you have given it the essential advantages of the city without depriving it of the essential advantages of the country.

There will be left the sweet and vitalizing country air, the isolation of broad acres, the beauty of hill and valley, woodland and meadow, and living, running water. The charm of the ripening grain, coming to its mysterious fullness in the warm embrace of the sunshine, the honest pride in the grazing flocks, and the affectionate interest in their growing young, will always be an inherent and uplifting element of life upon the farm. The rich blessing of unconscious health, the joy of wholesome work, that brings wholesome rest and wholesome appetite, are the natural rewards of this outdoor occupation. Nearness to nature, nearness to God, a truer philosophy, a keener human sympathy, higher ideals, greater individuality, will ever be stamped upon the life and character of the country home.

The new agriculture, the new education, new inventions will give added interest, larger profits, greater certainty of success. They will lighten its burdens, widen its sphere, and ultimately make agriculture the most desirable of all human avocations. A new day has already broken upon the tiller of the soil. The new life upon the farm will recognize not only the material value and dignity of labor, but the increasing necessity for greater leisure and a larger measure of recreation. It will not be only a life of industrious independence, high intelligence, and great culture, but it will have time for the aesthetic and artistic side of human affairs. Under these influences every farm will become a beautiful country home, provided with every comfort, every convenience, every rational luxury,—in close touch with the world, yet happily apart from it.

Wisconsin has been a pioneer in this advancement of American agriculture. Many of the distinguished leaders are here tonight. May their valued lives be spared yet many years to us to see the full measure of their great service to this noble industry and the fruition of our highest hopes for its future.

*Address, Farmers' Institute, Oconomowoc,
Wisconsin, March 19, 1902.*

The Farmer the Nation's Hope

Nearly one-half of all the people of this country are engaged in and directly dependent upon agriculture. The vital forces of every other business, I care not what its character, are drawn from and nourished by it. From the standpoint of economics purely and upon the strictest business principles the interests of agriculture are the interests of this Government. No other pursuit so universally and profoundly concerns every other citizen of the Republic—no other calling known to civilized man, where so entirely and completely the interests of one is the interest of all.

There are other considerations which are worthy the thought of those charged in part with the duties of government. Favored by the character of our institutions, almost all of the farm land in this country is held and owned by men who cultivate it. Ownership of soil means ownership of home, and I tell you that government whose people build and own their own homes lays broadest and deepest its foundations and bargains most surely and happily with time. Such homes, no matter how humble, are pledges of the perpetuity of the nation. Our little modest homes scattered over this land, reared by those who live in them, are the pillars of strength which lift this government above other nations of the civilized world. And it is well for us to remember here as elsewhere that the poorest home is just as great an element of strength to the state as the costliest mansion. To the state, to the government, there is no difference.

Now, sir, these rural homes are built on small margins, they are maintained only by industry and frugality. Every factor of strength and support about them is important to comfortable, decent existence.

Sir, I know something of life upon the farm; I know the value of little things in the economical system, in the sparing, cautious management practiced there. I know how the small things are used to fill up and round out the seasons as they go. There is little that can be safely spared.

I know, sir, the vital, the absolutely vital importance of the dairy to the maintenance not only of the home comforts, the sweetening of the home life, but its great value to that which makes the home possible—the farm itself. It is the one important element in almost the only system which can be adopted upon the small farms to sustain their soil and preserve their producing properties. To foreclose the farmer from this essential branch of his business is to greatly narrow the limits of his industry, lessen the number of farm products, and force overproduction in the few produced with all its consequent disasters to commerce and trade.

Speech on Bill to Tax Oleomargarine, House of Representatives, June 2, 1886.

Agriculture and Co-operation

Rural Economics Needs Attention

The high cost of living in cities compared with the prices received by farmers for their products requires our immediate attention; we denounce the suppression by special interests in congress of the investigation of the country life commission, and we favor a thorough investigation of the conditions of country and city life, as an aid in bringing the wage-earner and farmer closer together, eliminating the wastes of distribution, promoting co-operative selling, buying, storage, and warehousing, co-operative credit and knowledge of co-operative methods, collective bargaining and arbitration between employers and employees, and the encouragement of the ownership of homes by wage-earners and farmers.
Wisconsin Republican Platform, 1910.

Good Roads for Wisconsin Farmers

I am in hearty accord with all properly directed movements to provide good roads, not only to the people of Wisconsin, but to the people of the entire country. As governor of Wisconsin and as United States senator, I have aided in the enactment of legislation to secure good highways.

However, I believe that plans for highway construction should be so perfected as to secure to the people who pay the taxes a dollar's worth of road value for every dollar expended upon highways. We want good highways not only in name but in fact. Wisconsin roads should be constructed scientifically and economically. The initial cost of a road is no guarantee of its value. The road, the first cost of which is the least, may ultimately prove most expensive to the taxpayer.

There has been criticism of the highway taxes in Wisconsin. Some of it was justified, because of the character of the roads built in some of the communities. Some of this criticism was also justified because of the law which permitted a few men of large wealth who contributed a portion of the cost, to force road taxes onto a community unable or unwilling to bear such taxation.

The Good Roads Association of Wisconsin in promoting a better understanding of the value of scientifically constructed and co-related highways can supplement and aid the splendid work of the Wisconsin Highway Commission.

Such a service will be a real public service. It will build into the life of the state, highways of a lasting character and tend constantly to maintain better and higher standards of integrity in all public work.

It will be many years before Wisconsin has a complete and reasonably perfect system of highways. Your program of state trunk roads north and south and east and west is based on sound, economic principles. Such roads would materially aid the farmers and many of the small towns of the state. The beautiful lakes of the state would be made more accessible to the centers of population. Such improvements of our highways would bring thousands of tourists from other states, make better markets right at hand for the products of the dairy and farm. They will be followed by a greater incentive for the intensive cultivation of our land. This is

Agriculture and Co-operation

but one aspect of the economic value of good roads to the farmer., Another more general and far reaching lies in the better facilities thus afforded the farmer to reach all of his markets. The more grain or produce the farmers can haul at a single load, the greater the return per load. This not only benefits the farmer, but it also will benefit the residents of our cities.

I hope the good roads problem of our state will be worked out scientifically so as to secure the maximum of benefits to the state, to distribute these benefits equitably over the state and so that the financial burden may not fall too heavily in any one year or upon any one community. Our roads should be built for all time and the work should be carried forward on plans satisfactory to the taxpayers and the people.

La Follette's Magazine, August. 1916.

Why the Farmers are Organizing

Why, Senators, are you not able to see? Is there nothing that can arouse the statesmanship of this day from its lethargy? Can you not interpret this wonderful movement that is sweeping over the Middle West and going on to the Pacific and throwing out its feelers even into the New England territory—the movement of the Farmers' National Nonpartisan League? What is the cause? It is organized because there is a belief among the people that there is a power that puts them at a disadvantage by controlling the market price of what they produce and the market price of everything they buy. They have appealed to the Democratic Party and they have appealed to the Republican Party, and they have appealed in vain, for relief; for legislation to break the power that took out of their toil just what tribute it pleased; a power that forced them when they marketed their grain to take a low price and then took that grain into the great storage elevators and sold it to the consumer at a high price.

The great body of the agriculturists of this country decided that it had stood that thing long enough. They have protested; they have appealed to the various parties. They have gone before the various national committeemen; they have asked for this plank and that plank in the national platforms, but they have obtained no relief. Decade after decade has passed. They sweated to produce the crop; they sent it to market; they have taken out of it now enough to pay for the production and to carry the interest charges upon the capital invested in the farms. They have bought the supplies controlled by the Harvester Trust, the Beef Trust, the Fertilizer Trust, the Woolen Trust, and the Cotton Trust. The price of everything they had to buy has been controlled arbitrarily by selfish interests and is no longer controlled by competition.

Speech in U. S. Senate, Aug. 29, 1919.

XXIII

EDUCATION AND PUBLIC SERVICE

The District School

WHEN the educators of the state agree on the proposition that the district schools are inadequate for their work, and are steadily losing in usefulness and depreciating in popular favor; when this judgment is confirmed by a decreasing attendance upon the district school and corresponding removal to the cities for better common school advantages; when the best authorities give assurance that "for every hundred pupils now attending district school only one pupil reaches a high school," —then it must indeed be time to pause in praise of our colleges and city schools long enough to emphasize the necessity of more generous support and of more successful supervision for the long neglected country schools.

Wisconsin is an agricultural state. With comparatively few exceptions her cities are only centers of farm prosperity. The products of cultivated soil, always the most important factor in the development of the commonwealth, will gain rapidly in importance through the acquirement by farmers of the vast territory in the northern half of the state, following the clearing of the forests. Nowhere does education bring dividends more regularly than upon the farm. Nowhere is lack of it more extravagant in loss. The ignorant city laborer wastes only his own time and energy. An incompetent farmer may squander the productive power of the land which he occupies in addition to his misapplied efforts and labor. The valuable results of education in farm work are shown in the awakened interest and progressive methods which have come from the University dairy school and Agricultural college. I believe that this branch of educational work should be broadened in scope by adding elementary training in agricultural knowledge to the course of study in district schools.

Message to Legislature, 1901.

The Country Schools

For many years to come the district school must furnish education for the great mass of boys and girls born upon the farms. Probably no less than 75 per cent of these will never attend any other school. How vital it is, then, that we should make these long-neglected schools our first care and bestow upon them such attention and such aid as will insure the results so essential to agricultural prosperity and the welfare of the state.

Address, Annual Meeting State Board of Agriculture, 1901.

Public Service

Our state and our university are scarcely more than half a century old. Each is where it can begin to get a proper perspective of the other. The state was not created for the university, the university exists for the state. We, the children of this commonwealth, ought now to begin to appreciate the richness of our heritage and the full measure of our responsibility. It rests with us to do much to perpetuate it in all the plenitude of its power and greatness among the states of the union.

That university man or woman who fails, after leaving these portals, to render some distinct and valuable service to the state is a pensioner upon the state's bounty. The opportunity waits for all. Scarcely a day passes but brings with it the occasion and opens the way. It may require sacrifice. It may ask courage. It may provoke criticism. But the state has prepared us for this work, has developed our powers, enlarged our capacity for usefulness in the world, and we are in honor bound, whenever we can, to strike the blow and say the word which makes the state stronger, promotes a better public policy, and insures a better government.

Alumni Banquet, University, 1901.

On Elementary Education

It cannot be complained that the state has been negligent in the matter of financial aid to the common schools, but the official statistics of school attendance reveal the necessity of something more than money expenditure if the district school is to retain a degree of usefulness at all commensurate with its cost. Figures taken from the reports in the department of the state superintendent show that during the last six years with a steady, almost uniform, increase in the number of persons of school age in the state, there has been in the same period an equally steady decrease in the percentage or proportionate number of such persons enrolled in the public schools, without corresponding increase in the number of persons of school age attending private schools. The same statistics show that nearly one-half of the total number were enrolled in the country, village and small city schools, while the average daily attendance approximates less than sixty per cent of the enrollment. The attendance in many of the villages and small cities is comparatively high, and the inevitable conclusion is that the average daily attendance in the country schools is probably not more than fifty per cent of the total enrollment. The teaching force, accommodations, and equipment provided, were ample for a full attendance every day. Wholly disregarding the evil effect of such absences upon teachers and fellow pupils in a progressive school, the mere financial loss is worthy your most careful consideration. When approximately four million dollars is expended for school purposes throughout the state, outside the cities under city superintendents, a clear waste of nearly forty per cent of that expenditure through absence of pupils, who by right and by law should be in school, is not a matter to be neglected. It is pointed out by educators that this sum would much more than provide for comfortable transportation of all children in country districts to well built, well graded and well taught central schools. The legislature of 1901 enacted a law to provide for transportation of pupils in rural districts, and I commend to your attention the need of effort to improve these laws and

make them more effective in promoting the excellent work for which they were originally designed. The certain result will be larger attendance at the common schools with less expense to the commonwealth.
Message to Legislature, 1903.

Obligations of Citizenship

The state welcomes the ever increasing tendency to make the university minister in a direct and practical way to the material interests of the state. Agriculture, mining, manufacturing and commerce are already turning here for direct practical aid. On this material basis alone the university is paying back to the state an hundred fold every dollar appropriated to its support.

Standing here at the close of the first half century, we turn to meet the increasing responsibilities of the coming years. It is not enough that this university shall zealously advance learning, or that it shall become a great store-house of knowledge into which is gathered the accumulating fruits of research and all of the world's best culture, or that it shall maintain the highest standards of scholarship and develop every latent talent—all these are essential—but the state demands more than all these. The state asks that you give back to it men and women strong in honesty and integrity of character, in each of whom there is deeply planted the obligation of allegiance to the state. That obligation should meet them as they cross that threshold of this institution and go in and out with them day by day until it is a conviction as strong as life.

That obligation cannot be discharged by the passive performance of the merely normal duties of citizenship. Upon every citizen rests the obligation to serve the state in civil life as the soldier serves the country in war. To this high duty the children of the university are specially called. The state has prepared you for this work and you are honor-bound to strike the blow or say the word which will make the state stronger, promote a better public policy, insure a better government. To be silent when you should speak, to dodge, or evade or skulk, is to play the coward. To compromise with the opponents of just equal government for personal advantage or business gain is to betray the state and make barter of citizenship.

Fear has been expressed by endowed universities that state universities would be affected by politics. For fifty years politicians have come and gone in the state of Wisconsin, but the lamp of learning has never been trimmed, or turned down, or put out. The spirit of our university has continued to be democratic. In a state university every branch of learning stands on an equality. The state welcomes the efforts of the university to assist to the practical advantage of the people of the state. Every dollar invested in our university is returned in practical benefit to the people of the state one hundred fold. The state asks that you give back to it men and women strong in honesty and moral character, who shall appreciate the obligation they owe of loyalty to the state.

Address, Inauguration of President Van Hise, June 7, 1904.

Education and Public Service

Address to University Alumni

Rich in soil and scenery, with lakes and rivers unrivaled, rich in forests and mines and manufactures and the natural conditions for a remarkably diversified agriculture, Wisconsin has the attributes and elements which make for the highest material rank and power among her sister states. But the greatness of a state does not lie in its area, its commerce, its bonds and stocks and wealth and accumulated splendors. It lies back of all these in the character of her citizenship. It was just here that Wisconsin was most fortunate from the beginning. Our tempting forests and prairies and mines were opened to occupation and development at that period in the history of our country when the east could still furnish to the west, choice representatives of the rugged, original natures combined of puritan severity and quaint Yankee shrewdness. So that in our population today runs the blood of the sturdy pioneer from New England, Maine, New York, Ohio and Indiana commingled with that of the hardy emigrant from Europe, who came when the conditions abroad were likewise timely for giving to us the strongest types which the best foreign countries could possibly furnish.

I do not know to what extent in this new century the obligation of the student to the state is made part of the daily thought of university life, but I well remember when it found expression in every convocation and was heard from time to time in every classroom. It may be that in those dear old days, when the institution was poor and the support feeble, the appropriation looked larger, the opportunities offered more precious, and the obligation more exacting. But I do know that it was always present with us then and in some way we were made to feel, that as our Alma Mater was to us, so was the state to her; that we were within the bond, and as the state nourished and sustained the university, so should we ever serve and defend the state.

With the marvelous growth of the university, men and women go out from here each year into every section and corner of the commonwealth. They should bear with them as an abiding obligation, the thought that their first and foremost duty is to pay back in earnest, persistent, conscientious effort for good government, the debt due to the state.

I would not disparage scholarship, but venture to say that before all things, the university owes it to the state to give it good citizens—men and women who will fight the battles of the state, against all the combination of evil. I do say that the student should never be permitted to forget while here that he is primarily training for the duties of citizenship; and when he goes out, whatever may be his occupation or profession, it should be as one who has enlisted for life in the service of the state.

When this settles down as a conviction into the mind of every citizen and taxpayer, how direct will become his interest in the university! It will be his institution then, doing his service, equipping its graduates to protect his personal and property rights, as the advocates of clean and honest service in municipal and state government. When this mighty power for the general good is once fully felt throughout the state, when this sleeping giant is once awakened to his obligations and conscious of his strength, the university will not longer come cringing past an impudent and arrogant lobby, as a suppliant to the state for an appropriation that it may live and meet the increasing demands upon it; but, erect with a new dignity and a new power, knowing the value of its service to the citizen and to the state which supports it, secure in the affections of the whole people, receive their free offering to enlarge and expand its widening field of usefulness to the state.

With the university as a great recruiting station, the ranks of patriotic citizenship shall ever swell with increasing numbers, armed for the state's best service. O, you, who stand ready for the work today, are you fully conscious of your duty and your opportunity? Not since the days of the sixties have greater issues called for truer men. Upon you the state has bestowed the best training which fifty years of fostering care could develop. You go forth in her best armor with sword and sheaf upon which she has wrought with infinite pains for half a century. She is waiting for you in every community; she needs every arm. Strike always for the state and you will strike for the right. So shall the state grow stronger and stronger, so shall great and greater honor come to our university.

Address, University Alumni Dinner,
June 19, 1901.

To High School Pupils

It is a great pleasure to meet you for a few minutes this morning and give you a greeting. I congratulate you on behalf of the state for the work you are doing in your high school. It is a matter of pride to me to look over this splendid assembly this morning and to have impressed upon me as you impress me, the splendid work the state of Wisconsin is accomplishing through its school system. I am glad to be here personally for another reason. My earliest recollection of school work in its broad sense is associated with your principal (M. S. Frawley). My mind goes back to my boyhood days when he was county superintendent of that portion of Dane County in which I lived. Along through the years I have watched his career and have ever admired him, and I congratulate you on having at the head of this school so competent, earnest and honest a man as director of your work. May he long continue in the work here unless it be the fortune of the state to see him called to some higher place.

I am glad to be here for another reason. I like to look into the faces of the youth and to light again my own enthusiasm from that which is down in the minds of the young. You will go out from here in a little while when you have completed your work. You will go out with a well rounded education prepared to take up the work in the higher schools of Wisconsin and to meet the trials of life, for they will come to you, come to each one of you. You have possibly been told so many times that it has become trite and tiresome to you that these are your best days.

Education and Public Service

I do wish there was some way I could make you realize that the best of life is today. Get all the good, all the pleasure out of it that you can, because in a little while you will have to meet the serious side of life. Into the life of each of you there will come trouble. You will have your sorrows, your griefs, your disappointments and I am sure that the discipline that you are getting here now will help you to meet it, because I am confident that under this leadership you are getting a training in something more than books. Book knowledge is important. You must have it. You cannot get too much of it, but I am sure that the importance of character building is necessary in everything that you do. It is the highest essential of your life; you cannot accomplish anything without it, that is anything worth having, that will endure, and I say to you that character building is the most important part of education.

If it was a question of never opening the books, or of having the broad education closed to you, I should feel that it were better to have training of acts than the training of books. But if you have them both and I am sure that you carry into each day's work that spirit of honesty which is building up the best side of your life, you cannot cheat in a lesson or examination, for it leaves a scar on your character. You cannot do it without weakening the armor you are having fitted upon you now for the battle of life. Everything you do is simply putting another plate, another rivet in the armor you are wearing when you go out to fight for yourself, your state and your country, and every time you are tempted to evade duty or cheat a teacher you are putting a false plate, a weak rivet in that armor. We are such creatures of habit that the things we do once we are almost bound to do again, and so I say that the most important part of your education is in doing honestly and faithfully the task of each day, in equipping each one to meet each event, each requirement and each responsibility throughout life, and now let me say to you that I wish you everything good in your individual lives that can come to members of the human family, and I speed you Godspeed on your way.

To Eau Claire, Wis., High School,
October 2, 1903.

Moral Influence of a Great Teacher

It is difficult, indeed, to overestimate the part which the university has played in the Wisconsin resolution. For myself I owe what I am and what I have done largely to the inspiration I received while there. It was not so much the actual course of study which I pursued; it was rather the spirit of the institution—a high spirit of earnest endeavor, a spirit of fresh interest in new things, and beyond all else, a sense that somehow the state and the university were intimately connected, and that they should be of mutual service.

The guiding spirit of my time, and the man to whom Wisconsin owes a debt of gratitude greater than it can ever pay was its President, John Bascom.

I never saw Ralph Waldo Emerson, but I should say John Bascom was a man of much his type, both in appearance and character. He was the embodiment of moral force, and moral enthusiasm; and he was in advance of his time in feeling the new social forces and in emphasizing the new social responsibilities. His addresses to students on Sunday afternoon, together with his work in the class room were among the most important influences in my early life. It was his teaching, iterated and reiterated, of the obligation of both the university and the students to the mother state that may be said to have originated the Wisconsin idea in education.

He was forever telling us what the state was doing for us, and urging in return our obligation not to use our education wholly for our own selfish benefit, but to return some service to the state. That teaching animated and inspired hundreds of students who sat under John Bascom.

In those days we did not so much get correct political views, for there was then little teaching of sociology or political economy worthy of the name, but we somehow did get, and largely from Bascom, a proper attitude toward public affairs. And when all is said, this attitude is more important than any definite views a man may hold.

Years afterward when I was governor of Wisconsin John Bascom came to visit us at the executive residence at Madison, and I treasure the words he said to me about my new work:

"Robert," he said, "you will doubtless make mistakes in judgment as governor, but never mind the political mistakes so long as you make no ethical mistakes."

John Bascom lived to be 84 years old, dying in 1911 at his home in Williamstown, Mass. Up to the last his mind was clear and his interest in the progress of humanity as keen as ever. In his later years he divided his time between his garden and his books—a serene and beautiful old age. His occasional letters and his writings were always a source of inspiration to me.

In all my fights in Wisconsin the university and the students have always stood firmly behind me. In a high sense the university has been the repository of progressive ideas; it has always enjoyed both free thought and free speech. When the test came years ago the university met it boldly where some institutions faltered or failed.

Autobiography, 1913.

Greeting to Dr. John Bascom

I am accorded the high honor of extending to you here tonight a greeting and welcome on behalf of the state. Believe, me, sir, this welcome is deeply sincere and heartfelt.

Time has wrought many changes since that day, so well remembered by us all, when you left us fourteen years ago. The state has grown remarkably in numbers and wealth and power. It has made notable progress in its educational work and in its conduct of all its state institutions. While temporary delays and disappointments are encountered here as elsewhere, nevertheless through this commonwealth an increasing sense of the responsibilities of citizenship is everywhere manifest, and a well developed and powerful public sentiment must soon place Wisconsin high among her sister states in all that pertains to good government and the upbuilding of a noble statehood. It is fitting that you should be reminded of this progress, because you have been the source and the inspiration of so large a share of it. What we owe to you individually, each of us here tonight realizes more and more as the years go by. What this institution and this state owe to you can never be fully measured.

When first called to the university, you came from a state and from an institution old in educational methods; refined in educational taste; fixed in educational ideas; but your breadth, your comprehension, your wisdom, enabled you to establish in our institution the foundation of a great university. You valued our raw youth at its true worth, and saw in it strong material for future citizenship. The small numbers of students, the unpretentious buildings, the meagre accommodations did not bind you to the possibilities of the university. Our plain attire, country breeding, imperfect preparation, but earnest ambition for education and enlarged opportunities, enlisted your sympathy and inspired the deepest interest.

In the midst of the most trying circumstances and most discouraging situations you conquered opposition, maintained your faith in the institution, and kept constantly uppermost your high ideals of the mutual relationship of the state and the university. The obligation of generous support from the state and the corresponding obligation of the alumni to the state were daily impressed with great force and clearness upon all who came within your influence. No student ever left this university while you were its president, whose college education was not thoroughly seasoned with this sense of high moral obligation to serve the state upon every occasion with all that was best in him. Much of the enlarged scope, the harmonious development, the phenomenal growth of the university is due to the thorough inculcation of this idea upon the great body of students who passed in and out during all those years.

From its foundation down to this hour there was never a time when you could have rendered a greater service to the university and to the state than at the critical period which marked the beginning of your administration. The institution had just reached the most impressionable stage in its growth and development when you were called to the presidency. It was a fortunate day for the institution and for the future of the state. Youthful, plastic, yet full of lusty vigorous life, the time was ripe for some master mind to make an everlasting impression upon the character of the university, and through it upon the commonwealth. The hour was come, and, thank God, the man! For thirteen years —the most precious years of its life—this state had a great thinker, philosopher and teacher at the head of its highest educational institution.

Whoever shall set bounds, or fix limitations upon your noble work, let him look beyond executive orders and the presidential office. Let him look beyond the covers of any book and the walls of any class room. He will readily determine that everywhere, underlying all work, and all life in the institution, pervading its whole atmosphere, entering into the daily thought and being of each student was the mysterious power with which you laid hold of youth, grounded and established principles admitting of no compromise with error and evil, builded character of adamant, yet preserved individuality—in short, made well-rounded, full-orbed men and women, and finally gave them back to the state with a quality of citizenship which will run through all the generations to come.

The personality of a great teacher is greater than his teaching. Many of the written propositions of psychology and ethics are slipping away with the passing of the years, but you abide with us forever. May He, who orders all our lives, lengthen your days that your wisdom and your moral power may continue to be deeply impressed upon all who are so fortunate as to be near to you, and may we be so favored as to greet you here again and again.

University of Wisconsin, June 17, 1901.

On Academic Freedom of the State University

If there is any public institution in America that should be bulwarked and safeguarded against ignorant or covert attack, it is the University of Wisconsin. This university is famed throughout the world as "The Greatest State University." It has earned this distinction primarily because it has become truly THE PEOPLE'S University—because it has "served the time without yielding to it," because it stoops not to propagate the "theories" of any clique, class or interest, but ever explores the wide fields of knowledge and turns over, disinterestedly, to the people who maintain it, the fruits of its research.

Back in 1894, an enlightened, progressive board of regents issued this declaration of academic freedom:

"Whatever may be the limitations which trammel enquiry elsewhere, we believe that the great state University of Wisconsin should ever encourage that continual and fearless sifting and winnowing by which alone the truth can be found."

In devoting itself to this high and proper public service, it has kept strictly out of "politics;" hence it has developed no effective armor to shield it from the highly organized assaults of small but rich and powerful groups of interests who fear the truth—the truth, for instance, concerning the manner in which predatory business is systematically and unscrupulously exploiting the people.

During the past year the railroad, water power, insurance combination came temporarily into control in this state. This plunderbund promptly turned its weapons against the people's university into a propagandist and special pleader for their own "theories." As Governor Philipp—mouthpiece of this combination—expressed it in a recent speech: "I do not believe it wise to permit the teaching of half-baked theories of government that never have been demonstrated to be a success, that intimidate capital, and that close factory doors." The program laid down by the special interest combination is, to permit no investigation, no research nor teaching that has not first been censored by "capital." A program of abject academic slavery!

But intelligent alumni, irrespective of political affiliation, have come to the rescue. A conference was held at Madison, November 20, to consider means of maintaining the high standard of the university and of keeping unsullied its academic freedom against these plottings. Organized and sordid spreading of falsehood must be met by organized and unselfish spreading of the truth.

Here is an opportunity for real service to the people of Wisconsin. If this committee succeeds in working out a plan of reorganization that will enable Wisconsin alumni in every community quickly and effectively to register their convictions and influence, a notable chapter will have been added to the annals of educational freedom. A working and democratically organized association would be a medium through which the people who support the university could be kept constantly informed regarding the real services it performs, the real spirit of its teaching and investigation, exactly what it costs the state to maintain it, and the millions of money which it annually pays back to the taxpayers in better methods of farming, bigger crops, higher standards in the mechanic arts and a graduate body trained for the best service which the enlightened citizen can render the state.

So reorganized and re-vitalized, the alumni of the university will furnish the most intelligent body of criticism whenever honest, constructive criticism is necessary, and a powerfully organized defense whenever the best interests of the university are threatened. Such a live progressive alumni army always in the field will be ever ready to stand a tower of strength between the university and these business and political interests that attempt to censor and degrade its work.

The need for this is urgent. The step already taken by the alumni is reassuring. Let every loyal alumnus rally to this call to high service.
La Follette's Magazine, November, 1915.

Democratizing the Senate

In a great body like the Congress of the United States nearly all legislation is controlled by committees. The sanction of a committee goes a long way. The life of a congressman, a senator, is a busy one; he is worked early and late, and in some measure he must depend for the details of legislation upon the committees appointed for the purpose of perfecting the legislation. And as the business of the country grows and the subjects of legislation multiply, so committee action upon bills becomes more and more important. We spend a vast sum of money to print a Congressional Record in order that the public may be made acquainted with the conduct of their business, and then we transact the important part of the business behind the locked doors of a committee room. The public believes that the Congressional Record tells the complete story, when it is in reality only the final chapter.

Sir, I believe the time near at hand when we will change the practice of naming the regular or standing committees of the Senate.

It is un-American—it is undemocratic. It has grown into an abuse. It typifies all of the most harmful practices which have led to an enlightened

Education and Public Service

and aroused public judgment to decree the destruction of the caucus, convention, and delegate system of party nominations.

Under the present system of choosing standing committees of the United States Senate a party caucus is called. A chairman is authorized to appoint a committee on committees. The caucus adjourns. The committee on committees is thereafter appointed by the chairman of the caucus. It proceeds to alter the committee assignments of senators. This places the selection of the membership of the standing committees completely in the hands of a majority of the committee.

See now what has happened. The people have delegated us to represent them in the Senate. The senate, in effect, has delegated its authority to party caucuses upon either side. The party caucus delegates its authority to a chairman to select a committee on committees. The committee on committees largely defer to the chairman of the committee on committees in the final decision as to the committee assignments. The standing committees of the senate, so selected, Mr. President, determine the fate of all bills; they report, shape, or suppress legislation practically at will. Hence the control of legislation, speaking in a broad sense, has been delegated and redelegated until responsibility to the public has been so weakened that the public can scarcely be said to be represented at all. To make this control of legislation water tight, the trusted lieutenants assigned to the chairmanship of the committees have always exercised authority (1) to determine when a committee should meet (2) to appoint sub-committees for the consideration of all bills referred to the committee by the senate, and (3) to name the conferees to be appointed by the presiding officer of the senate. The action of committees, sub-committees, and conference committees on all bills, is conducted in executive session—that is to say, in secret session. As a member of the senate I have again and again protested against secret action of congressional committees upon public business, and against the business of congress being taken into secret party caucuses and there disposed of by party rule. I have maintained at all times my right as a public servant to discuss in open senate and elsewhere publicly all legislative proceedings whether originating in the executive session of committees or behind closed doors of caucuses and conferences.

The rules of the senate must be so changed as to provide for the election of members of committees by the senate pursuant to a direct primary conducted by each party organization under regulations prescribed by senate rules.

The chairmen of the committees should be elected by a record vote of the members of such committees.

The conferees on all bills should be elected by a record vote of the members of committees reporting such bills.

A permanent record should be made of the action of caucuses, standing committees and conference committees upon all matters affecting legislation.

All caucus proceedings touching legislation and the proceedings of sub-committees, committees and conference committees should be open to the public.
La Follette's Magazine, April 19, 1913.

Patriotism and Party Loyalty

I am not going to apologize for coming to New Jersey, I have a right to be here. Moreover, I am coming back here when you have a campaign, no matter what may be the outcome of this one.

Most men are ambitious, in different ways. I am ambitious. Some want to make money, some to be famous in various ways. My ambition is to write my name with the thousands who in this trial time of our country have enlisted for the redemption and restoration of representative government.

It is time for men to begin to work together for the welfare of the country. And I do not always urge democrats to vote the republican ticket. In Missouri I appealed to republicans to support Folk for governor. In these times there is something greater and better than simply standing blindly by party. Of course, I know the regulars, as they call themselves, will say: "There's that arrant demagogue advocating bolting the party," but that doesn't worry me much. I appeal to patriotism of country rather than partisanship. I love the Republican party, but when my work is done, I would rather have written on the little stone above my head: "He was a patriot" than "He was a Republican."

No one has any right to make war upon a corporation which receives only a fair interest upon its investment. We can't afford, by legislation, to impose upon or cripple corporations doing a legitimate business along legitimate lines, in a legitimate way. We want the best transportation we can get, and we ought to be willing to pay charges that will make investment in these enterprises profitable. But these are public-service corporations. It is the duty of the state to stand between the people and the corporations and see exact justice done to each—that the people don't pay too much and that the companies get a fair return, and only a fair return, on their investment. That is what the "new idea" in New Jersey stands for, so far as the railroads and public utilities are concerned.

Speech at Newark, N. J., Sept., 1906.

Importance of Character in Men Elected to Office

The most important thing of all is to send honest men to Washington—men in this time of stress who want to serve the public, and nobody else. The abler these men are, the better, but above all the people should see to it that their representatives are honest—not merely money honest, but intellectually honest.

If they have the highest standards of integrity and the highest ideals of service, all our problems, however complex, will be easily solved.

Autobiography, 1913.

The Future of the Republican Party

I believed then, as I believe now, that the only salvation for the republican party lies in purging itself wholly from the influence of financial interests. It is for this, indeed, that the group of men called insurgents have been fighting—and it is this that they will contend for to the end.

I here maintain with all the force I possess that it is only as the republican party adopts the position maintained today by the progressives that it can live to serve the country as a party organization.

Autobiography, 1913.

XXIV

ECONOMIC PROBLEMS

The Coal Strike

THE real issues of the coal strike have been obscured by the campaign of denunciation against the 450,000 miners who laid down their tools at midnight, October 31.

No one will deny that the closing of the mines at this time is deplorable.

But the vital question is: Who is responsible for the closing of the mines?—and the answer is not to be found in the extravagant statements of administration officials nor in the parrot phrases of the press.

The miners are asking for a six-hour day, a five-day week and a wage increase of 60 per cent. The miners contend that their present contract, entered into for the period of the war, terminated with the actual cessation of hostilities. With wages stationary during the past two years, they declare they are unable to feed and clothe their families in the face of advanced living costs.

The operators take issue with the miners.

They contend that the present contract is binding and insist that it shall remain in effect until the peace treaty is ratified, formally ending the war. They declare the demands of the miners for higher pay are unreasonable and that the shorter working day and

Economic Problems 315

week will curtail production. They warn the public that higher wages and curtailed production will mean increased cost of coal to the consumer.

In spite of the abuse which has been heaped upon the miners, the truth is on their side in the points at issue.

The validity of the present wage contract must remain a mooted legal question. Suffice it to say that the fuel administration many months ago suspended the war-time regulations governing fuel prices. The miners contend, with some logic, that if the war is over for prices, it should be over for wages.

Are the demands of the miners for a wage increase of 60 per cent unreasonable?

The present wage scale was adopted in November, 1917. Since that time, according to the figures of the department of labor, the cost of living has increased by more than 35 per cent. Meanwhile, the miners' wages have remained stationary.

During the past year, by reason of the curtailment of the normal number of working days, the miners have received an income less by 18 per cent than the income for the corresponding period in 1918, although living costs, by the government's figures, had increased 9 per cent over 1918 up to July 1 of the present year.

If the wage scale agreed upon in 1917 was sufficient to enable the miners to meet the cost of living at that time, it is now at least 35 per cent short of that standard.

In seeking a wage increase of 60 per cent, the miners are now attempting to bring their incomes up to the level of living expenses and they ask a margin of 25 per cent in their favor in order to meet the constant advance in prices from month to month. In view of their experience of the past year—when incomes dropped 18 per cent and living costs mounted 9 per cent—the margin asked by the miners is not unjustified.

The claim of the operators that a shorter working day and week will curtail production is unfounded.

In 1918, the operators caused the mines to be worked only 70 per cent of the time possible, and although 80,000 miners were in the military service, the peak production of 585,000,000 tons—more than enough coal for the normal needs of the country—was reached as the output of bituminous coal for the year.

During the present year, between January 1 and July 1, the mines have been worked but 50 per cent of the time.

Miner's Rights Taken Away

The granting of the full demands of the miners as to a six-hour day and a five-day week would not, therefore, necessarily affect production. It would have the wholly desirable effect of distributing the work evenly throughout the year, which is the object the miners have in view.

The operators, by a well-directed propaganda in the press, have attempted to convince the public that the miners are responsible for precipitating the strike and for the consequent closing of the coal mines.

The government has accepted this view and has declared half a million workmen violators of the law in leaving their employment.

Economic Problems 317

The true position of both sides may be seen in the statements issued on the eve of the strike. The miners' officers made the following statement:

"The mine workers' representatives are ready, willing and anxious to meet the coal operators for the purpose of negotiating an agreement and bringing about a settlement of the present unhappy situation. They will respond at any time to a call for such a meeting and will honestly endeavor to work out a wage agreement upon a fair and equitable basis."

Thomas T. Brewster, chairman of the scale committee of the Mine Operators' Association, made the following statement:

"The operators will resume negotiations with the miners and submit all disagreements to arbitration, provided the strike order be rescinded pending negotiations and the award of the arbitration board."

Thus the strike began November 1, and the United States was left with a fast dwindling supply of bituminous coal. The public may judge who is responsible for the existing shortage of coal and for the failure of the negotiations leading up to the strike.

The wisdom of the administration in using the courts and the military to break the strike, is open to grave question.

The right of workmen to strike has, up to the present time, been sustained by the courts. That this right exists is evidenced by the fact that legislation now pending is regarded as necessary to take that right away from one class of workmen—namely, the railroad employees.

It is not within the province of the government to decide, that "circumstances" justify interference with the exercise of an undoubted legal right.

The use of the great powers of the federal government on the side of men whose sinister aims against labor have best been expressed by Judge Gary—himself honored by the administration by appointment as a government delegate to the president's industrial conference—does not tend toward a healthy industrial situation in this country.

In the present controversy, the attempt to discredit half a million workmen, in order to protect the exorbitant profits of a handful of employers, will inevitab'y fall of its own weight.

The American people elected President Wilson in 1912, on the pledge that he would lower the cost of living.

The statistics of the United States department of labor show that the cost of living has increased 102 per cent since 1913, when President Wilson took office.

After mature reflection, the American people will not approve of the use of the machine gun and the injunction by the administration, in its effort to force 450,000 miners to continue at work against their will.

The administration which habitually fails to bring the profiteers to justice, in violation of its platform pledges, and which shows such extraordinary diligence in suppressing labor at the behest of employers, will, in the end, be discredited by the American people.

La Follette's Magazine, November, 1919.

On Life Insurance Companies

With the exception of the corporations which control the transportation facilities of a commonwealth, there is no class of corporations more in need of careful and economical administration than those which make a business of life insurance. It is the business which gathers the savings of youth and mature manhood to safeguard old age against poverty, and to provide sustenance and the shelter and comforts of home for the widow and the orphan. Infirm and unprovided old age, and helpless and unsupported childhood become a charge upon the state.

It is a shocking disclosure of the demoralized business integrity of the country when the admissions of the highest officials entrusted with the savings which the people have invested in life insurance and charged with the management of these funds show habitual violation of their trust to enrich themselves at the expense of policy holders. It ought not to be necessary to say that no officer, agent, or employee of any insurance company should be personally interested in the purchase or sale of any securities of that company, or have any personal or pecuniary interest in the making of loans of the funds of the company. The disclosures of the investigation of the New York legislative committee have demonstrated that the policy holders of at least three of the largest of the companies of the country have been systematically plundered by the operations of the officers of these companies. They have not only voted to themselves salaries out of all proportion to the services rendered, but this investigation establishes the personal financial interest of officers in the sale of securities to the companies, in the sale of securities by the companies, in the use of insurance funds in promoting industrial enterprises, in the loans of the funds of the companies, in the commissions paid for new business, in contracts for supplies, in the rentals of company property and in the payment of money of the policy holders as contributions to campaign funds and as salaries to legislative representatives.

It appears from the testimony taken before the New York investigating committee that one of the great sources of evil is the improper affiliation of insurance companies with other business enterprises, both through the personal connections of insurance officials with such enterprises, and through the holdings of stock and other voting securities of industrial and transportation companies by insurance companies. A conservative estimate places the par value of securities owned by insurance companies, which carry with them voting power, at over one hundred millions of dollars. To the extent to which these securities represent voting power insurance companies, acting through their officials, participate in the management of other business enterprises. This is beyond the legitimate province of life insurance companies.

It is questionable if insurance companies should invest in securities of this character at all, but if investments in selected shares of unquestioned value be expedient the voting power that they may carry should be invested in a public official not connected with an insurance company or any industrial or transportation company.

Governor's Message, Special Session, 1905.

Veto of Police Powers to Corporations

This bill is far-reaching in effect. It impinges the spirit of the constitution of the state, is subversive of the fundamental principles of good government, and vicious in principle. It authorizes street and other railway companies doing business in this state to appoint policemen empowered to arrest with or without warrant any person who in their presence shall commit upon or in or about their premises any offense against the laws of the state, or of the ordinances of any town, village or municipality, and clothes them with the authority of sheriffs in regard to the arrest or apprehension of such offenders in or about the premises or appurtenances of such companies.

Section nine of article thirteen of the constitution clearly prohibits the appointment of officers entrusted with the exercise of governmental powers by private individuals or corporations. The appointment itself must be made by a representative body of the state or some governmental subdivision or officer thereof; or the office must be filled by an election. The legislature cannot delegate the power to appoint or elect otherwise than to public authority. This is so even as to the officer exercising only in the slightest degree governmental functions. Neither the private individual nor corporation can be authorized to clothe with governmental power or authority any person whomsoever. Peace officers, policemen and sheriffs exercise in the highest degree the sovereign power of the government. They are very important factors in the administration of the criminal law of the state. Their duties are closely connected with the subject of the personal liberty and restraint of the citizen. They are state officers in that they exercise an important part of the sovereign power of the state. The constitution prohibits the exercise of this power to create and appoint its officers by private individuals or corporations. If it could delegate any part of the powers of government to private individuals all might be bestowed upon them. The state and its political subdivisions might be divested of all power over the subject and would lead to conflict, confusion, and anarchy. The policemen provided for in this bill are given the power and authority of sheriffs in and about all the property designated therein, which would include all the streets in each city through which street railway companies run or operate their cars, and all territory adjacent and appurtenant to their structures, buildings and property. If the legislature have the power to clothe these persons appointed by street or other railway companies with the authority of sheriffs, it could endow them with such authority as to constitutional officers He must be elected by a vote of the people. He can hold his office but one term, and hold no other office during that term. If the legislature could bestow upon policemen appointed by private individuals so important an authority and prerogative of the sheriff, it could divest him of all power and invest the individual with that power without limitation as to the tenure of, or regard to his qualifications for, the office. The constitution is a barrier to the enactment of this bill into law. To the citizen there is no subject of more vital importance than the one that touches the restraint of his personal liberty. The constitution of the United States as well as that of the state, has made this paramount and all-important. The fundamental law of the land forbids that the subject should be dealt with lightly, or that the citizen should be restrained of his liberty except by due form of law. It forbids that private or personal ends or private or personal interests should be a moving or controlling factor in compassing the arrest of any person, except through the instrumentality and by the authority of public officers. The machinery of the criminal code should not, and cannot be the fundamental law of the land, be operated, controlled, or moved solely by the interests of the private individual necessarily actuated and influenced by a sense of his own injury as distinguished from that of the general public. The power to arrest cannot and ought not to be delegated to the appointee of private interests. Such appointment would be subversive of the principles of representative government. The person appointed to exercise governmental powers would not be the representative of the state, but that alone of the private interests from which he derives his power and receives his compensation.

Every person guilty of a crime should be punished. All should be protected in their individual and property rights. It is the bounden duty of the state, and its political subdivisions, to give to both the individual and property rights the highest degree of protection. It should not, were it permissible under the constitution or the fundamental law of the land, delegate this power to the individual himself. Neither the state nor any political subdivision thereof can, without the most damaging admission of its weakness, lasting loss of its dignity, and grievous wound to its statehood and its government, county, city, town, and municipality, farm out its power to protect any or all within its borders from injury to either person or property. If one interest may be empowered to take into its own hands the independent administration of any part of the criminal code of the state, there is no reason why all interests and each individual should not be so empowered. The result would be the destruction of all governmental power and the substitution therefor of independent forces legal in form, but without constitutional authority in fact.

Veto Message, April 23, 1901.

Ship Subsidies—A Special Privilege

We are unequivocally opposed to the granting of shipping subsidies by the federal government, in the form of ocean mail subvention or otherwise. We hold that an American merchant marine cannot be upbuilt by appropriations from the tax-contributed treasury of the people for the enrichment of a special interest.

Republican State Platform, 1910.

Postal Bank Law

The postal savings bank law should be amended to compel the establishment of postal savings depositories throughout the country within easy reach of depositors, and to prevent the concentration of the postal savings in the large centers and their use in financial manipulations by the great corporate and banking interests in Wall street.

Republican State Platform, 1910.

XXV

CONSERVATION

Public Rights in Water Powers

FIVE hundred and sixteen laws granting franchises to dam navigable streams within this state have been passed since the organization of the territory of Wisconsin. Formerly many of these grants were for logging purposes. The great reduction in lumbering within the last few years has considerably decreased the number of grants made in aid of logging and lumbering. Notwithstanding this fact, the demand for franchises to build dams across the navigable streams of the state, seems to be increasing. It is, therefore, clearly manifest that capital has awakened to the opportunities which these water powers offer for permanent investment. It is certainly desirable that this should be encouraged in every proper way.

It has, heretofore, been the policy of the state to grant to any party seeking the same, the right to build dams across navigable streams anywhere within the limits of the commonwealth. Provided that its action does not conflict with the action of congress upon the same subject, the state has the undoubted authority to determine where and under what conditions dams may be constructed across its navigable waters. The only conditions which it has attached to grants of this character up to the present time, are the right to amend or repeal the same, and the requirement that fishways shall be maintained in all dams. It is the law that the structure must improve the navigation of the stream. Whenever those applying for these franchises have sought the authority, the legislature has freely conferred upon them the right to condemn and take the lands of others, and overflow the same, by providing effective statutory proceedings to that end.

Probably not more than half a dozen states in the union are so abundantly supplied with natural water power as Wisconsin and no state in the middle west is comparable to it in this respect. More than one thousand lakes, widely distributed within its borders, form natural reservoirs, furnishing sources of supply to the streams which flow through every section of the state.

In the early life of states and municipalities franchises are freely granted for the building of ferries and bridges, turnpikes, railroads, and street railways. Liberal donations of moneys and lands are frequently bestowed upon those receiving the franchises. Eager to secure rapid development, little thought is taken for the future, and no consideration given to the proper restrictions or limitations to be imposed upon those who are the beneficiaries of these valuable public grants.

Our navigable streams and rivers, like our streets and highways, are open to the free use of the people of the state. No one can acquire ownership in these waters. If the public through legislation, grants franchises, surrendering the use of any of its navigable waters to individuals or corporations, it is entitled to a reasonable consideration therefor. This it may not choose to take as a money consideration, but the state cannot do less than recognize the rights of the public, in making reasonable reservations at the time it confers the grants. The franchises so taken in many cases, grant rights of great and rapidly increasing value. The vast amount of power which these waters produce is a resource of a public nature, in the advantage and benefit of which the public should participate.

Water Powers Invested with Public Interest

Modern industrial development is making rapid progress. Already these water powers are extensively employed to generate electricity. The transmission of this power over considerable distances is successfully accomplished with little loss. It will, in the near future, be more widely distributed at a constantly diminishing cost. In manufacturing, in electric lighting in cities and towns and in the country, in operating street and interurban cars for the transportation of passengers and freight, and in furnishing motive power for the factory and the farm, electricity will eventually become of great importance in the industrial life of our commonwealth.

It is, therefore, quite apparent that these water powers are no longer to be regarded simply as of local importance. They are of industrial and commercial interest to every community in the state. Whether it be located in the immediate neighborhood of a water power will, in time, make little or no difference. While this is becoming more manifest year by year, it is probably true that we do not, as yet, approximately estimate the ultimate value of these water powers to the people of Wisconsin.

It must, therefore, be apparent that this subject, broadly considered, is of profound interest to the people of this commonwealth. If the policy of the state with respect to these franchises ought to be changed at all, it certainly ought to be changed now. Reserving the right to amend or repeal is not enough. When rich and powerful companies, availing themselves of these grants, acting in concert, seek to resist amendment or repeal, their influence will prove a very serious obstacle. Economic conditions are rapidly changing in this state and in the country. A legislative policy which grants franchises without substantial conditions amply protecting the public, and securing to it reasonable benefits in return, is neither right nor just, and ought no longer to be tolerated. The capital already invested, industries already established, may in a few years, find themselves quite at the mercy of power companies in combined control of the water power of the state.

Such investigations as I have been able to make of the subject plainly indicate that many of the grants to construct dams heretofore passed by the legislature, have been secured purely for speculative purposes. In such cases no improvements whatever have been made. The grants have been held awaiting opportunities to sell the same with large profit to the holders, who have not invested a dollar for the benefit of the state, or its industrial development. It is obvious that those franchises may be gathered up, and consolidated with others which have been granted where improvements have been made, and prices advanced until the state, municipalities, and the public will be compelled to pay an exorbitant rate for the power upon which we are likely to grow more and more dependent as time passes.

It is submitted to your honorable body that the time has come to give this subject the careful consideration which its great importance demands. I believe that the state should encourage the development of its natural resources, including its water power system, in so far as it may properly do so; but the obligation rests upon those charged with the responsibility and clothed with authority, to encourage this development under such conditions as will justly and fairly protect the public right in these great natural advantages.

Message to Legislature, April 12, 1905.

(Note: In this message Gov. La Follette is shown to have been a pioneer in the conservation movement, later capitalized by so many public officials and publicists. It was one of the first public notes sounded on the subject, and antedated the messages of President Roosevelt by several years.)

Indian Coal Lands

I believe that the time has come, Mr. President, for this government to declare a policy with respect to the ownership of coal lands by transportation companies; or to state the proposition more broadly, with respect to any transportation company going into competition with the producers who must ship over their lines. You cannot conceive of a highway being open and free to all shippers alike when those who are operating the highway are interested in reducing the profits or diminishing the holdings of competitors who ship over their lines of road.

For that reason I have incorporated in this amendment the proposition that not only the railroad company shall be barred from acquiring title to this land, but the deeds when executed shall contain a provision against the officials and stockholders of the companies becoming the owners of these coal lands.

It may be said here, Mr. President, as it was said in the committee on Indian affairs when I offered the amendment that if the railroads 'want these lands they will get them. But I desire to record here my protest against the doctrine that now or at any time in the history of this country it shall ever be said that the railroad companies can secure the mastery and control the ownership of any of the natural products of this country. In other words, to put it a little differently I believe that this government, however it may have appeared in recent years to the contrary, is stronger than any of its creatures; that this government is stronger than all the railroad companies in aggregation, stronger than all of the centralized power of this country represented in unlawful combinations and trusts.

So, Mr. President, I venture to ask senators to support the amendment which I have offered here and to write it into the statute books of the United States that railway companies shall be common carriers and nothing else, and to so write it as to make it effective.

First Speech in U. S. Senate, March 1, 1906.

Saving Alaska's Resources

The American people are waging a losing fight in Alaska. On the one hand are the 35,000 pioneers who are risking their lives and fortunes in the exploration and prospecting of its undiscovered resources. On the other hand are the millions of American people to whom this great storehouse of natural resources belongs. Between them is the enormous power of the greatest concentration of capital that the world has ever known.

Will the American people be so blind, so dull, as to permit this enormously rich field to become the property of Morgan and those allied with him, and thus force all the great western country and the millions who are to people it in the generations to come to pay such extortionate prices for coal as that power will certainly exact, or will the people of this country, who own Alaska, see to it that this great storehouse of wealth shall be used for the benefit of all the people, their children, and their children's children, for all time?

The American people are the owners of the resources of Alaska. The government should own and build the transportation facilities for the same reason that a private corporation, if owning the resources, would build and own them. The government itself should own and operate at least one great coal mine, to supply its naval and military needs, and to sell the surplus at a reasonable profit, as a check against extortion by private corporations developing other mines.

Speech in U. S. Senate, August 21, 1911.

Waste of Public Domain

Originally the public domain of the United States amounted in round numbers to 1,400,000,000 acres. Of this amount nearly all of the original domain available for agriculture and the greater part of our mineral wealth outside of Alaska have been disposed of, amounting in round numbers to more than 700,000,000 acres.

Out of the 571,000,000 acres disposed of to individuals and corporations there have been acquired through the exercise of the homestead right only 115,000,000 acres. The railroads and other corporations had bestowed upon them by congressional grants, without any return whatever to the government, in round numbers, 123,000,000 acres.

In addition to that, there has been conferred upon the railroads by state grants lands theretofore granted by the federal government to the several states, increasing the total grant to the railroads, in round numbers to 190,000,000 acres of land—enough to make the states of Ohio, Indiana, Illinois, Missouri, Iowa and Wisconsin.

And the government, through its executive departments, has sold at a mere nominal price, in round number, 182,000,000 acres.

The disposition of our mineral resources especially, and until recently our forests, forms a shameful chapter in the history of our nation. These mineral resources belonged to all of the people. In the early history this was recognized and we started out upon a correct basis. By an ordinance in 1785 the government reserved to itself one-third part of all gold, silver, lead and copper mines, to be sold or otherwise disposed of as congress shall hereafter direct.

But in 1829 cupidity and greed commenced to triumph, and the abandonment of this policy began. In 1845 congress repealed the leasing system of mineral lands. Had the policy of leasing been continued and applied to our coal, iron, oil, and copper lands and lands containing precious metals with suitable provision for control, the revenue from that source alone would today be almost sufficient to defray all of the expenses of our national government.

And what is more important, the trusts and monopolies which now exist and threaten the welfare of all of our people would not have been possible.

The statute of 1873 as to coal lands provided for the sale of known coal lands at "not less than $10 per acre," if more than fifteen miles from a complete railroad, and "not less than $20 per acre" for lands within fifteen miles of a complete railroad. The act made it perfectly clear, however, that the land should be sold for its full value.

This valuable property was sold from 1873, year after year down to 1906 just as if congress had written into that law a direction to the federal government that it must not charge more than $10 or more than $20 an acre in either of the cases defined by the statute.

Is it to be marveled at that the people of the country have waked up to a realization of their betrayal and demand some check upon those called upon to serve them who serve instead their own interests and that of others, and who betray the public?

Speech at Edwardsville, Ill., January 5, 1912.

Conserve Our National Resources

The Rooseveltian epoch in American history may have many or few things to make it memorable, but one alone is sufficient to give it place in history—the inauguration of the great movement for the conservation of our national resources. Men of foresight and penetration have for years been occasionally pointing out the enormous waste with which we are carrying forward our wonderful progress; but we have never awakened to the portentous situation until now—even if we are quite awake now.

We have looked upon the earth's resources as inexhaustible; but the truth is that they are in process of rapid exhaustion. We have felt that our rivers are not needed in the scheme of production and distribution; but we find that our railways are periodically clogged with a current of traffic too great for them to move, that we are handicapped in seeking the conquest of foreign markets by the superior facilities of nations which have improved their waterways, and that in the rivers and canal-routes left undone, we have neglected one of our great national assets, and one that we must use, or abandon the interior of the continent to an arrest of industrial development.

We have thought our farmers the best in the world; but we now learn that lands in the old world which have been farmed since the beginning of the Christian era are less exhausted than fields tilled by us for fifty years, that the best of our fertility is being washed away year by year through faulty tillage, and that the phosphate beds of our nation, in criminal disregard of the growing needs of our own soils, are being mined and sent to Europe to restore her fertility. We have thought of the coal and iron deposits of the United States as ample for all our imaginable future; but we now can see the end of all the available ones at the present increase in the rate of mining by the present wasteful methods.

In other words, we have acted like tenants-at-sufferance of a farm, "skinning" it of its best, and spoiling it for the next comer, with no apparent thought that the earth is given in trust only to the living, that the man or generation that robs posterity is the most reprehensible of robbers, and that "the next comer" will be our own children.

Roosevelt and the fine group of scientists and scholars and engineers who have been given a hearing by him on these great matters, have made us see our faults and realize our dangers. He has appealed to the national conscience. He has accepted the highest and wisest counsels, instead of the lowest and most sordid. If the tide of waste and destruction is turned back, and a better era ushered in, it will be the chief glory of the Roosevelt administration to have set in motion the good work.

La Follette's Magazine, February 6, 1909.

Keep Alaskan Coal Lands for People

The attempt of private monopoly to steal the Alaskan coal fields was defeated for the time being through the efforts of a few courageous officials, whose sacrifice and devotion to duty furnish an example worthy of emulation in every department and rank of the public service. Failing to secure the coal fields through perjury and fraud, special interests will exploit them through a monopoly of transportation. The title to the coal fields of Alaska should be forever retained by the government subject to lease under proper regulation. The situation of Alaska is exceptional. Transportation is the basis of control. It is the key to this vast territory of treasure. As exceptional conditions in Panama required the government of the United States to own and operate a railroad on the Isthmus in order to protect its interests and the interests of shippers, so we hold that exceptional conditions in Alaska require that the federal government should construct, own and operate the railroads, docks and steamship lines necessary to the opening up of the Alaskan coal fields and other natural resources.

For Control of Water Powers

We are unalterably opposed to the surrender to the state by the federal government of its control over water power sites still a part of the national domain.

The conservation of the natural resources of soil, forest, mines and water power and the settlement of the uncultivated lands suitable for agriculture, are the 'foundations of the prosperity of the state. We pledge legislation that shall encourage the earliest and highest development of these resources, while retaining all the rights of the people in them. A general law should be passed outlining a comprehensive plan for the development and operation of water power plants and providing proper restrictions under which water power franchises may be obtained, to the end that all persons holding water power rights may be made subject to the same general law. Private monopoly should be controlled by the leasing of water power on limited

permits subject to regulation, valuation and reasonable compensation. Prompt action should be taken to complete our forest reserves as soon as practicable and to preserve our forests from destruction by fire.
Republican State Platform, 1910.

Giving Away the Public Wealth

Legislation which has been permitted to be delayed in conference should put Congress on inquiry. In the closing hours, when appropriation bills involving billions upon billions of dollars must be considered, a measure like the pending bill, involving the disposition of the great public domain in which is treasured the coal, the oil, the gas, and other natural resources, is thrust in here, and we are expected to jam it through without time for proper consideration. This bill, if enacted, will dispose of all the resources that will furnish heat and energy to the people of the United States for all time to come, for there is practically gathered up within the four corners of this proposed legislation all that the people have left of the coal, the oil, and the natural gas underlying our public lands.
Speech in U. S. Senate, March 1, 1919.

XXVI

EQUAL SUFFRAGE

The Interests of Men and Women are Co-ordinate

IT has always been inherent with me to recognize this co-equal interest of women. My widowed mother was a woman of wise judgment; my sisters were my best friends and advisers; and in all the work of my public life my wife has been my constant companion.

I believe not only in using the peculiar executive abilities of women in the state service, but I cannot remember a time when I did not believe in woman suffrage. The great economic and industrial questions of today affect women as directly as they do men. And the interests of men and women are not antagonistic one to the other, but mutual and co-ordinate. Co-suffrage, like co-education, will react not to the special privilege of either men or women, but will result in a more enlightened, better balanced citizenship, and in a truer democracy.

Autobiography, 1913.

Equal Suffrage Bound to Come

Men would go out and be shot to pieces before they would surrender their ballot. It is their weapon, their shield, their only protection against tyranny and oppression in whatever form it may find expression in our modern life.

The ballot is an educator. The right to vote stimulates interest in public affairs and prompts the voter to an intelligent and critical study of administrations and the records of public servants.

The state could not afford to disfranchise one-half of its men. No more can it afford to refuse to enfranchise its women.

What the ballot is to working men it will be to the seven or eight million working women in this country, of whom Wisconsin has its share.

Women are tax payers; they are in business, they are mothers and teachers; they have shared equally with men in education.

The women of Wisconsin are especially well qualified to vote. They have long been interested in the struggle for a more truly representative government.

Equal Suffrage is bound to come. It is a part of the world's evolution in universal self-government.

La Follette's Magazine, November 9, 1912.

McGovern's Veto a Blunder

Governor McGovern's veto of the bill passed by the Wisconsin legislature submitting to the referendum vote in 1914 an amendment to the statute extending the right of suffrage to women, was a great surprise and disappointment.

A similar amendment was submitted in 1912 and defeated by ninety-two thousand majority. But the proposed amendment received more than one hundred and thirty-six thousand votes for its adoption. It was a splendid beginning.

Because of a large foreign population, traditionally conservative, and because of its great brewing interests and perfect saloon organization, the Wisconsin campaign for suffrage was handicapped at the outset by a lack of faith and enthusiasm. Organizing and conducting a state campaign was new work for the women of Wisconsin. But gradually inertia was overcome. As the campaign advanced there was a manifest awakening. It was soon apparent that the foreign element was open to conviction. The workers for suffrage grew confident. They became enthusiastic. The movement gained momentum. Late in the campaign the federation of women's clubs endorsed the proposed amendment. A few more weeks would have made a great difference in the vote for suffrage.

After the election it was found that the very failure to carry the amendment in Wisconsin which had been adopted in California, Oregon and Kansas, had aroused thousands of women and thousands of men, who had been indifferent, to a new sense of responsibility.

The suffrage leaders realized the advantage of the awakened sentiment and growing confidence of their perfected and harmonized forces, and of the great value of the training and experience gained in a state-wide campaign.

They called a state conference. That conference, composed of an earnest, intelligent, representative body of Wisconsin women, determined that another campaign following promptly would have cumulative educational power, that there must be no abatement of interest and zeal, that to hold off for four or six years means loss of the ground already gained, that the next forward step was to secure favorable action by the legislature and to carry the issue to the people at the next election.

It was in no spirit of child's play that the leaders of the suffrage movement resolved to secure the submission of a referendum vote in 1914. They had before them the example of the policy pursued in winning other great reforms in Wisconsin.

The governor is developing a bad memory. We lost our first campaign in 1894. We lost again in 1896, again in 1898. We won with the people in 1900 but lost in the legislature. We won again in the election of 1902, and again we lost in the legislature. Finally, we won with both the people and the legislature in 1904.

Where would Wisconsin have been today in this great era of progress if the leaders of reform had called a halt,—if they had thrown down their arms, abandoned the field, scattered their forces, and decided to defer action until—to quote the language of the governor's veto message—"there is a chance, at least, that the experience of other states similar in many respects to our own may furnish guidance not available now."

Fight for Right is Unending

The states of Platt and Quay, and Hinky Dink were then "similar in many respects to our own," but in those days we did not wait for them to "furnish guidance" for Wisconsin's future. Our flags were never lowered. Our arms were never stacked. Whether beaten before the people or in the legislature, our battered little army never faltered. We closed ranks, quickened the pace, and fought on to final victory.

There is no difference in principle in pressing the same issue before the people in successive campaigns, and in presenting the same issue to the legislature in successive sessions. Our direct primary, our equalization of taxation, our railway commission law, our control of public utilities and other advanced measures, were ultimately secured after a number of hard fought campaigns. And they were successive campaigns, too. It was for that very reason that they won so completely. We not only struck while the iron was hot; we made it hot and kept it hot by constant striking.

That is what the new spirit of American politics has taught us—if we will but learn never to be discouraged, never to know defeat in a good cause.

The governor urges that the suffrage issue would better be tried out in a presidential election. Common political experience teaches that any state issue receives more thorough consideration on its merits in a state campaign, than when subordinated to national issues in a presidential campaign. And even though the amendment were to fail of adoption in 1914, the people will be just so much better prepared to pass upon it in 1916.

Even the strongest opponents of the franchise for women no longer question that it will come. It is just a matter of education and enlightenment. Why cut out two years of education, why forego the chance to win now? The reasoning of the governor's veto is trivial. The legislature should pass the bill, the veto of the governor to the contrary notwithstanding.

La Follette's Magazine, June 7, 1913.

Marching in a Suffrage Parade

My knowledge of the great suffrage parade which took place in New York on May 4, was gained as a participant rather than as a spectator, for I walked from Eleventh Street to Fifth Avenue, where the representatives of the non-suffrage states other than New

York gathered, to Carnegie Hall on the corner of Fifty-seventh Street and Seventh Avenue. I did, however, get a chance to look on for a time for I did not get into the hall to attend the meeting, but stepping aside from the procession found a place on the steps of a near-by house. From this point I saw the ovation which was given to the one thousand men in the parade as they came into Fifty-seventh Street where suffrage enthusiasm was greatest. They deserved the ovation, and were doubtless glad of it, for while they had not been "guyed" in lower New York as were the eighty men who marched last year, they had braved no small measure of ridicule.

One remarkable thing about the parade was that in spite of its size, variously estimated at from 10,000 to 20,000 people, it started on time. Having found my place shortly before five o'clock when the procession was scheduled to leave Washington Square, I had settled myself for a long wait on the principle that processions never started on time. Suddenly, a very few moments after the hour the sound of music was heard, and the women on horseback who headed the procession came into view. They had left Washington Square on the moment. They were fifteen minutes late in reaching Carnegie Hall; not their own fault, but that of the police.

Where uniformity of dress had been adopted as it was by most of the marching clubs, the spectacle was most beautiful. White dresses were worn for the most part, and a regulation hat of white straw. Yellow sashes and scarfs were worn by some of the clubs, green and purple by others, and blue by one of the particularly well-drilled and dignified delegations from up-state. But even where there was no uniformity of dress, it was an impressive sight, not only because of floating banners and waving flags but because of the seriousness and moral fervor of the marchers.

Some of the inscriptions on the banners were:

We prepare children for the world; we ask to prepare the world for our children.

More ballots, less bullets.

Women vote in China, but are classed with criminals and paupers in New York.

Dr. Anna Shaw carried a flag with the inscription: "We are trying to catch up with China."

Best of all was a banner carried by The Men's Equal Suffrage League of New Jersey which bore this legend:

"La Follette is the only presidential candidate standing unequivocally for woman suffrage.

"Woman suffrage has passed the stage of argument; you could not stop it if you would, and in a few years you will be ashamed that you ever opposed it."

Mrs. R. M. La Follette, in
La Follette's Magazine, May, 1912.

XXVII

THE PRESS AND THE PUBLIC

The Modern Newspaper

NE would think that in a democracy like ours, people seeking the truth, able to read and understand, would find the press their eager and willing instructors. Such was the press of Horace Greeley, Henry Raymond, Chas. A. Dana, Joseph Medill, and Horace Rublee.

But what do we find has occurred in the past few years since the money power has gained control of our industry and government? It controls the newspaper press. The people know this. Their confidence is weakened and destroyed. No longer are the editorial columns of newspapers a potent force in educating public opinion. The newspapers, of course, are still patronized for news. But even as to news, the public is fast coming to understand that wherever news items bear in any way upon the control of government by business, the news is colored; so confidence in the newspaper as a newspaper is being undermined.

Cultured and able men are still to be found upon the editorial staffs of all great dailies, but the public understands them to be hired men who no longer express honest judgments and sincere conviction, who write what they are told to write, and whose judgments are salaried.

To the subserviency of the press to special interests in no small degree is due the power and influence and prosperity of the weekly and monthly magazines. A decade ago young men trained in journalism came to see this control of the newspapers of the country. They saw also an unoccupied field. And they went out and built up great periodicals and magazines. They were free.

Their pages were open to publicists and scholars, and liberty and justice and equal rights found a free press beyond the reach of the corrupt influence of consolidated business and machine politics. We entered upon a new era.

Rise of the Periodical

The periodical, reduced in price, attractive and artistic in dress, strode like a young giant into the arena of public service. Filled with this spirit, quickened with human interest, it assailed social and political evils in high places and low. It found the power of the public-service corporation and the evil influences of money in the municipal government of every large city. It found franchises worth millions of dollars secured by bribery; police in partnership with thieves and crooks and prostitutes. It found juries "fixed" and an established business plying its trade between litigants and the back door of blinking justice.

What Publicity Revealed

It found Philadelphia giving away franchises, franchises not supposedly or estimated to be worth $2,500,000 but for which she had been openly offered and refused $2,500,000. Milwaukee they found giv-

The Press and the Public

ing away street-car franchises worth $8,000,000 against the protests of her indignant citizens. It found Chicago robbed in tax-payments of immense value by corporate owners of property through fraud and forgery on a gigantic scale; it found the aldermen of St. Louis organized to boodle the city with a criminal compact, on file in the dark corner of a safety deposit vault.

The free and independent periodical turned her searchlight on state-legislatures, and made plain as the sun at noonday the absolute control of the corrupt lobby. She opened the closed doors of the secret caucus, the secret committee, the secret conference, behind which United States Senators and Members of Congress betrayed the public interest into the hands of railroads, the trusts, the tariff mongers, and the centralized banking powers of the country. She revealed the same influences back of judicial and other appointments. She took the public through the great steel plants and into the homes of the men who toil twelve hours a day and seven days in the week. And the public heard their cry of despair. She turned her camera into the mills and shops where little children are robbed of every chance of life that nourishes vigorous bodies and sound minds, and the pinched faces and dwarfed figures told their pathetic story on her clean white pages.

How the Press is Controlled

The control of the newspaper press is not the simple and expensive one of ownership and investment. There is here and there a "kept sheet" owned by a man of great wealth to further his own interest. But the papers of this class are few. The control comes through that community of interests, that interdependence of investments and credits which ties the publisher up to the banks, the advertisers and the special interests.

We may expect this same kind of control, sooner or later, to reach out for the magazines. But more than this: I warn you of a subtle new peril, the centralization of advertising, that will in time seek to gag you. What has occurred on the small scale in almost every city in the country will extend to the national scale, and will ere long close in on the magazines. No men ever faced graver responsibilities. None have ever been called to a more unselfish, patriotic service. I believe that when the final test comes, you will not be found wanting; you will not desert and leave the people to depend upon the public platform alone, but you will hold aloft the lamp of Truth, lighting the way for the preservation of representative government and the liberty of the American people.

Speech at Annual Banquet of Periodical Publishers' Association, Philadelphia, February 2, 1912

The Subsidized Press

The setting up of a new, invisible and all powerful government in this country, within the last twenty years, in open violation of fundamental and statutory law, could not have been accomplished under the steady fire of a free and independent press.

Where public opinion is free and uncontrolled, wealth has a wholesome respect for law.

Except for the subserviency of most of the metropolitan newspapers, the great corporate interests would never have ventured upon the impudent, lawless consolidation of business, for the suppression of competition, the control of production, markets and prices.

Except for this monstrous crime, 65 per cent of all the wealth of this country would not now be centralized in the hands of two per cent of all the people. And we might today be industrially and commercially a free people, enjoying the blessings of a real democracy.

La Follette's Magazine, April, 1918.

The Famous St. Paul Speech

Senator La Follette was widely quoted in the press as having said in a speech at St. Paul, Minnesota, September 20, 1917, that the United States had no grievances against Germany. At the request of the Minnesota commission of public safety an investigation of the charge was made by the senate and the matter finally dropped when the Associated Press admitted it had incorrectly quoted him.

What he actually said is shown by the duly certified transcript of the official stenographer who reported the speech for the Nonpartisan League. What the press reported him as having said is shown by the quotations from a few papers which are typical of hundreds of others.

The Chicago Daily Tribune of September 21st last quoted Senator La Follette as saying:

"I wasn't in favor of beginning this war. We had no grievance."

The Washington Post of September 22nd:
"I wasn't in favor of beginning this war. We had no grievance."

The New York Times, September 22nd:
"I was not in favor of beginning this war. We had no grievance."

Finally the Literary Digest for October 6, 1917, nearly a month after the speech was made, purports to gather up the comment of the papers throughout the country, and says that as reported in the press despatches, Senator La Follette said:

"I was not in favor of beginning this war. We had no grievance."

What was actually said by Senator La Follette as shown by the official certified transcript of his speech above referred to was:

"For my own part I was not in favor of beginning the war. I don't mean to say that we hadn't suffered grievances; we had at the hands of Germany, serious grievances."

La Follette's Magazine, November, 1917.

Retraction by Associated Press

The resolutions were referred to the committee on privileges and elections of the senate and by it they were referred to a sub-committee to investigate the accuracy of the report of the speech, the accuracy of the statements made in such speech and to report its findings to the full committee the first day of the next regular session in December, 1917. The sub-committee did not make any report to the full committee as provided in the resolution with reference to it.

Recently Gilbert E. Roe representing Senator La Follette appeared before the committee and asked for a dismissal of the proceedings, and in the course of his argument referred to the erroneous report of the speech as published in the newspapers. Thereupon the Associated Press published a retraction of its erroneous report, and said:

"The error was regrettable and the Associated Press seized the first opportunity to do justice to Senator La Follette."

Upon this retraction the New York Evening Post made the following editorial comment:

"The Associated Press has handsomely and promptly admitted its grievous fault in misreporting Senator La Follette. Whereas he said in his St. Paul speech that 'we had grievances' against Germany, and was so reported the next day in the St. Paul newspapers, some one slipped the fatal word 'no' into the sentence in the Associated Press report and made it read: 'We had no grievances.' Whether this was done maliciously or accidentally will probably never be known, but the fact remains that irreparable injury was done to the senator, and that a large part of the outcry against him was due to this misstatement in the one thousand newspapers which are served by the Associated Press. Senator La Follette declared at the time that the press had misquoted him, but the matter was never brought to the attention of the Associated Press until Mr. Gilbert E. Roe, his attorney, stated the fact before the senate committee of inquiry on Tuesday. Why the senator delayed so long is a mystery; but the serious wrong done by this error needs no expatiating. No amount of apology can undo it. The thought that unintentionally so extreme an injustice may be done to a public man is one to sober all responsible journalism."

Why the senator delayed so long in denying the false report should be no mystery because the senator did not delay such denial. He immediately publicly denied the correctness of the report of his speech, but the newspapers continued for months afterward to use the false report as a text upon which to base arguments condemning the senator and creating public sentiment against him. The senator had no adequate opportunity to give to the public the truth of the matter. The press was not open to him for that purpose. As the New York Evening Post says: "The thought that unintentionally so extreme an injustice may be done a public man is one to sober all responsible journalism."

La Follette's Magazine, June, 1918.

How the Press May be Russianized

Power vested anywhere in any office or court is always sooner or later abused; and here is a power the abuse of which is easy. Given an unscrupulous administration, or an honest one under the pressure of troublous times, and the law contended for in the Pulitzer and Smith cases lends itself to a press censorship as galling and ruinous to liberty as that of Russia. It may be that we have never had an administration capable of so using it; but he would be a bold man who would assert it. The publication of an accusation is always the more perilous as it is more grave. The administration, therefore, seeking to silence criticism by this new law, or this new application of an old law, would be safer in committing heinous crimes than in falling into slight errors. For the editor who might dare to call public attention to a merely questionable transaction at Washington, would not venture life and liberty so far as to allege a crime, no matter how clear the proof. His peril would be too great. Thus the press would be rendered most timid in those very exigencies in which the public safety calls for the most fearless denunciation.

Is the supposed case fanciful? Not at all. In the life of every nation come the crises when power of this sort is sure to be abused. The time to make the stand against it is now. The beginning of evil is like the letting out of water; and eternal vigilance is the price of liberty.

La Follette's Magazine, March 20, 1909.

Mission of a Magazine

La Follette's will be a magazine of progress, social, intellectual, institutional. Moreover, it will be progressive in the more distinctly political sense. It is founded in the belief that it can aid in making our government represent with more fidelity the will of the people.

This magazine recognizes as its chief task that of aiding in winning back for the people the complete power over government,—national, state and municipal,—which has been lost to them by the encroachments of party machines, corporate and unincorporated monopolies, and by the rapid growth of immense populations.

La Follette's will speak the truth. No eminence of position in party or government shall protect a servant of the people from deserved criticism; and its approval will be gladly given to all who commend themselves to it by brave and right action in any party or place.

Men and measures are both important. This magazine will discuss measures and political parties and policies impartially and fearlessly. It will not shrink from making estimates of men and will from time to time call the roll in order to disclose the exact position of those who are true and those who are false to public interest.

It is not enough to overthrow the political power of special interests. In the struggle for self-government throughout the nation every progressive movement will be critically observed and supported on merit. Constructive legislation wherever enacted will be so discussed as to give an intelligent conception of the actual progress made in the supremely difficult task of embodying progressive ideas and ideals in laws and institutions. We hope to be useful in constructive work, as well as in destructive criticism. We aim to be practical in our suggestions. We shall be just to every interest. Property rights are safe. The constitution guarantees security—a security which unanimous public opinion in America approves and supports.

We shall make mistakes. We assert no claim to infallibility. It is not expected that our readers will agree with all we have to say. But the co-

operation necessary to permanent progress can be
secured only through intelligent discussion. We
hope that this magazine may help to stimulate discussion and thought to the end that out of it shall
come better things into the life of this nation.
First Editorial La Follette's Magazine,
January 9, 1909.

Fooling the People

People who are here this afternoon may think
that the press of the country cannot fool them.
They may read what they know is a lie tonight in
the papers. They read it repeated tomorrow and
the next and the next day, and they say to their
families that there is nothing in it. That thing is
repeated time after time, day after day, it may be
when they see it in some special article elaborately
set up and illustrated, but finally it steals in upon
the judgment of the people.
Speech in U. S. Senate, Aug. 29, 1919.

Surrender of the Magazines

If you will study the editorial pages of newspapers through the years, beginning a little more than
20 years ago, you will find the trail of the serpent
that has control of the great newspapers of the
country. * * *

I spoke over at Philadelphia in 1912, and I warned
the magazine publishers that the day was at hand
when they, one after another, would be confronted
with the necessity of yielding to this mighty power
and ceasing the publication of articles of criticism

against the great industrial and commercial organizations in this country or they would be denied advertising and forced to the wall.

Mr. President, I stand here this afternoon to say that one after another of those magazines has succumbed to that influence. I stand here to say that it is impossible to secure the publication in those magazines today of articles denouncing this violation of law, this encroachment upon the liberties of the people, this overlordship that controls our industrial and commercial life. I say there is not one of these great periodicals, excepting four or five that I could number on one hand, left today the control of which has not been acquired by the special interests, the Standard Oil or like organizations. One after another of these magazines, periodicals, and publications has surrendered to that mighty power. There are only a few publications that reach, in all probability, more than 150,000 to 200,000 subscribers—which means probably not more than a million readers in the United States—that absolutely are free to publish criticism. That is the truth, and it is a terrible commentary on our Government.
Speech in U. S. Senate, Aug. 29, 1919.

On Public Opinion

Sir, I respect public opinion. I do not fear it. I do not hold it in contempt. The public judgment of this great country forms slowly. It is intelligent. No body of men in this country is superior to it. In a representative democracy the common judgment of the majority must find expression in the law of the land. To deny this is to repudiate the principles upon which representative democracy is founded.

It is not prejudice nor clamor which is pressing this subject upon the attention of this body. It is a calm, well-considered public judgment. It is born of conviction—not passion—and it were wise for us to give it heed.

The public has reasoned out its case. For more than a generation of time it has wrought upon this great question with heart and brain in its daily contact with the great railway corporations. It has mastered all the facts. It is just. It is honest. It is rational. It respects property rights. It well knows that its own industrial and commercial prosperity would suffer and decline if the railroads were wronged, their capital impaired, their profits unjustly diminished.

But the public refuses longer to recognize this subject as one which the railroads alone have the right to pass upon. It declines longer to approach it with awe. It no longer regards the railroad schedule as a mystery. It understands the meaning of rebates and "concession," the evasions through "purchasing agents" and false weights, the subterfuge of "damage claims," the significance of "switching charges," "midnight tariffs," "milling in transit," "tap-line allowances," "underbilling," and "demurrage charges." It comprehends the device known as the "industrial railway," the "terminal railway," and all the tricks of inside companies, each levying tribute upon the traffic. It is quite familiar with the favoritism given to express companies, and knows exactly how producer and consumer have been handed over by the railroads, to be plundered by private car and refrigerator lines, in exchange for their traffic.

Because it is a natural monopoly, because it is the creature of government, it becomes the duty of government to see to it that the railway company inflicts no wrong upon the public, to compel it to do what is right, and to perform its office as a common carrier.

Sir, it is much easier to stand with these great interests than against them. This was true when Adam Smith wrote his Wealth of Nations, and it is true in 1906.

Mr. President, I contend here, as I have contended upon the public platform in Wisconsin, and in other States, that the history of the last thirty years of struggle for just and equitable legislation demonstrates that the powerful combinations of organized wealth and special interests have had an overbalancing control in state and national legislation.

For a generation the American people have watched the growth of this power in legislation. They observe how vast and far-reaching these modern business methods are in fact. Against the natural laws of trade and commerce is set the arbitrary will of a few masters of special privilege. The principal transportation lines of the country are so operated as to eliminate competition. Between railroads and other monopolies controlling great natural resources and most of the necessaries of life there exists a "community of interests" in all cases and an identity of ownership in many. They have observed that these great combinations are closely associated in business for business reasons; that they are also closely associated in politics for business reasons; that together they constitute a complete system; that they encroach upon the public rights, defeat legislation for the public good, and secure laws to promote private interests.

Speech in U. S. Senate, April 19, 1906.

XXVIII
MISCELLANEOUS

Tribute to Albert R. Hall

FRIENDS: I have been requested to say a word respecting the life and character of our friend. All over this state today, in the homes throughout a sister state, in many throughout this union, to whose attention the work of Mr. Hall in public life had been attracted, there are sad hearts and bowed heads. We are gathered here to pay a last tribute to a great man whose life has been so simple, so modest, whose demeanor has been so humble that many of us perhaps have not been truly conscious of the greatness of his character. But into the history of this state and into the lives of its people there have come a new significance and a new meaning, high standards, better thoughts, better living, greater devotion to public interests than would have been known except for the life of Mr. Hall.

It is not easy to paint a portrait. It is much easier and requires a much lower order of ability to make a caricature. I know that he would have no friend of his say one word in exaggeration of his work and his life. But knowing him somewhat intimately since he has been in the public service of the state, I do not feel that it would be within my power to draw too strongly, to utter with any too great degree of emphasis expressions of praise on his life and public service.

He was a man of splendid courage; he feared nothing except to do wrong. In his heart he bore malice against none. I have seen him silent, his face quivering and working under the sting of unjust criticism, but I never heard from his lips an unkind word with reference to those who did not agree with him. I do not believe that Albert R. Hall ever consciously in his life did a wrong. He may have made mistakes, and who has not? He never took an advantage; he never worked in the dark; he stood out boldly before all men for what he believed was for the best interest of the public.

A life like his does not terminate with death. It lives on and on through the generations. In the higher ideals which he has established in this state, in the better regard for public rights which he has made plain as a public duty for all men, in right conduct with individuals in the community where he lived, in all his relations with all of his fellowmen, he has so impressed himself upon the day and hour of his time that his life should live and go on in the perfected life of the friends who knew him and have been made better by his presence.

We can take some little comfort in the thought that life has not been interrupted, that his great character is still working out the purposes of a higher and better life, and as we separate today, after performing the last sad duties, we can say to our friend "farewell but not forgotten." He will live in the lives of each of us while we are spared.

At Funeral of A. R. Hall, Knapp, Wisconsin,
June 4, 1905.

Advance Toward Higher Civilization

Gentlemen, the day of your admission to that profession which honors every man who honors it, is a day of royal triumph for you—but it is not a day of triumph for you alone. We all have a share in it. From the gilded home of the millionaire in the North, to the meanest hut in the rice swamps of the South, every man and woman in the land owns an interest in this event.

We are one people, one by truth, one almost by blood. Our lives run side by side. Our ashes rest in the same soil. The social order wraps us about altogether as the atmosphere envelops the earth. Each of us draws from it that which nourishes intellectual and spiritual life. Each one consciously or unconsciously gives back something of himself, clean or unclean, nourishing or poisonous to that social organization. It is snobbish stupidity, it is supreme folly, to talk of non-contact, or exclusion! Recognize it or not, it is a homogeneous mass, and each element is vitally interested in every other.

You stand upon the rim of an ever-expanding horizon. The morning breaks. Before you lies the waiting world of opportunity—behind you the long night of degradation, of ignominy, of human slavery. At your back stands a quick, responsive, capable, willing race, panting to be led to a higher civilization—above and beyond you the angel of human progress beckons you on and on. A new century is bursting upon you. There never was such an opportunity for leadership in the history of the hu-

man race. You are equipped for the mighty contest. Go to your work.
Address to Howard University Law Class, 1888.

On Transplanted Foreign Culture

Journeying across Wisconsin in any direction, one passes through cities and villages, counties and townships, changed, from unbroken prairies and vast forests, to thickly populated districts with beautiful homes, rich farms and great factories, by the hardy, courageous, but patient, industry of the German pioneer.

In that hour, fortunate for us, when emigration from the fatherland was at its full tide, the conditions invited most strongly toward this young commonwealth. Its productive soil, its low priced lands, its lakes and streams and forests, its climate, its liberal spirit, attracted alike the idealist, who dreamed of a German state within the Union, and the sturdy, practical homeseeker, who left his fatherland in the hope of larger opportunity in a new country.

Their industry, thrift, prudence and unyielding perseverance underlie much of our material development. Their native directness and honesty of thought, their resolute maintenance of right and justice and good order in every community have stamped their character upon the citizenship of our commonwealth. To this keen, eager, restless, commercial spirit of the Yankee, they have contributed calmness, repose, conservatism, a philosophic judgment, and a wise appreciation of the beneficence of leisure. We have become one people. Our lives run side by side; their living streams commingle; our ashes rest in the same soil.

No race of men has more enriched the artistic life of the world than the German. Into this new commonwealth they brought their native endowment of artistic temperament—a good leaven to our somewhat ascetic Puritan character.

As inherent as the love of music and flowers and children, is the German's love of home, his respect for law, his loyalty to country. Had they not been for generations imbued with patriotism and undying affection for the fatherland, they could not in nature have so soon become loyal American citizens; they would not have sustained, as they did with blood and treasure, this government in its darkest hour; they would not have proved such a bulwark of law-abiding sentiment for state and nation. The German-American's love for his native land, its heroic past, its majestic presence, its language, its traditions, its literature, its song, serves only to foster those elements of character which intensify his allegiance, his loyalty, his devotion to the land of his adoption.

Address Welcoming Prince Henry,
Milwaukee, March 4, 1902.

Welcome to Catholic Order of Foresters

I congratulate you upon this large gathering and the good work in which you are engaged. The foundation sentiment of your order appeals to the right side of human nature. Your ministration is that of helpfulness. You are not organized for investment or profit or gain, but for mutual benefit.

Yours is a benevolent order. You are bound together to relieve the sick and distressed, to comfort and sustain the widow, and to open the door of opportunity to the orphan. In the time of greatest trial, in the darkest hour of life, your word of good cheer is heard across the open grave, and the warm grasp of your fraternal hand takes away something of the chill of death.

I believe in this and other orders because they are American institutions, democratic in character. Every man is upon a level with every other man. Each bears his just share of the burden and receives his proportionate share of the benefits. The lessons which you teach are the lessons of equal rights for all; equal duties, equal responsibilities, equal privileges and equal voice. These are the foundation principles upon which the fathers established this government, and every organization such as I see before me here tonight is essentially democratic. It typifies representative government. It is a little republic and is a foundation of inspiration for patriotic citizenship.

Welcome to Catholic Foresters, June 11, 1901.

The Louisiana Purchase Exposition

Pity, indeed, the narrow soul which does not go out today in reverence to that tomb at Monticello where rest the ashes of him who framed the act of original inherent sovereignty, adopted by the people,—declaring that all men are created equal and that government must derive its just powers from the consent of the governed. Through his statesmanship we acquired half a continent within which that government might expand. He gave to higher education the first state university in America, dedicating it forever to freedom with this as its motto:

"And ye shall know the truth, and the truth shall make you free."

He and his compatriots were not the product of the eighteenth century any more than was their work for their day and generation alone. They were in God's plan for the liberty of the human race centuries before. When the declaration of independence was given to the world, it spoke for the great silent majority whose lives had been laid upon the altar of liberty through all the ages. It spoke for the millions yet unborn, whose precious heritage is American democracy.

And this great exposition of the progress and power of the nations of the world shall exert its liberalizing influence on all mankind, inspire mutual confidence and respect among established governments, quicken thought, stimulate endeavor, and promote peace and happiness. It shall do more than that. It shall bring the people of this country together in commemoration of great events in its history, charged with patriotic significance to every citizen of the republic.

Speech cannot express the indebtedness of the people of this nation to you who have wrought out in harmony the greatest work of its kind yet accomplished by man. Every worthy citizen should count it a great privilege and a patriotic duty to testify his appreciation by personally participating in this memorable event. No one can come here and not feel impelled to carry this message back to his neighbors and friends.

From a profound heart we thank you for the opportunity to come and the welcome we have received. We pledge you the most cordial support of the state of Wisconsin.

Speech at Louisiana Purchase Exposition,
St. Louis, 1904.

Not Influenced by Personal Abuse

I concede that, Mr. President. I have a habit which perhaps is not a matter of interest and I ought not to detain the senate to mention it—when I am speaking I see the face of every senator and every change of expression just as in practicing law I saw the face of every juryman, and used to think that I knew what was passing in the mind of each juror. It is a fault. Let that pass.

Mr. President, I return now to say that a great subject is before the senate. It is one that strikes deep down into the lives and the homes and will profoundly affect the prosperity and the happiness of all the people of this country. It does not affect merely manufacturers. It does not affect merely the people who work for the manufacturers and their interests. It ought to be weighed with very great care. I do not mean to say that the interests of the manufacturers and those who have invested their capital are not entitled to be weighed with as great care; but those who work for wages are entitled to have their interests carefully considered as well.

Mr. President, this bill will bear upon the people of this whole country—ninety millions of them—either fairly or unfairly, justly or unjustly. I tell you it is of tremendous consequence what we do here each day. We pass a paragraph or a schedule, and it is driven in on me all the while that we do not know just how our action is going to affect the people of our country. We do not know how much that is going to take out of the earnings or savings of this family or that family, and we ought to know.

The formation of public opinion is of tremendous importance in framing legislation.

Nothing ought to have a place in the debate upon this great measure except that which is germane to the bill. The issue involved should not be obscured by any personal controversy. It shall not be so obscured with my sanction.

Mr. President, it is one of the least concerns of my life how votes shall be cast in an election in so far as it affects me. I never have in my public life taken the easier pathway. I could have done so. I never have. What I am saying today is said from a deep conviction.

I have given fifteen years out of the best of my life to a great struggle in my state. I became deeply interested in certain things that seemed to me to go to the very foundation of this government. That interest possessed me; it took me out of my profession; it put me into a contest in Wisconsin to establish in that commonwealth, first of all, if possible, a government by the people and for the people.

Mr. President, I would not be provincial; I would not be boastful; but something has been accomplished in Wisconsin that draws to it the leading students of government from every state in this union. From every great university, from the economic departments of the great universities of Europe, they have come to the capital of Wisconsin to study the legislation of that state, especially concerning the government of corporations in their relation to the life of the people.

Principle Placed Before Individual

Mr. President, at every step in that long fight I was subjected to personal attacks of the most virulent kind—misrepresenting my character, attempting to destroy it, assailing my motives, lying about everything I did and everything I did not. But, sir, I early marked out a course for myself. I said: "If I permit myself to be drawn aside to answer personal attacks, this great struggle to bring government back to the people will be degraded to a petty personal issue." I turned neither to the right hand nor to the left. When assailed and misrepresented, my answer was· "The corporations in the state of Wisconsin are not paying their share of the taxes." To every personal charge I made one answer: "The public-service corporations shall not control in legislation. They shall serve the public impartially, and render services at reasonable rates."

So in respect to every assault made upon me, Mr. President, my answer was the great issue. As an individual I was insignificant, of little consequence. If I did anything for the state, in which I was born and live, it was simply as an humble instrument for the right settlement of the great issues over which we have, sir, so little control in our day and generation. We do not, we cannot, make the issues. Great ideas thrust themselves into the arena; they are antagonistic; one is right and one is wrong; and as the contest goes on the men who are drawn into that contest are but the instruments in those great ideas of evolution in the progress of the race.

Mr. President, does anybody suppose that I am to turn aside in this debate to answer some petty and contemptible attack upon me personally? No. The senate was occupied yesterday for five hours, at least, in the discussion of the cotton schedule. Certain facts were laid before this body. I may be wrong about it, but, in my judgment, they were important facts. An evening session followed. Some sensationalism developed in that evening session, and it claimed a space in the newspapers reporting yesterday's proceedings of congress to the exclusion of the debate upon the bill. So today, Mr. President, that might be repeated if personal controversy were again intruded into this discussion. It shall not occur with my consent.

As to the remarks of the senator from Pennsylvania (Mr. Penrose) last evening, Mr. President, the public is not greatly interested in individual senators and how they spend their time when away from the senate chamber. The people of Wisconsin will take care of me if I am an unfaithful servant without prompting from any senator upon this floor. I would suggest that he would render a more important service to the country and to the state of

Pennsylvania, were he to account for the way he spends his time when absent from this body, than in any effort to make any account of mine.

I might add, Mr. President, that no man could undertake to account for the whereabouts of the senator from Pennsylvania when absent from this body without transgressing the rules of the senate, and that I do not purpose to do in this debate.

Speech on Tariff, U. S. Senate, June 3, 1909.

Appreciation of a Fellow Fighter

One morning in December, 1909, there came into my office in the Capitol Building, a tall, bony, slightly stooped man, with a face bespeaking superior intelligence and lofty character. It was Andrew Furuseth.

He wanted to interest me in the cause of the American sailor. He was a sailor himself, he said, and he wanted to "be free." I did not know what he meant. I questioned him. Surely there were no slaves under the American flag. Bondsmen there were,—but Lincoln changed all that. And it had been written in the amended Constitution. "Yes," he said, "but not for the sailor. All other men are free. But when the amendments were framed, they passed us by. The sailor was forgotten."

I asked him to tell me about it. Sitting on the edge of the chair, his body thrust forward, a great soul speaking through his face, the set purpose of his life shining in his eyes, he told me the story of the sailor's wrongs. He said little of himself, excepting as I drew him on to speak of the long, long struggle of which he was the beginning, and is now finally the end. He spoke with a strong Scandinavian accent, but with remarkable facility of expression, force and discrimination.

He knew the maritime law of every country; the social conditions, the wage level, the economic life of every sea-faring nation. He was master of his subject. His mind worked with the precision of a Corliss engine. He was logical, rugged, terse, quaint, and fervid with conviction.

Born in Norway, the call of the sea came to him as a lad of sixteen. He stood upon the cliffs and looked out upon the infinite. The life of the sailor, like the ocean, must be wide and free. He felt its mysterious spell. He would be a "free seaman," with all the world an open door. New thoughts were stirring within him. He sailed away, thrilled with the idea that his was to be a free man's work.

His dream was shattered early by the hard realities of life before the mast. First in the boats of Norway and later on the decks of the merchant marine of every great maritime nation he served as a seaman, and everywhere conditions were the same. He found himself a common chattel! He was owned by the master of the ship!

In all the years of this historic struggle for human liberty, which finally culminated with President Wilson's signing of the Seamen's Law, March 4, 1915, Andrew Furuseth was the one man who had the faith, the vision and the courage necessary to sustain the contest. He launched the movement. He kept it afloat. Every moment of the twenty-one years he was at the helm. Through legislative storms and calms, over the sunken reefs of priviiege, across every treacherous shoal and past all dangers, he held his cause true to its course and brought it safely into port. Yet in all those long, disheartening years he has so effaced himself and lived his cause, that the public has had little opportunity to know the man. When history forgets many who now fill the public eye, with all who know the story of the sea he will be a great outstanding figure, from whose life others will gather hope and courage and inspiration to fight on and on to better living conditions and wider freedom.

Furuseth has done a great work. He has not acquired a monopoly of light, heat, or power. He has not endowed false educational foundations with money wrongfully extorted from an overpatient public. But he has won freedom for the American sailor, and made our country an asylum and a refuge for the oppressed seamen of the world. The gratitude of hundreds of thousands of human beings of this and future generations will accredit their liberty to his genius and devotion.

After the bill was signed by the president, in conversation with Furuseth one day, I touched upon his future. "When you can no longer work, what provision have you for old age?" I asked. "How much have you been able to lay up against failing power?" His keen eye mellowed, and a placid contemplative expression smoothed out the seams of his weather beaten face as he said, "When my work is finished, I hope to be finished. I have no provision against old age; and I shall borrow no fears from time."

La Follette's Magazine, April, 1915.

Poverty in the United States

Prof. E. A. Ross, of the University of Wisconsin, in a book published in May, 1918, has drawn for us a moderate but clear and brief statement of industrial conditions in this country, which it would be well for the Secretary of the Treasury and officials of this administration generally to study. Prof. Ross' book is entitled "Russia in Upheaval." Prof. Ross has been for many years a professor of sociology at the University of Wisconsin, and is the author of a number of standard works dealing with sociology and with history.

Let me say that Prof. King just before his death, which occurred a few years ago, published a work on the distribution of wealth. Prof. King was recognized among the statisticians and students of sociology and of the economists in this country as a very eminent man in his particular field. He was a member of the faculty of the Wisconsin University when he died.

Prof. Ross said—I quote from this work beginning at page 345:

> "Let it not be supposed that the United States, with its qualified political democracy, will prove immune to anticapitalist agitation. The fact is our society is one of the most vulnerable, because we have clung so long to the law and politics of an outworn individualism that the resulting distribution of wealth and of income would be grotesque were it not so tragic. According to the investigations of Prof. King, a statistician of unquestioned skill and impartiality, 65 per cent of our people are poor; that is, they have little or no

property, except their clothes and some cheap furniture, and their average annual income is less than $200 per capita."

That is—let me emphasize that—65 per cent of the people of the United States have nothing but their clothing and some cheap furniture and their average annual income is less than $200 a year per capita.

Thirty-three per cent of our people compose the middle class, in which each man leaves at death from one to forty thousand dollars worth of property. The remaining two per cent comprise the rich and very rich, who own almost one and one-half times as much as the other 98 per cent together

MR. KENYON. Mr. President—

The PRESIDING OFFICER. Does the Senator from Wisconsin yield to the Senator from Iowa?

MR. LA FOLLETTE. I do.

MR. KENYON. The figures the Senator quotes from Prof. King are so startling that I should like to ask the Senator a question. Did the Senator say that, according to Prof. King, 65 per cent of our people have an income of less than $200 per year?

MR. LA FOLLETTE. Per capita.

MR. KENYON. That is, a man with a family of four would figure each one in the income?

MR. LA FOLLETTE. Yes, sir.

Mr. President, I submitted as a part of the minority report in 1917 on the revenue bill fixing war profits taxes these very figures quoted from Prof. King, and I discussed them on this floor. I cited them over and over again, and tried to make them as impressive as possible. We are asleep; we treat as a joke the poverty of 65 per cent of the people of this country. Senators jibe and sneer and scoff and grin at the recital of these figures here tonight. You may, by pursuing that course long enough, invite into the Senate Chamber sometime or other a mob.

Speech in U. S. Senate, March 1, 1919.

Enlightening his Constituency

It was clear to me that the only way to beat boss and ring rule was to keep the people thoroughly informed. Machine control is based upon misrepresentation and ignorance. Democracy is based upon knowledge. It is of first importance that the people shall know about their government and the work of their public servants. "Ye shall know the truth, and the truth shall make you free." This I have always believed vital to self government.

Immediately following my election to congress I worked out a complete plan for keeping my constituents informed on public issues and the record of my services in congress; it is the system I have used in constantly widening circles ever since.

The task of building up and maintaining an intelligent interest in public affairs in my district and afterward in the state, was no easy one. But it was the only way for me, and I am still convinced that it is the best way. Of one thing I am more and more convinced with the passage of the years—and that is, the serious interest of our people in government, and their willingness to give their thought to subjects which are really vital and upon

which facts, not mere opinions, are set forth, even though the presentation may be forbidding.
Autobiography, 1913.

Where Some of the Salary Goes

It is not generally known that congressional speeches, reprinted from the Record for distribution, must be paid for by the congressman or senator ordering them at a cost equal to that of any first-class printing establishment. The size of the bills I paid the government printing office for many years was one of the reasons why I found myself so poor when I left congress. A congressman in those days received only five thousand dollars a year, and no secretarial or clerk hire whatever unless he chanced to be chairman of a committee. The result was that the bulk of the actual mechanical work of keeping up all this correspondence and pamphleteering fell upon Mrs. La Follette and myself. * * *
Autobiography, 1913.

On Answering Misrepresentations

I paid no attention to its (The Milwaukee Sentinel) misrepresentations and personal attacks. But finally, about 1904, I began holding a copy of it up to my audiences, telling them just what it stood for and appealing to the people of Wisconsin to drive it out of their homes; saying that the people ought to support only those papers that served the public; that the papers that were organs of corporations should depend upon the corporations for their support. And that is what the people of the country ought to do today. They ought to support the newspapers and magazines that are serving their interests. There must always be muckrakers as long as there are muckmakers, and the public owes it to itself to support those publications that stand for the public interest. It does not make any difference what good news service the organs of the corporations offer, turn them out; teach them that they can't prey upon the public and at the same time appeal to the public for support.

This law (anti-lobby) rests upon the principle that legislation is public business and that the public has a right to know what arguments are presented to members of the legislature to induce them to enact or defeat legislation, so that any citizen or body of citizens shall have opportunity, if they desire, to answer such arguments.

Since I came to the United States senate I have steadfastly maintained the same position. Again and again I have protested against secret hearing before congressional committees upon the public business. I have protested against the business of congress being taken into a secret party caucus and there disposed of by party rule; I have asserted and maintained at all times my right as a public servant to discuss in open senate, and everywhere publicly, all legislative proceedings, whether originating in the executive sessions of committees or behind closed doors of caucus conferences.

Autobiography, 1913.

Vacant Seats in the Senate

Mr. President, I pause in my remarks to say this. I cannot be wholly indifferent to the fact that Senators by their absence at this time indicate their want of interest in what I may have to say upon this subject. The public is interested. Unless this important question is rightly settled seats now temporarily vacant may be permanently vacated by those who have the right to occupy them at this time.

Speech "Regulation of Railway Rates," Senator La Follette's First Speech in the U. S. Senate, April 19-21, 1906.

APPENDIX

PLATFORM OF 1908

Submitted by the Wisconsin delegation at the Republican National Convention in 1908, and rejected by the convention.

THE Republican party has made progress toward a more effective control of the railroads engaged in interstate commerce, but it recognizes that much remains to be done in the public interest. We favor enlarging the powers of the Interstate Commerce Commission, clothing it with authority to institute proceedings upon its own motion, to establish classification, and whenever a proposed increase in the rate is challenged by shipper or consumer to determine whether such increase shall be allowed.

The problems submitted to the commission are so vast and complex and the demand for a better supervision of interstate commerce in the public interests so urgent, the work of the commission already so burdensome, that it is manifestly absurd to expect seven men to discharge the duty which the Government owes to the people in exercising control over common carriers engaged in interstate commerce. In response to the demand for better supervision of railway services and railway rates we favor enlarging the working force of the commission, dividing the country into districts and providing for commissions for each district and for appeals from such sub-commissions to the Interstate Commerce Commission at Washington.

The existing laws provide that the rates shall be reasonable and that any unreasonable rates shall be unlawful, but they wholly fail to provide any means by which the Interstate Commerce Commission can ascertain what is a reasonable rate. To this obvious defect may be charged the unwarranted advance made since the enactment of the law, and the increase recently announced by the railroads which will impose an additional burden of $100,000,000 a year upon the traffic affected.

Public interest demands that this defect in the law shall be remedied at once. To determine a reasonable rate it is desirable that the commission should know the value of the physical property of the railway company, the cost of maintenance and operation of the railway, and the income derived from the business. The interstate commerce law provides for the ascertaining of the cost of maintenance and the income derived from the business, but it fails to provide any means by which the commission can ascertain the value of the property of the railway company. The Interstate Commerce Commission has repeatedly urged upon Congress the importance of legislation to ascertain the value of the property and making the necessary provision to enable the commission to perform the work in the public interest. We, therefore, favor the authorization of the Interstate Commerce Commission to ascertain the exact physical value of all the property of every railway company engaged in interstate commerce, to the end that such valuation be made the basis of just and equal railway rates.

The Republican party proclaims its continued loyalty to the true principle of the protective tariff policy as established by Alexander Hamilton and advocated by Clay, Blaine and McKinley. Under this true principle of protection such duties were imposed on imports as equaled the difference between the cost of the production at home and abroad. From Hamilton to McKinley every great advocate of protection contended that a tariff so levied would establish and maintain American industries, and that free competition between producers would prevent monopoly and insure reasonable prices to all American consumers. Under this system so long as competition existed all classes shared in the benefits derived from the protective policy. But a great change has come. Through combinations of corporations competition between protected interests has been suppressed and the public compelled to pay prices dictated by monopoly. This condition is unjust, oppressive and intolerable.

It calls for prompt and effective remedy. No tariff and policy which contribute in any degree to place the control of prices and markets under the domination of monopoly can be maintained. To correct these abuses and permit a protective tariff system based upon this principle, we pledge the Republican party to the immediate revision of the tariff by the imposition of such duties only as will equal the difference between the cost of production at home and abroad, and whenever the control of any protected product by monopoly or the suppression of competition by agreement between the producers of protected articles limits production and controls prices and wages the collection of duties upon the similar imported article shall be suspended and abolished and such articles admitted free of duty, except where the cost of labor in the domestic article exceeds that in the imported article, in which case such article shall be subject to a rate of duty equal only to the difference in the cost of labor in the domestic and the imported article, in which case such article shall be subject to a rate of duty equal only to the difference in the cost of labor in the domestic and the imported article.

To ultimately place our tariff schedules upon a just, scientific and more equitable basis there must be a thorough and impartial investigation of the ever-changing conditions affecting labor, and the cost of production at home and abroad. For this purpose we favor the early establishment of a permanent tariff commission, to be appointed by the President. Such commission to be composed of men from civil life who represent all sections of our country and who are specially equipped by training and experience for this important work.

For twenty years in its national platforms the Republican party has opposed trusts and combinations whose purpose it is to prevent competition and restrain trade. In its platform of 1900 it says: "We recognize the necessity and propriety of the co-operation of capital to meet new business conditions, and especially to extend our rapidly increasing foreign trade, but we condemn all conspiracies and combinations intended to restrict business, to create monopolies, to limit production or to control prices, and we favor such legislation as will effectively restrain and prevent all such abuses and promote competition and secure the rights of producers, laborers and all who are engaged in industry and commerce."

We declare that no additional legislation has been enacted, pursuant to that declaration. It is established upon the highest authority that trusts and combinations have within the last four years made the greatest growth for the centralized control of business and the suppression of competition in the entire history of consolidation. The increase in trust capitalization and consolidation of industrials, franchises and transportation alone aggregates more than 55 per cent. This enormous growth in unlawful combinations places in jeopardy every independent industry in the land. It exercises control over production and prices in manufactures, for service and rates in transportation. No political party loyal to the public interests can ignore this monstrous evil.

The administration of President Roosevelt has in notable instances prosecuted such unlawful combinations under the antitrust law of 1890, and no act of his Republican administration has been more highly commended by the public. But we believe that existing conditions demand at this time more control than in 1900, and the enactment of such legislation as will effectively restrain and prevent all such abuses and promote and protect competition.

The Republican party, represented in this National Convention, demands the most rigid enforcement of the existing law and the enactment of a statute prohibiting any individual, co-partnership, corporation or association from engaging in interstate commerce whenever such co-partnership, individual, corporation or association is a party to any agreement, understanding or contract for the suppression of competition, the control of prices and markets and the restraint of trade, and imposing imprisonment as a penalty for the violation of its provisions. We demand that Congress shall go to the full extent of its constitutional authority to give force and effect by statutory enactment to the declarations herein set forth.

We strongly protest against any attempt, however disguised, to weaken or destroy the Sherman Anti-Trust Law as applied to trusts and combinations organized to control production and prices, and we favor strengthening the law by providing imprisonment as the penalty for its violation and the strict enforcement of all of its provisions. The anti-trust law was not designed, as declared by its author or advocates in Congress when enacted, to apply to labor organizations, and we favor legislation which Congress may enact within the Constitution to exempt trade unions from the statute.

And the minority of said committee further respectfully submits and recommends the adoption of the following paragraph, to be added to the report of the majority of this committee:

Publicity of campaign contributions and expenditures. Certain expenses are inseparable from the conduct of political campaigns; and these expenditures may be made by voluntary contributions from citizens devoted to the cause for which a candidate or a party stands. Experience has shown, however, that the largest contributions are not made to further the cause, but in some special or personal reason corruptly to influence the nominations, platforms, administration and legislation. If those contributions were known they would be promptly condemned by the public. The relation of them to subsequent favors sought in return would be recognized and understood, and their purpose thwarted. Therefore we propose that the Republican Congress and President shall enact and enforce a law to require those charged with the management of campaigns for the nomination or election of a President of the United States, Senator or Representative in Congress to publish at stated times during the campaign the name of each contributor and the amount contributed or promised by him—and the amounts and the purpose of such disbursement and the name of the person to whom paid.

We pledge the Republican party to the enactment of a law to regulate the rates and services of telegraph companies engaged in the transmission of messages between the states.

We are unalterably opposed to ship subsidies and to granting privileges in any form to special interests at the public expense. (Applause.)

We pledge the Republican party to the enactment of a law to prohibit the issuance of injunctions in cases arising out of labor disputes, and such injunctions would not apply when any labor dispute exists, and providing that in no case shall injunctions be issued when there exists a remedy by the ordinary process of law.

And which act shall provide that in the procedure for punishment for contempt of court, the party cited for contempt shall be entitled to trial by jury, except when such contempt was committed in the presence of the court or so near thereto as to interfere with the proper administration of justice.

We pledge the Republican party to the enactment of a law creating a Department of Labor separate from existing departments, with a secretary at its head, having a seat in the Cabinet, and for the erection of a Bureau of Mines and Mining under the proposed Department of Labor, and the appropriation of sufficient funds to thoroughly investigate the cause of mine disasters, so that laws and regulations may be recommended and enacted which will prevent the terrible maiming and loss of life in mines.

We pledge the Republican party to the enactment of an amendment to the existing eight-hour law for government employees and all workers whether employed by contractors or sub-contractors, when they are doing work for or on behalf of the United States Government.

We pledge the Republican party to the enactment of a law by Congress as far as the federal jurisdiction extends for a general employer's liability act for injury to body or loss of life of employees.

PLATFORM OF 1912

Submitted by the Wisconsin delegation at the Republican National Convention in 1912, and rejected by the convention.

Banking and Currency

ORE dangerous even than the industrial trusts is that subtle, concentrated power exercised over money and credit, by what is ordinarily called the "Money Trust." It can make and unmake panics. But of far greater significance is its constant, all-pervading influence exerted from day to day over the commercial life of the nation in times of prosperity and of adversity alike. Through control of capital it dominates practically all important business. Without its consent few large enterprises, public or private, can be carried to success. Against its opposition the strongest struggle is vain. To it, great corporations, cities, states, and even the nation must pay tribute in order to obtain needed loans. Yet this dominance of the few is not due to their own wealth, vast as that wealth is. In other days, the power of the money lender arose from the vices or weakness of the borrower. But the despotic power of the money trust rests rather upon the virtues,—the thrift and virility,—of a great people. We are subjugated by means of our own savings, for the money trust controls the banks and the life insurance companies, reservoirs into which the savings of the nation naturally drain. The money trust controls likewise the avenues through

Platform of 1912

which these savings are invested so as to become remunerative. Therefore the enterprise and initiative of our people, qualities which ordinarily emancipate men, increase our dependence, since each new demand for capital enhances the power of the few who control it.

The resources of our national banks designed for the protection of depositors, are now permitted, under cunningly devised provisions of our patch-work currency system, to be transferred and re-transferred, until finally placed in speculative banks controlled by the money trust, and used to promote its own selfish interests and augment its power.

Under our present currency system the people's bank deposits are forwarded to the reserve city banks to help finance the trusts, destroy independent producers, promote speculative markets, and foist inflated securities on the public.

Panics which the money power itself has created are used to force government to come to its aid and competitors to give up their property. The vice of the system lies in the privilege of using the money and credit of the people for speculation, thus depriving legitimate business of support. This vice is now admitted by the money power itself, but the legislation proposed, however sound in certain respects, carried in its "jokers" the intent to deceive the people. Pretending to offer support to commerce, it creates preferences for speculation that lead to inflation and rising prices instead of elasticity and stable prices. Realizing that the people's only means of effective control is power to revoke the charter, they create a vested right for fifty years with a semblance of power of revision by Congress once in ten years. On the pretext that this is merely a business question, they strive to prevent the people from putting their candidates on record regarding it.

We are opposed to the so-called Aldrich Currency plan. We pledge our candidate that under no circumstances shall the federal government come to the aid of high finance, but shall support those banks that extend a genuine preference to strictly commercial, as against speculative, loans and to the millions of real producers who depend on those banks. We favor a carefully worked out and scientific emergency circulation under control of the government, backed by proper reserve, issued only against commercial paper that represents actual transactions, and adopted only after the people have thoroughly discussed and intelligently approved of thoroughly discussed and intelligently approved of it.

To free the country from this thralldom all the powers of the nation and of the state should be invoked. Means must be devised for diverting from the money trust the millions of savings which flow freely from city and farm to its banks and insurance companies. The people should be enabled to control the banks in which their own money is deposited.

Federal Trade Commission

In the enforcement and administration of federal laws designed to curb and control the powerful special interests of the country there is much that may be committed to a Federal Trade Commission.

thus placing in the hands of an administrative board responsible to Congress many of the functions now exercised by the courts, promoting promptness in the administration of law and avoiding delays and technicalities incident to court procedure.

Among the matters which should be handled by such a board is the determination of the differences in the cost of production at home and abroad for the purpose of protective tariff legislation; an investigation into the character of great combinations of capital and the trusts of the country; a determination of the facts which may be declared by law to be a violation of the anti-trust laws; enforcing the laws which may be passed with reference to the reasonable use of patents, and to co-operate with the proposed Department of Labor in enforcing regulations for the health, safety and hours of labor of the employees of protected manufacturers; requiring a uniform system of accounting and cost-keeping for monopolistic protected industries and combinations, and such other powers as may be conferred from time to time by other laws of Congress. We believe that all of these functions, some of which are now performed ineffectively by separate agencies of government and by the courts, may be brought together in a single organization, able to cope with the combined power of special privilege. Such commission should be composed of men peculiarly qualified for the discharge of such duties and should be drawn from the various walks of life and supplied with an adequate staff of experts, accountants and engineers, to enable it to properly discharge the duties conferred upon it. In subsequent planks of this platform, dealing with the subjects of tariff, trusts and patents, more specific suggestion is made of the duties which appropriately may be conferred upon such commission. We pledge the establishment of such commission, the members to be appointed by the President and subject to recall by concurrent resolution of Congress.

The Tariff

The tariff has been instrumental in building up American industry, but it has been seized upon by powerful interests to take advantage of consumers and wage-earners. We favor a continuation of the protective policy for the benefit of the producing classes, but demand that the tariff schedules be reduced to the ascertained difference in the labor in this country and abroad, and so adjusted as to assure its benefit to labor and not to protect inefficient management nor place a premium on the further exhaustion of our limited natural resources. The investigation of these facts and the revision of schedules should be made by the proposed Federal Trade Commission, subject to the action of Congress, but such schedules as are generally recognized to be excessive shall be immediately reduced.

Patents

Inventions should be fully developed and utilized for the public benefit under reasonable regulation by the proposed Federal Trade Commission. We pledge the enactment of a patent law which will protect the inventor as well as the public, and which cannot be used against the public welfare in the interest of injurious monopolies.

Trusts and Monopolies

The special interests, the railroads, the harvester trust, the United States steel trust, and all industrial combinations are planning to secure some action by the government which will legalize their proceedings and sanction their fictitious capitalization. Already there has been one powerfully organized attempt in Congress to enact legislation approving all railroad combinations heretofore perfected in violation of law, and validate all the watered stocks and bonds with which corporate greed has sought to burden the commerce of the country. The situation is critical. It may be expected from the attitude of the Supreme Court, as shown in the Standard Oil and Tobacco Trust cases, that any act on the part of the executive or legislative branch of government giving countenance to these unlawful combinations will be construed as an approval of the thousands of millions of watered stocks and bonds issued, and will fasten upon the people for all time the speculative capitalization of public service and industrial combinations. The time is at hand to declare for a statute that shall make it everlastingly impossible for any president, or any congress, or any court, to legalize spurious capitalization as a basis of extortionate prices, and we pledge the Republican party to the enactment of such a law. By the enactment of the Sherman Anti-Trust Law, in 1890, the American people declared their belief that monopoly is intolerable, and their determination that competition, the natural law in trade, should be maintained in business. The will of the people embodied in this law, has been frustrated because the administrations charged with the responsibility failed to enforce the law. But the wisdom of that law has been confirmed by the bitter experience of recent years. Within the last dozen years trusts have been organized in nearly every branch of industry. Competitors have been ruthlessly crushed, extortionate prices have been exacted from consumers, business development has been arrested, invention stifled, and the door of opportunity has been closed except to large aggregations of capital. In the few cases where consolidation resulted in great efficiency, greedy monopoly has retained all its fruits. The public has not received any of the resultant economies and benefits of combination which have been promised so profusely. But ordinarily, the combinations have demonstrated merely that the hand of monopoly is deadening, and that business may as easily become too large to be efficient, as remain too small.

In order to restore and preserve competition, as the people have willed, new and adequate legal machinery must be provided. The present law is uncertain of application, since the Standard Oil and Tobacco cases have decided that only unreasonable restraints of trade are prohibited, and later proceedings in those cases have shown that the present law is impotent to destroy monopoly. Legitimate business halts, because the law-abiding merchant and manufacturer doubts what he may legally do. Law breaking monopoly flourishes, because this same uncertainty increases the difficulty of enforcing the statute and making it secure in wrong-doing.

Platform of 1912

Supplemental legislation should be enacted to remove this uncertainty by specifying and prohibiting methods, practices and conditions which experience has shown to be harmful. Supplemental legislation should be enacted to facilitate the enforcement of the law, by imposing upon those who combine to restrain trade (and particularly upon those who combine to control more than thirty per cent. in any branch of business) the burden of proving that their action has been consistent with the public welfare. Supplemental legislation should also be enacted by which proceedings for the dissolution of trusts shall become effective to restore competition. To this end courts should be empowered to prevent any person from owning shares in more than one of the companies into which a trust has been divided by decree.

The control of limited sources of raw material, like coal, iron, ore, and copper should be broken up and these resources opened to all manufacturers on equal terms. And to afford an actual remedy for injuries suffered by innocent competitors and consumers, decrees obtained in such suits instituted by the government should be made to inure to their benefit, and they should be permitted to seek in such suits, damages for wrongs done and protection against future abuse of power so illegally acquired. The proposed trade commission should have power to condemn all contracts, agreements, and practices found to be discriminatory and oppressive, and to compel the substitution of such as are found to be reasonable. It should enforce prohibition of criminal practices which should be specifically defined by law. We denounce that interpretation of the anti-trust law which uses it to suppress the unions and co-operative efforts of wage-earners and farmers in protecting their labor against moneyed monopolies and we pledge a revision of the law making such construction impossible.

Injunctions

We pledge the Republican party to the enactment of a law to prohibit the issuance of injunctions in cases arising out of labor disputes, when such injunctions would not apply where no labor disputes existed, and providing that in no case shall an injunction be issued when there exists a remedy by the ordinary process of law, and which act shall provide that in the procedure for contempt of court the party cited for contempt shall be entitled to a trial by jury, except when such contempt was committed in the actual presence of the court or so near thereto as to interfere with the proper administration of justice.

Department of Labor

We pledge the enactment of a law creating a separate Department of Labor with a secretary at its head having a seat in the President's cabinet. We pledge ourselves to employ all the powers of the federal government, including the power over interstate commerce and internal revenue taxation, in order that the benefits intended for American labor from tariff protection shall actually reach the laborer. To this end we favor federal legislation providing for workmen's compensation for accident, protection of women and child labor, safety and sanitation in work places and reasonable hours of labor according to standards to be fixed and enforced by the Department of Labor.

Health

We favor the strengthening of the various agencies of the government relating to pure foods, quarantine and health, and their union into a single United States Health Service not subordinated to any other interest, commercial or financial, but devoted to co-operation with the health activities of the various states and cities of the nation, and to such efforts as are consistent with reasonable personal liberty, looking to the elimination of unnecessary disease and to the lengthening of human life.

Conservation

We pledge the preservation of the mines and water powers in this country to the whole people and particularly the beneficial control by the government of our coal supply whether in public or private possession. We pledge an appropriation for the further exploration for phosphate beds, to be taken over and operated by the government. We pledge the increase of the forest domain and the extension of scientific forest development. We pledge a thorough investigation into living conditions and especially into the conditions of rural life, and legislation to encourage rural co-operation and credit, land purchase by actual settlers, with the aid of long-time favorable government loans, the increase of rural education, and to prevent the growth of monopoly and monopoly values in land, all looking to the encouragement of the tiller of the soil and to the reduction of the cost of living.

Alaska

Alaska contains untold wealth in coal, lumber, copper, and other natural resources, for the upbuilding of industry and commerce and for the conquest of the markets of the Orient and South America. The government still has it in its power to save this vast storehouse of supplies from the interests which have monopolized the natural resources of the nation. Before the monopoly of the anthracite coal of Pennsylvania in the days of free competition, that coal sold at from $2.50 to $3.00 a ton at the seaboard. Independent producers were destroyed by discriminations and rebates and the oppressive methods exercised by monopoly of transportation. Today, 96 per cent. of the anthracite coal mines are owned and controlled by great railroads. The coal costs at the mouth of the mine, $1.84 per ton, and sells at the Atlantic seaboard at $6.00 to $7.00 per ton.

To preserve Alaska for all the people, to develop its untouched resources, we should adopt the plan so successfully carried through in Panama, where the government has built and now maintains a railway and Atlantic steamship line. We should utilize the Panama Commission, a highly trained, efficient body of men, which has mastered almost every conceivable engineering emergency, to build government owned and operated railways, terminals, docks, harbors, and to operate coal mines to the end that the last remaining patrimony of the nation shall forever be free from the control of monopoly.

We should own and operate a government line of steamships, running from Alaska by way of Pacific ports through the Panama Canal to New York, thus relieving the Atlantic and Pacific seaboard from the oppression of transcontinental lines. And we favor the immediate enactment of such legislation as will preserve this remaining heritage of the nation, and develop it for the benefit of all the people.

Panama Canal

The construction of the Panama Canal was designed to give the public the benefit of water competition as a protection against excessive transcontinental railway rates. The American people assumed the enormous burden required for the greatest of all engineering projects at a total cost, with purchase of treaty rights, of $375,000,000. Already the interests are organized to secure the exclusive benefits to flow from the construction of the Panama Canal. In order to preserve their present high railway rates, they seek to make the water rate by the canal expensive by imposing a heavy tax upon domestic commerce through the canal. These interests must be made to keep their powerful hands off this canal and the steamship lines as well. The people have paid for its construction, as they have paid for improving the rivers and harbors, and should resist now any further attempt on the part of the railroads to rob the public of all advantages resulting from a reduced rate by water.

We favor such legislation as will insure the domestic commerce of this country, when carried in American ships, passage through the Panama Canal free of all tolls.

Interstate Commerce

The life of the nation is close-woven with the means of transportation upon which communities must depend in trade and commerce. The railways, which are clearly defined by law to be public servants, have become more powerful than their creators. Two thousand independent competing companies have merged into a half dozen groups controlled by a handful of men. They have issued billions of securities that represent no investment by their owners. Thousands of millions have wrongfully been extorted from consumers and invested in permanent improvements and extensions, and thereupon capitalized and made an excuse for still greater extortions. The gross railway earnings of the country have reached the enormous total of more than two billion eight hundred million dollars annually. This transportation tax is mainly levied upon the necessaries of life. Railway rates and charges are not adjusted to the cost of the service. They are fixed by what the traffic will stand. The sacrifice and the hardships of the farmer and the worker, because of this unchecked power to collect such tribute as the masters of transportation dictate will never be known. No effective regulation of railways is possible until we know the cost of service, and the cost of service depends upon the value of the property used in the business, the cost of maintaining the property, and the cost of operation. We favor the reasonable valuation of the physical properties of interstate railroad, telegraph, telephone and other public utility companies, justly inventoried and determined upon a sound economic basis, distinguishing actual values from monopoly values, derived from violations of law, and making such discriminating values, so ascertained, the base line for determining rates. With such a valuation the country would know how much of the total value of railway property represented by the eighteen billions of stocks and bonds issued against that property was contributed by those who own the railroads, and how much by the people themselves, in excessive rates. The Interstate Commerce Commission is wholly unable to deal with the problem under existing law. It can at present do no more than check some of the most flagrant abuses. We should recognize the magnitude of the undertaking to control and regulate interstate commerce. We favor such amendment and revision of existing law as shall provide for a nation wide supervision of railway transportation and services by the division of the country into districts, in each of which a subsidiary commission should be established to regulate and control the railways within its jurisdiction, retaining the present interstate commerce commission to which appeals should lie from the orders of the subsidiary commissions. Only by such comprehensive control can the shippers and consumers of the country be assured adequate protection.

Joint Control of Production and Transportation

Common ownership, operation or control of mines or manufactories and public railroads, is inseparable from discrimination and resulting extortions. We oppose all combinations whereby, through joint ownership or control, the public-service corporations engaged in transportation, including pipe lines, operate in conjunction with coal, iron ore, oil, or other private agencies of production.

Parcels Post and Express

We pledge the extension of the postal service to include a parcels post, offering, against the service of the private express monopoly, a cheap and direct means of transportation between the producer and the consumer, upon a charge based upon distance and the actual cost of operation.

Good Roads

Recognizing the demand and necessity for Good Roads, we favor state and national aid for their construction and maintenance, under a plan which will insure its benefits alike to all communities upon their own initiative.

Ship Subsidy

We are unequivocally opposed to a ship subsidy in any form as vicious and indefensible in principle. Once entrenched, it would become another corrupting influence in our politics.

War Expenditures

We are opposed to further extravagance on the advice of interested persons only in building battleships and political navy yards, and favor the establishment of an unprejudiced commission to investigate and report what is required in the way of national defense.

"Dollar Diplomacy"

We condemn the "dollar diplomacy" which has reduced our state department from its high plane as a kindly intermediary of defenseless nations into a trading out-post for Wall Street interests, aiming to exploit those who would be our friends.

Income and Inheritance Taxes

We collect the revenues to maintain our national government through taxing consumption. These taxes upon the consumer are levied upon articles of universal use. They bear most heavily upon the poor and those of moderate means. Other countries tax incomes and inheritances at a progressive rate. The burdens of our people should be equalized; wealth should bear its share.

We favor the adoption of the pending income tax amendment to the constitution and thereupon the immediate passage of a graduated income tax law, and we pledge the enactment of a law taxing inheritances at a progressive rate.

Initiative, Referendum and Recall

Over and above constitutions and statutes, and greater than all, is the supreme sovereignty of the people. Whenever the initiative, referendum and the recall have been adopted by state governments, it has stimulated the interest of the citizen in his government and awakened a deeper sense of responsibility. If it is wise to entrust the people with this power in state government, no one can challenge the extension of this power to the national government. We favor such amendments to the federal constitution, and thereupon the enactment of such statutes as may be necessary to extend the initiative, the referendum and the recall to representatives in Congress and United States senators.

So long as judges are the final makers of statute and constitutional law, government by the people becomes government by a judicial oligarchy. The people are the source of all power, and we favor the extension of the recall to the judiciary with safeguards as to lapse of time between the petition and the vote.

Amending the Federal Constitution

Under a democratic form of government, the right to amend and alter their Constitution is inherent in the sovereignty of the people. But the methods of amendment prescribed in the Constitution, framed when this government was a small community with a total population of only four million, render it almost impossible of application by a nation of ninety million people, divided into forty-eight states, with a most complex social and industrial life. For more than fifty years an overwhelming majority of all the voters have struggled in vain so to amend the Constitution to insure the election of United States Senators by direct vote of the people. The public interest demands that this should be remedied.

We favor such amendment to the Constitution as will permit a change to be made therein by a majority of the votes cast upon a proposed amendment in a majority of the states, provided a majority of all the votes cast in the country shall be in favor of its adoption. An amendment may be initiated by a majority in Congress, or by ten states acting either through the legislators thereof or through a majority of the electors voting thereon in each state.

Presidential Primaries

In the conflict with privilege now on, much progress has already been made through the direct primary. We favor the enactment of a federal statute providing for the nomination of all candidates for President, Vice President, and Representatives in Congress, by direct vote of the people at a primary election held in all states upon the same day, the question of closed or open primaries to be determined by each state for itself.

The law should provide that, after the nomination of candidates for president and vice president by the primary, national platform conventions shall be held for each political party recognized by law, the expenses of attendance by members to be paid from the public treasury.

Corrupt Practices

We pledge legislation providing for the widest publicity and strictest limitation of campaign expenditures and the detailed publication of all campaign contributions and expenditures, both as to sources and purposes, at frequent intervals before primaries and election as well as after.

Direct Election of Senators

We pledge support of the pending amendment to the Constitution for the election of Senators of the United States by direct vote.

Equal Suffrage

We favor the extension of the suffrage to women.

Legislation and Publicity

We pledge the enactment of a law requiring all congressional committee hearings to be public and providing for a permanent public record of all appearances and votes at committee meetings and for the strictest regulation of the acts of all persons employed for pecuniary consideration to oppose or promote legislation.

Legislative Reference Department

The growth of statute law, resulting from the increasing economic problems, urgently requires increased attention to the facilities for the enactment of legislation, in the most effective and serviceable form.

We pledge the establishment of a non-partisan federal legislative reference and drafting bureau.

Civil Service

We pledge the extension of the civil service law to all branches of the federal service and the abolition of useless sinecures, and pledge the strengthening and enforcement of the law prohibiting the use of federal employees to perpetuate the power of an existing administration. Justice and efficiency require an extension to all classes of civil service employees of the benefits of the provisions of the compensation act, and a provision by law for a direct petition to Congress by civil service employees for redress of their grievances.

LA FOLLETTE'S PERSONAL PLATFORM IN 1912

Published on the eve of the presidential primaries in 1912 in La Follette's Magazine under the title, "The Republican Party Faces a Crisis."

THERE is just one overmastering issue in this campaign. What are we going to do with the railroads, the trusts and the money power?

The trusts and the money power are making their final stand to perpetuate their power. The supreme court is with them. They only need a president and a congress that will legalize their capitalization; that, under the guise of regulation by government will fix their prices and wages so as to earn a profit on these illegal values; that, under the guise of providing elasticity in our currency system, will perpetuate their control of the people's deposits and savings.

Let the people not be misled. Let no mistake be made at this time, which, under the pretense of putting control in the hands of the people will really take away from them the chance of ever getting control.

I am opposed to anything like federal incorporation, federal license, the Aldrich currency scheme or any other scheme that looks towards clinching the illegal power that has now been concentrated in a few hands. I demand a physical valuation that will gradually squeeze out the water. I demand a clear definition of monopoly and restraints so that business that is not a monopoly shall know where it stands under the Sherman law.

I demand protection of wage-earners and farmers in their right to organize and to defend themselves by means of unions.

All other issues are subordinate to this great issue. They are methods and means. As such, I demand the initiative, referendum and recall—national as well as state—direct primaries, income and inheritance taxes, parcels post and government ownership of express companies, government ownership and operation of Alaskan railroads, coal mines and a steamship line, free use of the Panama canal to American ships, a national policy of internal waterways, a tariff based on the difference in the labor costs of production and conditioned on labor receiving its benefits.

Industrial and commercial tyranny destroys individual freedom. We may have the privilege of the ballot. We may have the form and semblance of democracy, but in the end industrial servitude means political servitude.

We are building up colossal fortunes, granting unlimited power to corporations and consolidating and massing together business interests as never before in the history of the world—but the people are losing control of their own government. Its foundations are being sapped and its integrity destroyed.

The republican party is facing a crisis in its history. Two courses are open before it. The rank and file of the party, organized to restore human rights and preserve free institutions, will tolerate no further temporizing with existing conditions.

The republican party cannot ignore the social injustice, the industrial and commercial oppression which everywhere prevails. It can honestly face these conditions and with firmness and patience and wisdom make an end of them.

For 20 years I have pursued an uncompromising course whose goal was liberty and equality, an even chance for every man, woman and child—the right to buy, the right to sell our labor and the products of our labor in a free, open American market. For 20 years I have fought for real representative government, fought to make the will of the people the law of the land. I do not now propose to abandon that course, and today, as well as at the Chicago convention and always, I shall struggle for these practical reforms which, as I see it, will achieve social justice and human welfare.

La Follette's Magazine, April, 1912.

PLATFORM OF 1916

Submitted by the Wisconsin delegation at the republican national convention in 1916, and rejected by the convention.

Tariff

E favor a protective tariff the schedule of which shall be based upon the ascertained difference in the labor in this country and abroad and which shall be so adjusted as to assure its benefit to labor and yet not tax the consumer to cover inefficient management nor place a premium on the exhaustion of our national resources. The investigation of these facts and the revision of these schedules should be made by a nonpartisan tariff commission, subject to the action of Congress.

Patents

Inventions should be fully developed and utilized for the public benefit under reasonable regulation by the Federal Trade Commission. We pledge the enactment of a patent law which will protect the inventor as well as the public, and which cannot be used against the public welfare in the interest of injurious monopolies.

Ship Subsidies

We are unequivocally opposed to ship subsidies. We believe the American merchant marine can be builded upon a stable basis by equalizing the cost of building and the costs of operation. We commend the enactment of the so-called Seamen's Law which gave freedom to seamen and equalized the labor costs of ship operation between vessels of the United States and foreign countries. We insist upon the proper enforcement of that act and demand legislation to equalize the cost of ship construction.

Social Welfare

A well nurtured, well developed, loyal citizenship is essential to National defense. Without such a body of citizens, physical resources are of little value. The nation best commands an adequate defense that most efficiently safeguards against exploitation and most adequately provides for the material and physical well-being of its citizens. We favor laws to assure the greatest possible safety to workmen from industrial accidents and vocational diseases, to provide compensation for occupational accidents and diseases, to facilitate and encourage safe provisions for dependents and for old age, to strictly regulate and control the employment of women and children, to secure the fullest inquiry and publicity with regard to living conditions and conditions of employment, to encourage the organization of workmen and farmers to co-operate in the distribution of products and the elimination of unnecessary expense, loss and waste and to promote their education, efficiency and general welfare.

Health

We favor the strengthening of the various agencies of the government relating to pure foods, quarantine and health, and their union into a single United States Health Service not subordinated to any interest, commercial or financial, but devoted to co-operation with the health activities of the various states and cities of the nation, and to such efforts as are consistent with reasonable personal liberty, looking to the elimination of unnecessary disease and the lengthening of human life.

Government Manufacture of Munitions

We favor a comprehensive survey by the government of the industries, transportation and other resources of the United States and such organization thereof in times of peace, that in time of war every resource of the country shall be available immediately for the needs of the government. National defense should involve equal sacrifice and there should be no private profit from war or preparation for war. The private manufacture of munitions of war furnishes a direct incentive to war. Government manufacture of munitions by eliminating private profit, does away with the desire for war. We pledge the government manufacture of all munitions and vessels of war in time of peace, and in time of war the requisition and operation by the government of privately owned plants so far as needed.

Naval Supplies

We pledge ourselves to the acquisition and operation by the government of coal mines and oil wells upon the Atlantic and Pacific Coasts and in Alaska for the supply of the Navy and other governmental departments with fuel and oil.

Taxation

Great fortunes have been gained through the manufacture and sale of munitions of war to belligerent European countries. We believe that those who have directly profited by the European war should contribute a portion of such profits to pay the increased expenses of our government caused by expansion of our military program. We therefore favor paying for such increased expenditures by increasing the sur-tax upon incomes, levying a tax upon all manufacturers of munitions of war, and a graduated Federal Inheritance Tax with reasonable exemptions.

Strict Neutrality

We insist that this country shall maintain strict neutrality toward nations engaged in war, thus preserving friendly relations with all belligerents and keeping open the door of opportunity to service in promoting just terms of peace. We pledge to so amend our neutrality laws as to make it the duty of the President, by Executive order, to preserve the perfect balance of our neutrality even at the sacrifice of profits to the money power and the manufacturers of arms and ammunitions.

Conference of Neutral Nations for Peace

We favor a conference of neutral nations with a view to a permanent organization to promote peace, prevent wars and aid in the settlement of international questions and the adjustment of differences between nations at war.

International Peace Tribunal

To compose the differences of nations and to maintain World peace, we favor the creation of an international Tribunal to which shall be referred for final settlement, all issues between nations, and upon the establishment of such a Tribunal we favor action by our government toward general disarmament of the nations of the World; and that an adequate International Army and Navy be maintained under the command of such Tribunal to enforce its decrees.

Referendum On War

We favor a law providing for a popular expression of opinion by the voters for or against war with any foreign government with which the President shall have severed diplomatic relations.

Foreign Relations

We denounce the un-American and undemocratic secret diplomacy which continually threatens the honor, peace and security of our country, and we favor full and immediate publicity in all our relations with foreign governments.

Dollar Diplomacy

The natural resources of our country have been largely monopolized by privileged interests. These interests have formed monster combinations in every important industry, controlling production and prices and creating a vast surplus wealth. This excess capital which might otherwise be loaned at reduced interest rates to the people from whom it has been wrongfully exacted, has been withdrawn from the country by the masters of finance and used to secure concessions in oil, coal, timber and mineral lands in Mexico, Central and South American countries, and loaned in China and elsewhere at usurious rates and extortionate commissions, thus enabling these interests to control the natural resources of the weaker nations and exploit their helpless peoples.

In support of this system in recent years there has been an attempt to establish and maintain a foreign policy of "Dollar Diplomacy" that would make our government the guarantor for the private investments of our privileged interests in foreign countries.

Back of this foreign policy lies in large part the demand for a big army and a big navy to enforce the collection of the private claims and protect the concessions and investments of these interests.

These same interests own the munition plants which fatten off the great government contracts to supply the big army and build the big navy maintained by taxing our people.

We denounce this mercenary system of a degraded foreign policy which has at times reduced our State Department from its high service as a strong and kindly intermediary of defenseless governments into a trading outpost for those privileged interests and concession seekers engaged in exploiting weaker nations.

We pledge ourselves against "Dollar Diplomacy" and the identification of the government with the claims of concession seekers, financiers and privileged interests operating in weaker countries.

Woman's Suffrage

We favor the extension of suffrage to women.

Initiative, Referendum and Recall

Over and above constitutions and statutes and greater than all, is the supreme sovereignty of the people. Whenever the initiative, referendum and the recall have been adopted by state governments, it has stimulated the interest of the citizen in his government and awakened a deeper sense of responsibility. If it is wise to entrust the people with this power in state government, no one can challenge the extension of this power to the national government. We favor such amendments to the federal constitution and thereupon the enactment of such statutes as may be necessary to extend the initiative, the referendum and the recall to representatives in Congress and United States Senators.

Legislation and Publicity

We pledge the enactment of a law requiring all congressional committee hearings to be public and providing for a permanent public record of all appearances and votes at committee meetings and for the strictest regulation of the acts of all persons employed for pecuniary consideration to oppose or promote legislation.

PLATFORM OF 1920

The following platform was issued by the La Follette Progressive Republican candidates for seats in the Republican National Convention in 1920. The primary on April 2, 1920, resulted in the election of twenty-four out of a possible twenty-six delegates. The platform was submitted at the Republican national convention but was rejected by the convention.

I. We favor the immediate conclusion of peace and resumption of trade with all countries.

II. We are opposed to the League of Nations as a standing menace to peace, and we denounce the Treaty as a violation of the pledges made to the world and a betrayal of the honor of this nation. It would make us a party to the enslavement of Egypt and India, the rape of China, and the ruthless oppression of Ireland.

III. We would favor a League for Peace, composed of all the nations of the world, provided they were mutually pledged by binding convenants, with proper guarantees, to abolish compulsory military service, and provided further, that the several nations mutually bind themselves to a speedy disarmament, reducing the land and naval forces of each nation to the strict requirements of a purely police and patrol service.

IV. We demand the immediate restoration of free speech, free press, peaceable assembly, and all civil rights and liberties guaranteed by the constitution. We favor the repeal of the Espionage and Sedition Act, and denounce the attempt to write such laws into the permanent statutes of the country.

V. We oppose all legislation conferring upon the Postmaster General, or any other governmental agency, the power to deny the mailing privilege to any person without judicial hearing, and the right of appeal.

VI. We oppose compulsory military service in time of peace. We denounce the use of our soldiers in countries with which we are not at war, and we favor the speedy reduction of world armaments.

VII. We oppose the exile of any person lawfully admitted to this country, except for crime fixed by law, and then only upon trial and conviction by jury.

VIII. We demand the abolition of injunctions in labor disputes.

IX. We favor laws permitting labor and farm organizations, for the purpose of collective bargaining, in industry, trade and commerce.

X. We favor such legislation as may be needful and helpful in promoting direct co-operation and eliminating waste, speculation and excessive profits between producer and consumer, as offering some measure of relief from the oppressive and intolerable economic conditions under which the farmer, the wage-earner, and people generally suffer at this time.

XI. We favor repeal of the Esch-Cummins railroad law, by which the people are forced to guarantee railroad profit, while such railroads are privately owned, and declare for the ultimate public ownership of railroads, and the gradual acquisition of stock yard terminals, large packing plants, and all other natural resources, the private ownership of which is the basis of private monopoly.

XII. We demand economy in government, to replace the extravagance run riot under the present administration. The expenses of the present year of peace, it has been estimated, will be approximately $11,000,000,000, or ten times the annual pre-war expense.

XIII. We condemn the system that permits 18,000 millionaires to be produced from war-profits —one millionaire for every three American soldiers killed in France. We demand that taxes be laid upon wealth in proportion to ability to pay, in such manner as will prevent such tax burdens being shifted to the backs of the poor, in higher prices and increased cost of living.

XIV. We denounce the alarming usurpation of legislative power, by the federal courts, as subversive of democracy, and we favor such amendments to the constitution, and thereupon, the enactment of such statutes as may be necessary, to provide for the election of all federal judges, for fixed terms not exceeding ten years, by direct vote of the people.

XV. We favor such amendments to the Constitution, and thereupon the enactment of such statutes as may be necessary to extend the initiative and the referendum, to national legislation, and the recall to Representatives in Congress and United States Senators.

XVI. We favor paying the soldiers of the late war a sufficient sum to make their war wages equal to at least civilian pay, and this as a matter of right, and not as charity, or bonus. We favor other laws liberally recognizing the patriotic devotion of our soldiers in all our wars.

XVII. We favor a deep waterway from the Great Lakes to the sea. The government should, in conjunction with Canada, take immediate action to give the Northwestern states an outlet to the ocean for cargoes, without change in bulk, thus making the primary markets on the great lakes equal to those of New York.

XVIII. We favor a platform for the Republican party, embracing these principles, and a candidate for president whose public record is a guaranty that he is in full accord therewith.